Understanding China's Behaviour in the South China Sea

Klaus Heinrich Raditio

Understanding China's Behaviour in the South China Sea

A Defensive Realist Perspective

palgrave
macmillan

Klaus Heinrich Raditio
University of Sydney
Sydney, NSW, Australia

ISBN 978-981-13-1282-3 ISBN 978-981-13-1283-0 (eBook)
https://doi.org/10.1007/978-981-13-1283-0

Library of Congress Control Number: 2018950397

Cover illustration: © Pomogayev / Getty Images
Cover Design by Tom Howey

This Palgrave Macmillan imprint is published by the registered company Springer Nature Singapore Pte Ltd.
The registered company address is: 152 Beach Road, #21-01/04 Gateway East, Singapore 189721, Singapore

For Indonesia

Foreword

Albert Einstein once said that "peace can only be achieved by understanding". In a world full of suspicion and distrust, his word is very relevant. Our knowledge and understanding on other countries, particularly the emerging power like China, are indeed of paramount importance. For some, the rise of China offers plenty of opportunities, and success awaits those who can take advantage of it. However, for others, China is still a mystery. Its behaviour in the South China Sea, for instance, is perplexing—and sometimes considered worrying.

This book—which offers the perspective of defensive realist—is meant to deepen our understanding on China and its behaviour in the South China Sea. This fruitful research serves Indonesia's diplomacy which consistently promotes inclusiveness and habit of dialogue. Indonesia's foreign policy aims at alleviating great powers rivalry, maintaining peace, stability, and prosperity.

This research was successfully conducted and wins acclaim from prominent scholars in international relations. I congratulate Klaus for presenting his original idea on China's behaviour in the South China Sea. I am confident that this book contributes to enhancing our understanding on China and the current stage of international affairs.

Director General for Asia-Pacific and African Affairs of the Ministry of Foreign Affairs, Jakarta Republic of Indonesia

Desra Percaya

Preface

I have conducted this research under the Australia Awards Scholarship (AAS) scheme. I dedicate this research to my country and hope this research can help everyone, especially my fellow Indonesians and Australian friends, to understand China better.

This research is conducted with generous support from my principal supervisor Associate Professor Jingdong Yuan and associate supervisor Dr Justin Hastings. I am grateful also for support from the staff and colleagues at the University of Sydney's Department of Government and International Relations.

I would also like to thank the National Institute of South China Sea Studies in Haikou, China, and the Centre for International Law, National University of Singapore, where I conducted my fieldwork in November and December 2015.

My deepest appreciation goes to the Foreign Ministry of the Republic of Indonesia to which I belong, for giving me the opportunity to serve my country in the scholarly field. I thank the Indonesian Consulate in Sydney and all the staff for their support and care while I have been undertaking this research, in particular Mr and Mrs Yayan Mulyana, and Mr Novan Ivanhoe Saleh.

I thank Dr Desra Percaya, the Director General for Asia-Pacific and African Affairs, for giving me the opportunities to develop my skill in diplomacy and scholarly field. I am most grateful for my colleagues' support, particularly Yvonne Mewengkang, Rifky Akbar, Raka Pamungkas, Gina Virginianty, Diah Setyorini, and Junaedi.

This research could not have been completed without moral support from my family, who created a positive atmosphere and helped me to be a better person.

Ad Maiorem Dei Gloriam!

Sydney, NSW, Australia
April 2018

Klaus Heinrich Raditio

Contents

Abbreviations

ADIZ	Air Defence Identification Zone
ARF	ASEAN Regional Forum
ASEAN	Association of the Southeast Asian Nations
CCP	Chinese Communist Party
CMS	China Marine Surveillance
CNOOC	China National Offshore Oil Cooperation
DoC	Declaration on the Conduct of Parties in the South China Sea
DRV	Democratic Republic of Vietnam
ECS	East China Sea
EDCA	Enhanced Defence Cooperation Agreement
EEZ	Exclusive Economic Zone
FONOP	Freedom of Navigation Operation
ICC	International Criminal Court
ICJ	International Court of Justice
ITLOS	International Tribunal for the Law of the Sea
JMSU	Joint Marine Surveillance Undertaking
LSG	Leading Small Group
NATO	North Atlantic Treaty Organization
OBOR	One Belt One Road
PCA	Permanent Court of Arbitration
PLA	People's Liberation Army
PLAN	People's Liberation Army Navy
PRC	People's Republic of China
RIMPAC	Rim of the Pacific Exercise
ROC	Republic of China
RVN	Republic of Vietnam
SCS	South China Sea

SRV	Socialist Republic of Vietnam
TAC	ASEAN's Treaty of Amity and Cooperation
THAAD	Terminal High Altitude Area Defence
UNCLCS	United Nations Commission on the Limits of the Continental Shelf
UNCLOS	United Nations Convention on the Law of the Sea

List of Figures

List of Tables

CHAPTER 1

Introduction

1.1 Background

The dispute over the South China Sea (SCS) is one of the hottest territorial and jurisdictional disputes in modern history. This resources-rich area is claimed by China and four other countries in the Southeast Asian region (Vietnam, the Philippines, Malaysia, and Brunei), and by Taiwan. There have been numerous incidents in the SCS since the mid-1970s. In most of the high-profile incidents—such as the 1974 Paracel Islands incidents, the 1988 Johnson Reef incidents, the 1995 Mischief Reef incidents, and the 2012 Scarborough Shoal incidents—they have all involved China vis-à-vis other claimant states. Neither the incidents among non-China claimant states themselves receive high-profile coverage nor are they considered significant. China's behaviour has been at the centre of gravity with regard to stability in the region. This might be because China is the latecomer in establishing a presence in the SCS, especially in the Spratlys, regardless of the fact that its claim dates back to a time before the founding of the People's Republic of China in 1949. This research's primary interest is to analyse the nature of China's SCS behaviour, its rationale, and development that has led to its defection in the early part of the twenty-first century.

Prior to the recent tension, China's behaviour in the Southeast Asian region was described as relatively self-restrained, accommodating, and reassuring. Ralf Emmers describes this period as one of de-escalation which lasted from the aftermath of the 1995 Mischief Reef incident to between 2007 and 2009.[1] During this period of de-escalation, however,

K. H. Raditio, *Understanding China's Behaviour in the South China Sea*, https://doi.org/10.1007/978-981-13-1283-0_1

the situation in the SCS was not completely free of conflict. Some skirmishes between maritime law enforcement ships and fishing boats from China and other claimants did take place, but overall, the disputes were low profile and no dramatic tension occurred.[2] Until the late 1990s, the SCS tension was reduced, and the parties concerned seemed content to keep the status quo.[3] China itself became more open to discussing the SCS issue in the context of ASEAN.[4] The friction among the claimant states was reduced in the early 2000s because of China's adoption of a reassurance policy towards its ASEAN counterparts—stressing the peaceful nature of its ascent.[5] China realised that without regional stability, development and modernisation of the country would be hard to attain. This reassurance policy towards ASEAN was adopted as the good neighbour (*mulin waijiao wending zhoubian*) guideline gained prominence in Chinese foreign policy.[6]

This conducive situation contributed to the signing of the Declaration on the Conduct of Parties in the South China Sea (DoC) in November 2002. The following year, China signed the Treaty of Amity and Cooperation (TAC) in Southeast Asia, which prevents the signatories from using a military approach in dealing with disputes in the region. In the following years, these two agreements were effective in restraining the claimant states from making any provocative moves. In March 2005, China, the Philippines, and Vietnam signed an agreement, the Joint Marine Seismic Undertaking (JMSU), which was applauded as a breakthrough in the dispute.[7] In brief, the SCS experienced a period of tension de-escalation in the mid-1990s until between 2007 and 2009 due to China's reassurance policy towards ASEAN countries.

However, with the recent conditions in the SCS, it is easy to consider that such a situation no longer applies due to a series of events such as China's stand-off with the Philippines in the 2012 Scarborough Shoal incident, China-Vietnam tension in the 2014 HSY Oil Rig incident, and China's massive reclamation in the SCS, which all reflect the heightened tension. In the aftermath of the Scarborough Shoal incident, the Philippines initiated a United Nations Convention on the Law of the Sea (UNCLOS) Tribunal in January 2013, which was unofficially supported by Vietnam and Malaysia; the other claimant state, Brunei, seems to keep a low-profile attitude towards the disputes.[8]

In addition to the dispute between claimant states, the US plays a significant role in the SCS. It has officially been involved in the SCS since the then US Secretary of State Hillary Clinton affirmed that the US has an interest in maintaining freedom of navigation in the SCS in the ASEAN Regional Forum (ARF) in Hanoi, July 2010[9]—which seriously irritates Beijing. The US pivot to Asia in 2011–2012 also contributes to tension between China and the US in the SCS. The US has also increased its assistance to the Philippine military in the framework of the Enhanced Defence Cooperation Agreement (EDCA) in 2014. On 5 February 2014, the US Department of State issued an official statement dismissing China's nine-dash line claim to the SCS, calling it "inconsistent with international law".[10]

The above-mentioned cases have contributed to re-escalation of tension in the SCS. In view of China's status as the rising power in the region, this research is interested in whether the nature of China's behaviour in the SCS is changing, from reassurance and self-restraint in the period of de-escalation to the opposite.

This research attempts to uncover the nature, rationale, and development of China's recent behaviour in the SCS from the perspective of defensive realist theory. Regarding policy, this research is significant because as a paramount power in the region, China's behaviour will have a great impact on regional order and stability. China's behaviour in the SCS is a "litmus test" for the whole of its foreign policy.[11] This means that China's behaviour in the SCS will determine how it pursues its national interest externally, in both the present and the future.

1.2 Literature Review

1.2.1 Is the Nature of China's SCS Behaviour Changing?

Most of the literature does not discuss much about the nature of China's behaviour in the SCS. Studies indicate the events that signify China's changing behaviour in the SCS. They differ in presenting the timing of the behavioural shift, ranging from as early as 2007 up to 2012. Table 1.1 summarises the various views on the timing and events that signify China's changing behaviour in the SCS.

Some of the events mentioned above still need factual clarification, for instance, whether China has begun to see the SCS as its core interest. If China has definitively asserted the SCS as a core interest alongside with Taiwan, Tibet, and Xinjiang, this can also be considered as well as the changing of China's stance on the SCS issue. The confusion of whether China has elevated the issue to its core interest list began when the US media reported the meeting in Beijing in March 2010 with senior US

Table 1.1 The events that signify China's changing behaviour

Authors	*Events*
2007	
Carlyle A. Thayer[12]	• China's intimidation towards US energy companies to end joint cooperation with Vietnam in the SCS • China's unilateral fishing ban in the SCS • China's protest against a claim for extended continental shelves and renewal of its claim, which covers 80% of the SCS
Tran Truong Thuy[13]	• China's intimidation towards US energy companies to end joint cooperation with Vietnam in the SCS • The establishment of the city of Sansha for administering the Paracel and Spratly Islands in December 2007
Peter Dutton[14]	• China's intimidation towards US energy companies to end joint cooperation with Vietnam in the SCS • China's assertive behaviour towards the SCS claimants in 2007, and towards the US in 2009
Bonnie Glaser[15]	• China's intimidation towards US energy companies to end joint cooperation with Vietnam in the SCS • An incident involved Chinese naval patrol and a Vietnamese fishing boat, killing one fisherman
Clive Schofield & Ian Storey[16]	• The establishment of the city of Sansha for administering the Paracel and Spratly Islands in December 2007 • China's intimidation towards US energy companies to end joint cooperation with Vietnam in the SCS
Tridib Chakraborti[17]	• China's intimidation towards US energy companies to end joint cooperation with Vietnam in the SCS • An incident involved Chinese naval patrol and a Vietnamese fishing boat, killing one fisherman • The establishment of the city of Sansha for administering the Paracel and Spratly Islands in December 2007
2009/2010	
M. Taylor Fravel[18]	• China's submission of the nine-dash line map to the UN Commission on the Limits of the Continental Shelf (CLCS) on May 2009 • The expansion of the unilateral fishing ban (2009) • The PLAN exercises in the SCS throughout 2010
Alastair Iain Johnston[19]	• The increasing presence of Chinese paramilitary in the SCS in unprecedented numbers
Michael Yahuda[20]	• The *Impeccable* incident • The increasing Chinese naval exercises in the SCS
Sarah Raine[21]	• The *Impeccable* incident
Pek Koon Heng[22]	• China's assertion of the SCS as its core interest

(*continued*)

Table 1.1 (continued)

Authors	*Events*
Thomas J. Christensen[23]	• The *Impeccable*
Zhang Jian[24]	• China's submission of the nine-dash line map to the UN CLCS on May 2009
Irene Chan & Li Mingjiang[25]	• China's submission of the nine-dash line map to the UN CLCS on May 2009

officials, NSC Asia Director Jeffrey Bader and Deputy Secretary of State James Steinberg. The report said that an American official involved in the meeting referred to China's intolerant stance to foreign interference in the SCS, which is viewed as a part of "China's core interest of sovereignty".[26] Secretary Clinton also mentioned this issue, confirming that China views the SCS as a core interest in an interview with Greg Sheridan of the *Australian*.[27] Nonetheless, a thorough examination of the Chinese official documents reveals there is no hint in them of the SCS as a core interest.[28] The Chinese Foreign Ministry also did not clarify the ambiguity nor confirm the status of the SCS. As a matter of fact, when the press demanded a confirmation on the status of the SCS as a core interest, Foreign Ministry Spokesperson Jiang Yu during a press conference on 21 September 2010, responded inconclusively.[29]

Furthermore, Swaine suggests three points concerning the SCS' status as its major territorial Chinese core interest. First, Beijing has been equivocally determining the SCS as its core interest, unlike the cases of Taiwan, Tibet, and Xinjiang. Second, even if the SCS is defined as a core interest, especially during the May 2010 Strategic and Economic Dialogue, this was uttered in an unofficial tone. Third, China deliberately averted making a confirmation on the status of the SCS, which creates an impression of distancing itself from international fuss.[30] Indeed, the thing that differentiates the SCS from Taiwan, Tibet, and Xinjiang is the nature of the negotiability of the issue. Whilst China regards Taiwan, Tibet, and Xinjiang as non-negotiable, the country anticipates negotiations for the SCS disputes, with applied terms and conditions (only limited to the parties directly concerned).

Regarding its military presence in the SCS, Swaine and Fravel contend that there is no clear indication that China has increased its presence in the disputed waters, including those of the State Oceanographic Administration and Fisheries Administration, since 2005.[31] They state that activities mentioned above have occurred as a response to what China regards as the growing assertiveness of other claimants since 2007.[32]

On the establishment of Sansha as a new city with the responsibility of administering the Paracel and the Spratly Islands, scholars argue that this came into effect in July 2012, not 2007.[33] The idea was considered in 2007, but due to several considerations, it was postponed for five years. The establishment of Sansha as a governing city over the Paracels and Spratlys could be a sign of China's assertiveness in consolidating its claim in the SCS.[34] However, one month earlier, Hanoi passed a law that claims sovereignty over the Paracels and Spratlys.[35] Thus, the creation of Sansha as the administering city of the Paracel and Spratly Islands could be Beijing's response to Hanoi's move.

Another case is the Chinese imposition of a fishing ban in 2009—mentioned by several scholars above—that cannot be considered a sign of policy departure. The fishing ban is supervised by the South Sea Region Fisheries Administration Bureau (SSRFAB) under the Ministry of Agriculture. It has, however, been imposed since 1999 annually, and China merely extended its effectiveness in 2009.[36] It is simply a continuous practice.

One event that is considered as a sign of China's behaviour departure is the *Impeccable* incident in March 2009. In this incident, five Chinese vessels "shadowed and aggressively manoeuvred in dangerous proximity to USNS Impeccable, in an apparent coordinated effort to harass the US ocean surveillance ship while it was conducting routine operations in international waters", according to a written statement by the Pentagon.[37] However, it is doubtful that this incident represents a change in China's behaviour in the SCS.[38] China took some actions that the US considered "harassment" before the *Impeccable* incident. In 2002, the US hydrographic survey ship USNS *Bowditch* was confronted by a Chinese vessel while steaming in international waters.[39] Earlier, in 2001, a Chinese fighter pilot collided with a US EP3 reconnaissance aircraft in international airspace.[40] The US aircraft was damaged, and its aircrew was detained, while China lost its pilot. These actions, however, can be interpreted as China's attempts to defend its territorial sovereignty. On the other hand, the US, due to its different interpretation of the 1982 UNCLOS, considers it did not violate China's sovereignty.[41] The frequency of similar incidents demonstrates that the 2009 *Impeccable* incident cannot represent a departure from China's usual behaviour.

Last but not least is China's *nota verbale* in response to the two separate submissions by Vietnam and Vietnam/Malaysia to the UN Commission on the Limits of the Continental Shelf (CLCS) on 7 May 2009. In this,

China attached the so-called nine-dash line map that demarcates China's territorial claim in the SCS. It was the first time that China had asserted its maritime territorial claim in the SCS by using such a map in the international forum. Interestingly, China only enclosed the briefly sketched map despite having other laws and regulations that serve as the legal basis to support its claim. Jerden argues that there was an adjustment change, that is, a qualitative change in the level of effort made when China responded by submitting this nine-dash line map internationally for the first time.[42] This seems to support the argument that China's submission of the map to the UN CLCS is an event that signifies its change in behaviour in the SCS.

So far, China has submitted three documents iterating its claims over the SCS: a *nota verbale* to the Secretary General of the UN and a preliminary declaration of claims to an extended continental shelf—both submitted in May 2009 and a second *nota verbale*, submitted to the UN in April 2011.[43] The first document was presented in response to a joint submission to the UN's CLCS by Malaysia and Vietnam.[44] The second document was presented in response to a UN request to present claims for an extended continental shelf by 13 May 2009. The third document was submitted in response to the Philippines' *nota verbale* in April 2011 objecting to China's May 2009 *nota verbale* and the nine-dash line map.[45] According to Swaine and Fravel, the contents of China's documents are consistent with China's long-term stance, in terms of the territorial coverage and the wording.[46] Having said that, these researchers contend the submission of the *nota verbale* attached with the nine-dash line map only signifies an increasing level of effort in consolidating China's claim in the SCS and does not represent a departure from China's previous behaviour.[47]

From the cases mentioned above, we can conclude that they are not convincing enough to be considered representative of a departure from China's behaviour. The claim about China's elevation of the SCS as a core interest lacks evidence; the increase in Chinese military presence is debatable (since other claimant states also do this); the imposition of a fishing ban is a regular practice; the establishment of Sansha city is apparently a response to another claimant's move; the *Impeccable* incident has a defensive character and is an event regarding which China was expected to behave in the same way in the past and the future; and the 2009 *nota verbale* to the UN CLCS is merely the result of an increasing level of effort over China's longstanding claim.

While this research argues that China has changed the nature of its behaviour in the SCS, these events do not signify any substantial change. To find the events which actually do signify changes, one needs to probe the development process and the rationale for China's SCS behaviour with the guidance from international relations theory.

1.2.2 *The Rationale for China's Changing Behaviour in the SCS*

The above-mentioned events indeed contributed to the heated tension in the SCS. A review of the literature indicates that this tension grew from 2007. However, to lay the blame solely on China for the deterioration in the SCS is contestable. It is understandable for China to react against actions by other claimants that were considered as "encroachment" in the claimed territory. Failing to do so would be regarded as a tacit recognition of other states' territorial claims. This applies to other claimants as well. Assertiveness is not exhibited solely by China since other claimant states also demonstrate the same attitude.[48] The situation in the SCS among all claimant states is extremely vulnerable and volatile, even during a period of de-escalation as tension can rise anytime due to their overlapping territorial claims.

This chapter discusses the various scholarly views on China's SCS behaviour, in particular, the motivation and rationale for China's changing behaviour in this region. Michael Yahuda contends that China's "new assertiveness" has risen from four factors: First, China's perception of the shift of power balance towards its favour; second, its growing national interest that covers the maritime domain in nearby seas and trade routes; third, its advanced military capability in consolidating its claim more powerfully; and fourth, the rising patriotic sentiments among the Chinese elite as well as its ordinary citizens.[49] Timothy Glogan underscores China's attempts in the SCS to secure hydrocarbon resources and energy, opining that these are by no means meant to be expansive.[50] Glogan also points out domestic factors such as growing nationalist sentiment within the Chinese society and the enhancement of the regime's legitimacy as the driving force for its assertive behaviour.[51] All in all, Glogan affirms that in almost all events pertaining to the SCS issue, Chinese assertive behaviour was in response to others' assertiveness, not vice versa.[52]

Alastair Iain Johnston contends that suggesting patriotic sentiment as a motivation for China's behaviour, as Yahuda and Glogan did, is quite flawed.[53] His doubts are mainly due to the Chinese political system which does not involve public participation in installing the leadership. For this sort of system, some questions inevitably arise: (1) How does public opinion matter to foreign policy making? (2) How does the regime perceive that anti-foreign sentiment is potentially turned into anti-regime sentiment? (3) How can nationalistic sentiment be used to confront other frictions in internal political intrigues?[54]

Besides, nationalism has been nurtured in the elites and ordinary citizens' minds throughout the history of the PRC. It is problematic to assume a new rising nationalistic sentiment and deduce that this factor is a driving force for China's assertive behaviour, since the sentiment has always been pervasive and is likely to motivate Chinese behaviour, be it assertive, aggressive, or even passive.

From the strategic point of view, Peter Dutton suggests that China is pursuing three main objectives in the SCS: regional integration, resource control, and enhanced security.[55] China had been oozing its charm in the Southeast Asian region to promote peace and stability in the aftermath of the Mischief Reef incident in 1995. Dutton marks a period of the late 1990s until 2007 when the economic and political cooperation between China and its Southeast Asian counterparts has been fruitful.[56] This strategy of oozing the charm has been successful to promote China's economic development. On the other hand, this tactic is also meant to create a conducive situation to advance its SCS interests. With the intention of eventually dominating the issue and substantiating its SCS claim,[57] the Chinese leadership considered that by benefiting Southeast Asian countries with economic development, it will eventually earn gratitude from and leverage over other claimants and may end up with voluntary abandonment in China's favour.[58] Recently, considering the development in the SCS, this view seems to have become mere wishful thinking.

Second, Dutton contends that China also aims at controlling abundant resources in the SCS, mainly energy and hydrocarbons to feed its 1.3 billion population.[59] As the country becomes more dependent on foreign oil and gas, the offshore exploration in the SCS will bring a positive contribution to China's energy replenishment.

Third, Dutton contends that security concern has become China's objective in the SCS to create a buffer zone that protect China's eastern coastal area.[60] In addition, by advancing its military power, China has a trump card to deter any party to strengthen its own claim in the disputed territory.

Michael D. Swaine and M. Taylor Fravel argue that China's recent behaviour in the SCS is largely reactive to other claimants' action, noticing four main activities recently: (1) the imposition of fishing regulations that require foreign vessels to obtain permission prior to conducting activities in the disputed territory; (2) regular maritime surveillance activities (primarily by the State Oceanic Administration and the Chinese Fisheries Administration), which are sometimes followed by detention of foreign fishermen; (3) political and diplomatic manoeuvres; and (4) scientific surveys or naval exercises in the disputed area.[61]

Swaine and Fravel contend that there is clear indication that China has increased its military and paramilitary presence in the disputed waters, including that of its State Oceanographic Administration and Fisheries Administration since 2005.[62] However, they argue, the above-mentioned activities have occurred as a response to what China regards as the growing assertiveness of other claimants since 2007.[63] In addition to that, China's more intense activities are a logical consequence of its developed capacities to support its longstanding claim in the SCS.[64] Overall, Swaine and Fravel regard China's behaviour in the SCS as assertive, considering that this also applies to other claimants and that China does not seem to seek military means to resolve the disputes.[65]

Ralf Emmers analysed the situation in the SCS from the early 1990s to the first five years of the twenty-first century, arguing for an initial escalation followed by a de-escalation after the 1995 Mischief Reef incident.[66] He identified six factors contributing to the de-escalation: (1) there was a shift towards moderation in the overall Chinese foreign policy due to its concern over US military presence in the region and the difficult situation with Japan; (2) China's PLAN has a relatively weak military posture to exert control over disputed waters; (3) Vietnam's accession to ASEAN gives the organisation a more sound reason to discuss the SCS issues vis-à-vis China; (4) the other claimant states in the SCS have demonstrated self-restraint in not arousing patriotic sentiment over the SCS issues; (5) there is limited evidence of proven oil reserves in the SCS; and (6) the US made a statement to maintain neutrality in the disputes, following the Mischief Reef incident.[67]

From the six above-mentioned points made by Emmers, China's initiative played a dominant role in de-escalation of the SCS disputes. Interestingly, the then Chinese Foreign Minister Qian Qichen prior to the ARF meeting in August 1995 made a concession to the ASEAN members by affirming that China was prepared to hold multilateral talks on the Spratly issues based on the 1982 UNCLOS.[68] It is not clear why this signal was not followed up by China and other ASEAN members, particularly the claimant states in the SCS.

Emmers contends that given the conflict-prone nature of the SCS issues, the de-escalation period after the 1995 Mischief Reef incident will somehow turn into another period of escalation. In particular, he suggests this would be because of China's display of its naval capabilities in the area, the worsening Sino-US or Sino-Japanese relations and new findings of a new abundant hydrocarbon reserves. It is argued these factors will spark a new escalation in the SCS.[69]

Among Chinese scholars, the analysis of China's motivation for its recent behaviour in the SCS is thought to be mainly caused by a deteriorating situation which was not initiated by China. Wu Shicun notices the shift from territorial dispute to jurisdiction disputes over the SCS, particularly in the Spratly/Nansha Islands.[70] From the history of dispute arbitration, there is a clear indication that the principle of effective occupation decides the winner of each case. Therefore, Wu Shicun calls on Beijing to enhance its administration in terms of economy and tourism over the disputed territory to bolster China's claim in the SCS.[71] Other reasons for China's recent behaviour in the SCS are varied. Chu Hao identifies that China feels anxious about the exploration activities by other claimants and their foreign multinational companies. He also points to the rising military budgets of other claimants which creates arms competition in the region.[72] Moreover, as Chu Hao and Wu Shicun advise, the return of the US to the dispute with its excuse to secure freedom of navigation only adds more complexity to the issue.[73] These Chinese researchers contend that all of these factors combined put China in a cornered position and therefore lead the country to adopt more assertive behaviour in the SCS.

This examination of the literature shows that scholars do not say much about the changing of the nature of China's behaviour, generally, discussing strategy shifting and behavioural change superficially. Scholars also do not place much emphasis on discussing the process that leads to the change of such strategy and behaviour. This causes the discussion on the rationale of China's behaviour to be detached from a theoretical framework and placed merely at the level of strategic behaviour.

1.3 The Contributions

This research is meant to fill the gap in the literature surrounding China's behaviour in the SCS. From the author's observation, there are at least three contributions that this research is attempting to make.

1.3.1 Contribution 1: Theoretical Analysis

This research comprises a theoretical analysis of defensive realism which differentiates the nature of assertive behaviours, whether they are offensively or defensively realist. A solid theoretical framework in this research provides guidance on the nature of each behaviour as to whether it is a defection, potential defection, or merely an assertive behaviour; and determines the significance of the behaviour in relation to the situation in the SCS. In addition, this research also discusses the process and the dynamic of the security dilemma between China vis-à-vis other claimants and China vis-à-vis the US.

1.3.2 Contribution 2: Systematic Explanation

Most of the literature of China's behaviour in the SCS does not agree on any particular event that signifies China's departure from its earlier behaviour, due to a lack of systematic explanation. Researchers do not differentiate between action and reaction (by China and other claimants) treating all actions as if these have the same significance. They do not differentiate the stages of the SCS tension's development and the process that led to the raising of this tension.

This research offers a systematic framework to perceive China's behaviour in the SCS and to elaborate its development and rationale. The framework is also important to explain the development that may lead to defection or the changing of the status quo.

The research makes a clear distinction between the actors involved in the SCS. In a nutshell, China, other Southeast Asian claimant states (especially the Philippines and Vietnam) and the US are the primary actors in the SCS. However, a distinction should be made between Chinese behaviour towards other claimant states and towards the US. The US is not a claimant state and its involvement in the SCS has motives other than territorial disputes or maritime rights. The rival claimant states and the great power are perceived differently by China and have disparate capabilities. This differentiation should be kept in mind when examining China's SCS behaviour.

1.4 Research Questions

Solid research design begins with good and meaningful research questions. This introductory chapter defines such questions as those which have a sound basis theoretically. As demonstrated in Sect. 1.1, the shift in

China's SCS behaviour from accommodating to assertive in the first decade of the twenty-first century has prompted some questions regarding the specific event which signals China's shift in behaviour. However, its theoretical framework guides this research to inquire for more substantial and meaningful questions.

In the context of the SCS, China and other SCS claimant states do not have an agreed dispute resolution mechanism. Any move to assert one's perceived territory or rights is seen as a violation of others' rights—which contributes to the escalation of tension. In other words, the escalation of the tension is inevitable, it will happen anyway sooner or later. Furthermore, this leads to a seemingly never-ending spiral of action and reaction in asserting claims.

As discussed further in Chap. 2, a security dilemma develops through some stages, from dormant to activated and then spiralling. An acute security dilemma could lead to a defection—which means one or all parties involved defect from a defensive realist code and start adopting offensive realist measures. Defection is when one of the parties involved changes the status quo in its favour. Therefore, finding a point of defection is more relevant than finding the specific event that escalates the tension.

This research is aimed at finding if China has defected in the SCS and if so, what event signifies the point of defection. This question is meaningful because first it will test whether China is a peaceful rising power as claimed by Beijing. Theoretically, it will determine if China is a defensive realist state as posited by Chinese scholars like Tang Shiping. Second, it will explore how far China—the rising power in the region—could act at the expense of different stakeholders in the region, that is, rival claimants and an external power like the US. Third, it will demonstrate the explanatory power and the relevance of defensive realism in international relations. In sum, the research is conducted to answer the following questions:

1. Is the nature of China's SCS behaviour changing/defecting from defensive realist to offensive realist?
2. If so, how the behaviour develops to defection?
3. What is the rationale for the defection?
4. What are the limitations of China's behaviour in the SCS for the foreseeable future?

1.5 The Structure of the Book

This research is about China's behaviour in the SCS and consists of nine chapters. Chapter 1 begins with an introduction to the research and presents the main research questions. Chapter 2 discusses the concept of the security dilemma, presenting a rigorous definition of the concept according to its original meaning so that it may help to answer the research questions convincingly. It attempts to clear the theoretical underbrush of security dilemma as the core logic of defensive realist theory and explains that the application of the concept of security dilemma should meet some conditions.

Chapter 3 reviews some historical evidence, examining if China can be viewed as an expansionist state as its economy and power have grown enormously in the last decades, and also its interests. It is concluded that China's interests in the SCS are primarily non-expansionist.

These growing interests fuel China's anxiety and insecurity, as explained in Chap. 4. Furthermore, this chapter discusses China's SCS interests from different perspectives such as resources, security, geopolitics, Taiwan issue, and the legitimacy of the Chinese Communist Party (CCP). The mounting evidence shows that China's interests in the SCS are primarily defensive.

Having cleared the doubt that China does not harbour expansionist motives in the SCS, this research continues to explore whether the country performs any defensive realist qualities in the region, which is discussed in Chap. 5. This chapter provides evidence to suggest that even though China performs some defensive realist qualities in the period of de-escalation, it also defects from a defensive realist code, especially in its recent behaviours: the seizure of the Scarborough Shoal in 2012 and the resulting blockade of access to Philippine fishermen, and secondly the massive building of artificial islands in 2014–2015.

In brief, from Chaps. 3, 4, and 5, this research focuses on explaining China's SCS behaviour shifting from a defensive realist position to an offensive realist one. The research then elaborates on the formation of the two security dilemmas in the SCS. Chapter 6 describes the security dilemma between China and other claimant states, particularly Vietnam and the Philippines. Chapter 7 outlines the security dilemma between China and the US. Chapter 8 concludes the major findings of the research.

Notes

1. Ralf Emmers, "The De-escalation of the Spratly Dispute in Sino-Southeast Asian Relations," in *Security and International Politics in the South China Sea: Towards a Cooperative Management Regime*, ed. W. S. G. Bateman and Ralf Emmers (New York: Routledge, 2009).
2. Erik Beukel, *China and the South China Sea: Two Faces of Power in the Rising China's Neighborhood Policy* (DIIS Working Paper, 2010), 13.
3. Ibid., 14.
4. "NIDS China Security Report 2011" (Tokyo: The National Institute for Defense Studies, 2012).
5. Bonnie S. Glaser, "Tensions Flare in the South China Sea," Online paper. *Center for Strategic and International Studies*, 30 June 2011.
6. Jian Zhang, "China's Growing Assertiveness in the South China Sea: A Strategic Shift?," in *The South China Sea and Australia Regional Security Environment*, 5 September 2013 (Canberra: National Security College, Australian National University, 2013), 19.
7. Clive H. Schofield and Ian Storey, *The South China Sea Dispute: Increasing Stakes and Rising Tensions* (Jamestown Foundation, 2009), 24.
8. Tessa Jamandre, "Brunei Snubs ASEAN Spratly Claimant's Meeting to Forge One Stand on China," *VERA Files*, 4 March 2014, http://verafiles.org/brunei-snubs-asean-spratlys-claimants-meeting-to-forge-one-stand-on-china/ (accessed 5 May 2014).
9. US Department of State, "Remarks at Press Availability," 23 July 2010, Hanoi, http://www.state.gov/secretary/20092013clinton/rm/2010/07/145095.htm (accessed 8 July 2016).
10. Jeffrey A. Bader, "The US and China's Nine-Dash Line: Ending the Ambiguity," The Brookings Institute, http://www.brookings.edu/research/opinions/2014/02/06-us-china-nine-dash-line-bader (accessed 11 November 2016).
11. Timothy Glogan, "China's' Assertive' South China Sea Policy and Rhetoric: Proactive, Reactive or Myth?," (2011).
12. Carlyle A. Thayer, "The United States, China and Southeast Asia," *Southeast Asian Affairs*, 2011, no. 1 (2011): 16–25.
13. Truong Thuy Tran, "Recent Development in the South China Sea: Implications for Regional Security and Cooperation," in *Maritime Security in the South China Sea* (Washington, DC: Center for Strategic and International Studies, 2011).
14. Peter Dutton, "Three Disputes and Three Objectives: China and the South China Sea," *Naval War College Review*, 64, no. 4 (2011): 42.
15. Glaser, "Tensions Flare in the South China Sea."

16. Schofield and Storey, *The South China Sea Dispute: Increasing Stakes and Rising Tensions.*
17. Tridib Chakraborti, "China and Vietnam in the South China Sea Dispute: A Creeping 'Conflict–Peace–Trepidation' Syndrome," *China Report*, 48, no. 3 (2012): 283–301.
18. M. Taylor Fravel, "China's Strategy in the South China Sea," *Contemporary Southeast Asia*, 33, no. 3 (2011): 292; "Maritime Security in the South China Sea and the Competition over Maritime Rights," in *Cooperation from Strength: The United States, China and the South China Sea*, ed. Patrick M. Cronin (Center for a New American Security, 2012).
19. A. I. Johnston, "How New and Assertive is China's New Assertiveness?," *International Security*, 37, no. 4 (2013): 7–48.
20. Michael Yahuda, "China's New Assertiveness in the South China Sea," *Journal of Contemporary China*, 22, no. 81 (2013): 446–59.
21. Sarah Raine, "Beijing's South China Sea Debate," *Survival*, 53, no. 5 (2011): 69–88.
22. Koon Heng Pek, "The "ASEAN Way" and Regional Security Cooperation in the South China Sea," in *EUI Working Paper RSCAS 2014/121* (European University Institute, 2014).
23. Thomas J. Christensen, "Advantages of an Assertive China-Responding to Beijing's Abrasive Diplomacy," *Foreign Affairs*, 90 (2011): 54.
24. Zhang, "China's Growing Assertiveness in the South China Sea: A Strategic Shift?".
25. Irene Chan and Mingjiang Li, "New Chinese Leadership, New Policy in the South China Sea Dispute?," *Journal of Chinese Political Science*, (2015): 1–16.
26. Edward Wong, "Chinese Military Seeks to Extend Its Naval Power," *New York Times*, 23 (2010).
27. Greg Sheridan, "China Actions Meant as Test, Hillary Clinton Says," *The Australian*, 9 November 2010, http://www.theaustralian.com.au/national-affairs/china-actions-meant-as-test-hillary-clinton-says/story-fn59niix-1225949666285 (accessed 6 May 2015).
28. Michael D. Swaine, "China's Assertive Behavior—Part One: On 'Core Interests'," *China Leadership Monitor*, no. 34 (2011).
29. Foreign Ministry of the People's Republic of China, *Foreign Ministry Spokesperson Jiang Yu's Regular Press Conference on 21 September 2010*, http://www.fmprc.gov.cn/eng//xwfw/s2510/2511/t756092.htm (accessed 15 August 2016).
30. "China's Assertive Behavior—Part One: On 'Core Interests'".
31. Michael D. Swaine and M. Taylor Fravel, "China's Assertive Behavior—Part Two: The Maritime Periphery," Ibid., no. 35.
32. Ibid.

33. June Teufel Dreyer, "Sansha: New City in the South China Sea," in *China Brief XII:16* (The Jamestown Foundation, 2012).
34. Zhang, "China's Growing Assertiveness in the South China Sea: A Strategic Shift?," 23.
35. Michael Martina and Ben Blanchard, "China Says Vietnam Claim to Islands 'Null and Void'," *Reuters*, 21 June 2012, http://www.reuters.com/article/2012/06/21/us-china-vietnam-sea-idUSBRE85K0EM20120621 (accessed 5 May 2016).
36. Fravel, "China's Strategy in the South China Sea," 292.
37. Yuli Yang, "Pentagon Says Chinese Vessels Harassed US Ship," *CNN* (9 March 2009), http://edition.cnn.com/2009/POLITICS/03/09/us.navy.china/index.html?_s=PM:POLITICS.
38. B. Jerden, "The Assertive China Narrative: Why It Is Wrong and How So Many Still Bought into It," *Chinese Journal of International Politics*, 7, no. 1 (2014): 47–88.
39. Bernard D. Cole, "Beijing's Strategy of Sea Denial," in *China Brief*, 6, no. 23 (The Jamestown, 2006).
40. Ibid.
41. For more comprehensive explanation with regard to this different interpretation, see Ronald O'Rourke, "Maritime Territorial and Exclusive Economic Zone (EEZ) Disputes Involving China: Issues for Congress" (2012).
42. Jerden, "The Assertive China Narrative: Why It Is Wrong and How So Many Still Bought into It," 47–88.
43. Swaine and Fravel, "China's Assertive Behavior—Part Two: The Maritime Periphery."
44. Ibid.
45. Ibid., 3.
46. Ibid., 4.
47. Jerden, "The Assertive China Narrative: Why It Is Wrong and How So Many Still Bought into It," 47–88.
48. Swaine and Fravel, "China's Assertive Behavior—Part Two: The Maritime Periphery"; Timothy Glogan, "China's 'Assertive' South China Sea Policy and Rhetoric: Proactive, Reactive Or Myth?," (2011): 73.
49. Yahuda, "China's New Assertiveness in the South China Sea," 446–59.
50. Glogan, "China's' Assertive' South China Sea Policy and Rhetoric: Proactive, Reactive or Myth?".
51. Ibid., 63.
52. Ibid., 73.
53. Johnston, "How New and Assertive Is China's New Assertiveness?," 7–48.
54. Ibid., 38.

55. Dutton, "Three Disputes and Three Objectives: China and the South China Sea," 42.
56. Ibid.
57. Valencia, Mark J., Jon M. Van Dyke, and Noel A. Ludwig. *Sharing the Resources of the South China Sea*, Vol. 31 (Cambridge, MA: M. Nijhoff Publishers, 1997), 87 quoted in Ibid., 56.
58. Ibid.
59. Ibid.
60. Ibid., 57.
61. Swaine and Fravel, "China's Assertive Behavior—Part Two: The Maritime Periphery."
62. Ibid., 7.
63. Ibid.
64. Ibid.
65. Ibid.
66. Emmers, "The De-escalation of the Spratly Dispute in Sino-Southeast Asian Relations."
67. Ibid., 134–38.
68. Sheldon W. Simon, "ASEAN Regional Forum," in *Asian Security Handbook: An Assessment of Political Security Issues in the Asia Pacific Region*, ed. William M. Carpenter and David G. Wiencek (New York: M.E. Sharpe, 1996), 47 quoted in Ibid., 131.
69. Ibid., 138.
70. 吴士存, "海域争端与海洋行政管理改革—南海问题面临的挑战与应对思考," *行政管理改革* [Wu Shicun, "Maritime Dispute and the Reformation of Maritime Administrative Control: Some Thoughts to Cope with the South China Sea Issue," *Xingzheng Guanli Gaige*], no. 7 (2012): 14–19.
71. Ibid., 18.
72. 褚浩, "南海问题的新形势与新发展," *国际资料信息* [Chu Hao, "The New Situation and Development of the South China Sea Issue," *Guoji Ziliao Xinxi*], 6, no. 12 (2010).
73. Ibid., 吴士存, "海域争端与海洋行政管理改革——南海问题面临的挑战与应对思考," [Wu Shicun, "Maritime Dispute and the Reformation of Maritime Administrative Control: Some Thoughts to Cope with the South China Sea Issue," *Xingzheng Guanli Gaige*], 14–19.

CHAPTER 2

Theoretical Framework: Security Dilemma Reconsidered

One of the most important concepts in international relations (IR) is that of the security dilemma. In fact, the security dilemma is the core logic of defensive realist theory.[1] A defensive realist state is one which recognises the existence of a security dilemma as a feature of anarchy.[2] Many scholarly works have been devoted to clarifying the concept of the security dilemma; however, there is no consensus on its definition and application in international politics. Some scholars argue that the confusion and ambiguity surrounding the concept is due to a lack of definitional rigour.[3] This chapter aims to enrich this debate by providing a rigorous definition and offering new ideas on the origins of the concept by discussing the concepts of spiral, deterrence, and defection.

2.1 Security Dilemma: The Concept

The idea of a security dilemma finds its foundation in the work of British historian Herbert Butterfield:

> The greatest war in history could be produced without the intervention of any great criminals who might be out to do deliberate harm in the world. It could be produced between two powers both of which were desperately anxious to avoid a conflict of any sort.[4]

Even though Butterfield did not mention the term "security dilemma" in his writings, his idea of a potential for conflict laid the foundation for

K. H. Raditio, *Understanding China's Behaviour in the South China Sea*, https://doi.org/10.1007/978-981-13-1283-0_2

the concept of security dilemma in international relations. John Herz coined the term "security dilemma" and elaborated as follows:

> Groups and individuals living in such a constellation [anarchic society] must be and usually are, concerned about their security from being attacked, subjected, dominated, or annihilated by other groups and individuals. Striving to attain security from such attack, they are driven to acquire more and more power in order to escape the impact of the power of others. This, in turn, renders the others more insecure and compels them to prepare for the worst. Since none can ever be entirely secure in such a world of competing units, power competition ensues, and the vicious circle of security and power accumulation is on.[5]

Butterfield revealed the potential for conflict in the absence of harmful or criminal intention; Herz described the security dilemma as a process which is rooted in fear in an anarchic society. From Herz's description, we can derive that the main elements of a security dilemma involve anarchy, fear, power competition, and a vicious circle. Inadvertency and tragic consequences, as mentioned by Butterfield, are also highlighted in the attempt to define the concept since security dilemma applies only between non-expansionist states where no one intends to harm others' interests or becoming aggressive.[6]

Other notable scholars have also offered their definitions of the security dilemma. Jervis explains that "the security dilemma exists when many of the means by which a state tries to increase its security decrease the security of others".[7] By saying this, Jervis emphasises the zero-sum nature of the anarchic society. Other scholars put the emphasis on the paradoxical or self-defeating nature of an attempt to improve security, which appears to end up threatening others and eventually weakens one's own security or even causes conflict.[8]

In particular, Booth and Wheeler warn readers not to be confused between "paradox" and "dilemma".[9] They criticise definitions of the security dilemma that distort the concept by recasting it as a "security paradox". They claim that their definition of a security dilemma is derived from Butterfield and Herz whom they acknowledge as the "pioneer theorists" of the concept. Booth and Wheeler write:

> The security dilemma is a two-level strategic predicament in relations between states and other actors, with each level consisting of two related lemmas (or propositions that can be assumed to be valid) which force

> decision-makers to choose between them. The first and basic level consists of a dilemma of interpretation about the motives, intentions and capabilities of others; the second and derivative level consists of a dilemma of response about the most rational way of responding.[10]

By this definition, Booth and Wheeler indeed highlight the nature of the concept. Here, there is a sense of overemphasising the "dilemma" from a strategic perspective. Another study considered helpful in explaining the security dilemma was conducted by Tang Shiping. Building on the work by Butterfield, Hertz, and Jervis, he proposed the "BHJ Formula" in clearing the theoretical underbrush of the security dilemma. Tang describes the concept as follows:

> Under a condition of anarchy, two states are defensive realist states. The two states however cannot be sure of each other's present and future intentions (because they live under anarchy). As a result, each tends to fear that the other may be or may become a predator. Because both believe that power is a means toward security, both seek to accumulate more and more power. Because even purely defensive capability will inevitably contain some offensive capability, many of the measures adopted by one side for its own security can often threaten, or be perceived as threatening, the security of the other side, even if both sides merely want to defend their security. Consequently, the other side is likely to take countermeasures against those defensive measures. The interaction of these measures and countermeasures tends to reinforce their fears and uncertainties about each other's intentions, leading to a vicious cycle in which each accumulates more power without necessarily making itself more secure, through a self-reinforcing or positive feedback mechanism. This vicious cycle can also lead to unnecessary conflicts—threats of war or war. The severity of the security dilemma can be regulated by both material factors and psychological factors.[11]

Here, Tang puts the security dilemma in the context of structural or defensive realism, explicitly indicating three main and necessary elements: anarchy, defensive realist states, and a power contest.[12] Tang includes anarchy in his definition of security dilemma because he believes in the evolutionary nature of international society.[13] This corresponds to Barry Buzan's interpretation of the anarchic nature of the international system, where he differentiates between "immature" and "mature" anarchy.[14] However, identifying anarchy as one of the constitutive elements of the security dilemma is redundant, since the theory of structural realism assumes that states always operate in a constant state of anarchy.

2.2 The Root of the Security Dilemma

Butterfield's idea that war can occur from anxiety between states in the absence of any criminal motive laid the foundation for the concept of the security dilemma. According to Butterfield, this predicament results from "Hobbesian fear", which finds its root in the "universal sin of humanity".[15] This corresponds to Morgenthau's idea about international relations which attributes the dynamic between nations to human aggression. Morgenthau holds that international relations are a matter of struggle for security where nations are motivated by a lust for power and their options are to conquer or be conquered. These views were closely aligned to those of Niebuhr, a major American theologian and political thinker in the mid-twentieth century. Niebuhr contended that a human is always tempted to establish her/his own security, yet hiding behind the will-to-live is the sinful will-to-power.[16] This is the source of injustice that humans often ignore. Furthermore, Niebuhr attributes humans' ignorance of understanding the root of the vicious dynamic in international politics to the failure to understand the Christian doctrine of original sin. He explains original sin as a condition where a human is helpless to liberate him/herself from the vicious circle of sin regardless of whether s/he recognises it or not.[17]

The explanation of the root of international relations—which is attributed to human sin by Butterfield, Morgenthau, and Niebuhr—is derived from the Reformed Tradition. According to the Reformed Tradition, all human beings have fallen to wickedness due to original sin. This is explained through the concept of "total depravity". The concept teaches that a human has inherent vileness and innate hostility towards anything good and spiritual.[18] The argument continues that ever since the beginnings of his very existence, the human being is not morally neutral but evil, and preoccupied with anything vicious, such as a desire for conquest, a tendency towards violence, selfishness, and lack of any benevolent motivation or ability to do good.

The "human sin" explanation of the root of struggle for security, especially if applied to the security dilemma—as done by Butterfield—is challenged by Tang. He questions whether everyone suffers from the effects of human sin, as if programmed to exploit others, and argues that if that were the case, then there would be no real uncertainty because everyone would be basically malign.[19] In particular, Tang challenges Butterfield's concept of the security dilemma as something inadvertent and with tragic consequences due to the proposition that every human being was afflicted by human sin. Tang contends that the confusion concerning the root of the security dilemma is resolved by Herz and Jervis when they attributed it to the social aspect of international politics, that is, anarchy. Herz stated:

> Whether man is by nature peaceful and co-operative, or aggressive and domineering, is not the question.... It is his uncertainty and anxiety as to his neighbours' intentions that places man in this basic [security] dilemma, and makes the 'homo homini lupus' a primary fact of the social life of man. Basically it is the mere instinct of self-preservation which, in the vicious circle leads to competition for ever more power.[20]

Herz's explanation of the root of the security dilemma as demonstrated above is not merely social. The "instinct of self-preservation"—which he claims as the foundation of social life—is by itself an anthropological problem. Therefore, this chapter contends that anarchy as social structure is not sufficient to explain the root of the security dilemma.

The question posited by Tang with regard to Butterfield's explanation of the root of the security dilemma is valid. It is inconsistent to apply the idea of the universal sin of humanity to explain the security dilemma, a dilemma which incorporates uncertainty. The idea of the universal sin of humanity seems more coherent to explain offensive realism which advocates that a state can guarantee its security by accumulating the maximum possible, even if it has to harm other states.

However, ruling out the human factor and merely applying anarchy in explaining the root of the security dilemma—as suggested by Tang—seems insufficient to explain this root. There are two reasons for this: first, the failure of a particular theological concept, that is, taking into account original sin/total depravity in explaining the root of the security dilemma is not a reason to ignore human factors, given that uncertainty and fear are major elements of the security dilemma. Second, the security dilemma does not apply only to states but also to different ethnic groups which sometimes are not operating in an anarchical society.[21] The security dilemma itself is a concept which is much discussed in a non-anarchical IR tradition, such as constructivism.

In contrast to the doctrine of total depravity—where original sin is believed to radically pervert humans and strip their freedom—the Council of Trent (1546) taught that original sin is a "deprivation of original holiness and justice, but human nature has not been totally corrupted; it is wounded in the natural powers proper to it… and inclined to sin".[22] Furthermore, Thomas Aquinas taught that original sin is a state of loss of original justice and does not in itself lead humans to evil or induce them to sin in any active way. Aquinas defined original justice as a state when a human is able to realise her/his spiritual being and maintain a relationship with God, therefore, s/he does not become a subject of human disorder and frailty.[23] Original sin, according to Aquinas, causes a lack of original justice and an inclination towards disorderly behaviour, which can be called concupiscence.[24]

Therefore, we can say that the fear caused by uncertainty of others' intentions is a result of every person's inclination towards malign intention, although by one' free will, one can choose not to give into such an inclination. This explanation answers Tang's objection to Butterfield's attribution of human factor in causing the security dilemma and to Hobbesian fear of the "universal sin of humanity". Due to the universal sin of humanity or to original sin, humans are inclined to evil but they are not programmed or induced to give in to it. Butterfield is correct to attribute the Hobbesian fear to the "universal sin of humanity", yet the elaboration of the "universal sin of humanity" cannot refer to the doctrine of total depravity. Uncertainty is pervasive as nobody knows for sure how humans will respond to his inclination to disorder. To conclude, original sin—which leads to concupiscence not total depravity—is the root of uncertainty, human fear, and all problems in struggle for security including the security dilemma.

2.3 Security Dilemma: The Constitutive Elements

To have a rigorous definition of the security dilemma, what one needs to do is accurately indicate the constitutive elements of the concept. This chapter argues that uncertainty, lack of malign intention, and self-defeating policies are the key elements of the security dilemma. These elements must exist for the security dilemma to apply.

In the international sphere, where there is no single authority above states, no state can guarantee its own survival. Uncertainty has been prevalent among nations throughout the ages because no state can perfectly know the intention of other states, particularly with regard to the accumulation of power. There is no assurance that the accumulation of power is expansionist in motivation or merely motivated defensively. This is well described in term the "known unknown" as opposed to the Donald

Rumsfeld's "unknown known".[25] The uncertainty is what differentiates defensive realism from its cousin, offensive realism.

Offensive realism—derived from the same context of anarchy—assumes that strong states do what they have to do and the weak accept what they have to accept. For offensive realists, war is the fate of every nation, because they will accumulate power to improve their security and, by so doing, generate fear. Thucydides described this as follows: "It was the rise of Athens and the fear that this inspired in Sparta that made war inevitable." Uncertainty about other states' intention does not play a significant role in the logic of offensive realism.[26]

This idea of the inevitability of war and the prevalence of expansionist ambition is rather out of date, although these phenomena still exist in contemporary international politics. Bluth even contends that as the Cold War has concluded, most states are living in relatively peaceful circumstances and no longer fear being conquered or attacked by other states.[27]

In reality, although war is not as threatening as in the past, some states are still facing challenges with regard to their survival. While states in North America and Western Europe are facing no threat with regard to survival or territorial integrity, we cannot deny that the Ukraine, Japan, China, and littoral states in the South China Sea (SCS) are facing a serious problem in relation to their territorial integrity. China even declared territorial integrity to be its core interest.[28]

Tang explains international politics as "social evolution" from a position of offensive realism to defensive realism, where contemporary international relations can be interpreted more convincingly by using a defensive realist perspective.[29] Therefore, uncertainty, as one of the main tenets of defensive realism, prepares the ground for the application of the security dilemma.

In many definitions of the security dilemma, the lack of malign intention is clearly mentioned.[30] Tang even contends that the lack of malign intention is the most crucial constitutive element of the security dilemma and cannot be replaced with other criteria.[31] Malign intention refers to offensive motives which aim to attain security by deliberately harming others.[32] This could be manifested in expansionist or hegemonic ambition. Mearsheimer describes the offensive motive as an ambition to "establish hegemony in their region of the world while ensuring that no rival great power dominates another area".[33] Lack of malign intention is considered an essential element of the security dilemma, but this is problematic since no state can ever be sure about other states' intentions. Lack of malign intention as a constitutive element of the security dilemma seems inconsistent with another posited element, that is, uncertainty.

However, here, lack of malign intention refers to the original motive of the states involved. It is possible that due to some regulators (technology or psychology), state(s) can adopt an offensive posture and start becoming malign and/or expansionist. But, for the security dilemma to apply, one should be able to assess the initial motive of every state. In other words, one should be sure that the states involved in the security dilemma are originally defensive realist.

Paradoxical or self-defeating policy is another prerequisite for the security dilemma. This means that an attempt made by a state (especially in defence) does not put it in an advantageous position vis-à-vis other state(s), but causes it to be less secure instead.[34] Glaser explains how paradoxical policy occurs under three conditions: first, a state's accumulation of power will provoke its adversary to offset or even surpass this attempt and the net effect would be a reduction in the state's security; second, a state's military build-up causes its adversary to be less secure and this condition increases the value the adversary places on expansion—since this measure may increase security—and by so doing invites a greater threat to itself; third, an arms build-up simply wastes a state's limited resources.[35]

These three elements (uncertainty, lack of malign intention, and paradoxical policy) together constitute the necessary conditions in which the security dilemma has been theoretically argued to apply. Therefore, the security dilemma can be defined as a situation where states are uncertain of each other's motivation in their attempt to improve security—although it is for defensive purpose—which leads to self-defeating behaviour.

2.4 The Actors within the Security Dilemma

The security dilemma occurs only between those states with a lack of malign intention. However, the literature has been quite confused regarding the labelling of states with the absence of such an intention. Some have referred to status quo states as the antithesis of revisionist states[36] or predatory states[37]; some have called them genuine security seekers vis-à-vis relative power seekers[38]; and some have labelled states which are not greedy or security-seeking states as the antithesis of greedy states.[39] Those labels are sometimes also used interchangeably.

The security dilemma can only operate if the states involved are defensive realist states and not a single one is an offensive realist state. It goes without saying that defensive realist states are the states whose behaviour is guided by defensive realism. Contrary to offensive realist states, defensive realist states pursue strategies of deterrence, reassurance, and cooperation. Tang defines a defensive realist state by proscribing three criteria. First, a defensive realist state is one which acknowledges the pervasiveness of balancing behaviour and the security dilemma. Second, a defensive realist state accepts the constraints from itself or an external actor.[40] Above all, a defensive realist state does not pursue security by harming others' interest deliberately, let alone harbour an expansionist ambition.[41]

Furthermore, offensive realism suggests that security is scarce, because resources are scarce.[42] According to this assumption, when states struggle for scarce security, the most reasonable behaviour for a state to ensure its survival is to be offensive. Those who are offensive will gain the lion's share of the scarce resources and survive in the system. Based on this premise, offensive realism assumes that conflict is inevitable, because states have to seek access to resources and this could mean expansion or hegemonic behaviour.[43] In other words, the gain of one state is a loss for another and the zero-sum is the rule of the game.

Whilst acknowledging the anarchic nature of the international system, defensive realism suggests that resources are manageable for all states and conflict is avoidable. Currently, states exist in an environment where expansion is no longer easy. States are constrained by international laws, norms, and long-term interests. Those who appear to be aggressors are most likely to confront a balancing coalition that eventually decreases rather than increases their chance of survival.[44] Technology and markets also make resources more accessible and resource scarcity is no longer an excuse for expansionism.

Regarding the power–security relationship, offensive realism holds that power maximisation is necessary to enjoy security. It follows then that the more power a state accumulates, the more secure it is. According to this premise, greater military power will provide more security to a state; and if a state wins the arms race, it will rise as a hegemon in the system, which eventually guarantees its survival.[45]

However, defensive realism contends that power maximisation can be a "risky business" since more power does not necessarily mean more security.[46] Having either limited or excessive power propels insecurity, since the former attracts conquest and the latter provokes a balancing act from other states.[47] The goal of states therefore according to this outlook is not power but security and the maintenance of states' position in the system;

therefore, states should have an "appropriate amount" of power in order to achieve their goals.[48]

In a situation of security dilemma, defensive realist states are preoccupied with the uncertainty of others' intention. This sense of fear and anxiety is exacerbated by other states' accumulation of power—even though this may be for defensive purposes. This fear and uncertainty exist because most defensive realist states behave from the perspective that other states see themselves as defensively motivated; therefore, any hostile behaviour will be interpreted as offensive.[49]

Defensive realist states assume that states should pursue an appropriate amount of power.[50] It has been seen that the accumulation of power can be a "risky business" since more power does not necessarily support national security.[51] However, it is difficult to reach a certain level of appropriateness in power accumulation. First, let us consider the amount of spending for military purposes. For instance, which one is more appropriate: China, which increases its military spending by double digit increments almost annually, or the US, which spends about four times as much (according to the official exchange rate)? How does one compare Singapore and Malaysia which spend 3.3 and 1.5% of their respective GDPs on defence,[52] although Singapore has a smaller population and territory? These questions are difficult to answer and become the source of fear and uncertainty among states. Second, it is difficult to distinguish offensive weapons from defensive ones. This makes a state uncertain about another state's intention. If there were a straightforward way to distinguish offensive weapons from defensive ones, uncertainty could be reduced significantly.[53]

The case is entirely different with offensive realist states. There is no uncertainty for offensive realist states, since states will harm other states' interest if they have the capability to do so and the only means to enhance a state's security is by pursuing as much power as possible. Offensive realist states always attempt to undermine others' security and leave no room for uncertainty. This is why the security dilemma cannot operate if one or more states harbour malign intentions. For example, many think that the Cuban missile crisis in 1962 presented a security dilemma. But since Nikita Khrushchev intended to install missiles in Cuba with the purpose of putting pressure on the US in West Berlin, the USSR harboured offensive motives against the US, and so this was not a security dilemma.[54] A state's original intention becomes the litmus test for deciding whether a situation presents a security dilemma.

Having said this, to label a state as defensive realist or offensive realist does not mean the state cannot change its behaviour. A defensive realist state can change to become an offensive realist state and vice versa.[55] China under Mao Zedong was an offensive realist state but started to evolve into a defensive realist state when Deng Xiaoping assumed office.[56] Even, China cannot be perceived solely as either a defensive realist or offensive realist state. In facing the US and other potential great powers in the region, that is, India and Japan, China's behaviour bears a resemblance to that of offensive realism, while on the other hand its attitude towards its Southeast Asian neighbours is best explained by defensive realism[57] (Table 2.1).

In other words, to establish whether a situation represents a security dilemma, one needs to gauge the state's intention on a particular issue in a given period. Unfortunately, this is not an easy task, as history has demonstrated that the necessary information about a given state's intention can only be obtained after decades; for example, information about the USSR's intentions during the Cold War could only be obtained after the collapse of the country.[58]

2.5 Security Dilemma, Spiral, and Deterrence

Another important way to clarify the concept of the security dilemma is by differentiating it from other related concepts, that is, the spiral model and the concept of deterrence. This is urgent because the terms—

Table 2.1 Offensive and defensive realist states in brief

	Offensive realist state	*Defensive realist state*
International system	Anarchy	Anarchy
The primary goal	Security	Security
View on security	Security is scarce because resources are scarce	Security is not scarce and resources are manageable
Strategy to achieve security	Power maximisation	Accumulating an appropriate amount of power
The best position in the system	Hegemon	Appropriate position, self-content
View on expansion	Beneficial	Counterproductive
View on war	Likely	Avoidable
View on other states' intention and behaviour	All states are offensive realist states	Uncertain, they could be offensive or defensive

"security dilemma" and "spiral model"—are often used as if they were interchangeable.

The spiral model explains how states—driven by their fear and uncertainty of other states' intentions—become involved in a seemingly endless action-reaction dynamic of power competition.[59] The relationship between the security dilemma and the spiral model is sequential, that is, the spiral model can be seen as the continuum of the security dilemma.[60]

The security dilemma becomes a spiral model when regulators (psychological and material) begin to operate. A psychological regulator—generally manifested as incorrect judgement or misperception—regulates the severity of the security dilemma. But it can neither create the security dilemma nor is it required for the maintenance of the security dilemma.[61] A material regulator, according to Jervis, consists of four elements: geography, polarity, military technology, and the ability to distinguish between defensive and offensive weapons. Tang adds another three elements: foreign allies (third parties), unbalanced power, and distribution of ethnic groups. In correspondence with a psychological regulator, material regulators do not play an indispensable role in the security dilemma—they only regulate its severity.

Regarding the spiral model, Kydd argues that the model envisioned by Jervis and Butterfield—where the states involved lack malign intention—is a "tragic spiral" because it arises out of a misperception.[62] Kydd calls a spiral model in which at least one side is malign "non-tragic", because the fear is at least justifiable and conflict would have been unavoidable. Furthermore, Kydd argues that a tragic spiral is less likely since the states will eventually get access to accurate information and are able to judge the situation correctly. Basically, Kydd's non-tragic spiral is the equivalent of a deterrence model and the tragic spiral is the equivalent of a Jervisian spiral.

Kydd differentiates between two categories of spiral model, tragic and non-tragic, because according to the Bayesian realism that he develops, "convergence on correct beliefs is more likely than convergence on incorrect beliefs".[63] The researcher further argues that although the learning process is tortuous and misjudgements may arise, eventually time will reveal everything when the real motives and intentions of other states will become known to all parties. Furthermore, Kydd believes that since conflict is more likely to arise due to an expansionist or untrustworthy motive by at least one party involved, it is less likely that conflict arises between defensive realist states. In other words, the non-tragic spiral model is less likely to occur and lead to conflict. Here, Kydd's understanding of the spiral model diverges from Jervis' model and undermines the role of misperception as psychological regulator in exacerbating the security dilemma.

Tang sees the spiral model as a continuum of the security dilemma, describing the model as "a process of progressive deterioration or simply a situation that gets worse and worse"—a definition that is derived from the *American Heritage Dictionary*. Tang contends that the spiral model is universal whereas the security dilemma is conditional, the purported reason being the lack of malign intention between the states involved. However, Tang's definition of the spiral model allows for it to occur between states without the absence of malign intention, which shows flawed logic. Jervis and other scholars, on the other hand, contend that the spiral model occurs between defensive realist states or in the absence of malign intention.[64] Therefore, the spiral as well as the security dilemma is not universal but conditional.

Tang explains the relationship between the security dilemma and the spiral model as a reversible continuum. Contrary to the mainstream understanding of the spiral model, Tang mistakenly asserts that the spiral model begins to operate when one or more states begin to have a malign intention.[65] By so doing, Tang is inconsistent with the Jervisian perspective of the spiral model, and of deterrence, which describes the two concepts as dichotomous. That is to say, the mainstream Jervisian perspective holds that the spiral model occurs only between two defensive realist states, while deterrence applies when one or both states have malign intention. This chapter argues that when one or more states begin to have malign intention, the situation enters into defection, instead of a spiral as Tang suggests.

Furthermore, distinguishing the spiral model from the deterrence model has strategic meaning. In a situation of uncertainty and heightening tension, policy makers are required to make a prudent judgement as to which strategy to adopt. If a situation is judged to represent a spiral, then reassurance will be the main strategy to pursue each other's interest and alleviate tension. On the other hand, if a situation is perceived to represent deterrence, a state has no other option but to deter the other state's expansionist intention. A mistaken judgement may well result in a disastrous outcome.

2.6 Are There Variants of Security Dilemmas?

The security dilemma is not perceived as a uniform concept. In explaining an event in international affairs, scholars tend to make some adjustment to the concept which leads to the development of variants. However, the validity of these variants does not depend on their relevance to a particular issue or their explanatory power but on their consistency with the constitutive elements of the security dilemma, that is, uncertainty, lack of malign intention, and paradoxical policy.

Based on the actors involved, Roe classifies the security dilemma into three categories: tight, regular, and loose security dilemmas.[66] The third grouping basically equates with a security problem or security tension; there is no rigorous definition of the conditions of the states involved. Therefore, the loose security dilemma is irrelevant here and will not be discussed.

According to Roe, the tight security dilemma is Butterfield's and Jervis' version of the security dilemma. It occurs because of an illusory perception of incompatibility by the actors involved in pursuing their own security. The tight security dilemma also incorporates inadvertency, which means states end up with insecurity for unwarranted reasons—a situation that is undesirable by any party. Wheeler and Booth label Roe's tight security dilemma an inadvertent security dilemma.[67]

The second variant of the security dilemma according to Roe is the regular security dilemma. In this security dilemma, the states involved are not greedy according to Roe, a term he borrows from Glaser.[68] Not greedy states, however, are not status quo states because in a certain situation they can be insecure. In the situation of insecurity, a not greedy state can pursue an aggressive and/or expansionist policy to increase its security. In other words, the regular security dilemma operates among not greedy states which have expansionist intentions as their security motive. In the regular security dilemma, the states involved do not necessarily harbour misperceptions, because the incompatibility among them is real, not illusory—at least one of the parties involved has a real expansionist intention.

Wheeler and Booth differentiate between an inadvertent and a deliberate security dilemma. As mentioned above, an inadvertent security dilemma is basically the same as Roe's tight security dilemma. However, Wheeler and Booth categorise the deliberate security dilemma into two types. First, there is a deliberate action they call an "offensive" measure, which is intended to deter other states but not meant to challenge the status quo. The "offensive measure" is adopted merely from a security motive. Second, there is a deliberate action to change the status quo by revisionist states.

Snyder (1984) proposes a typology of security dilemmas.[69] He categorises the concept into system-induced, state-induced, and imperialist security dilemmas.[70] Judging by the label, the imperialist security dilemma is not a security dilemma as identified by Collins and therefore not relevant to the current discussion.

The system-induced security dilemma equates to the traditional security dilemma as defined by Jervis and Herz, and recognises anarchy as the source of uncertainty. In this type of security dilemma, neither of two actors has any intention to be the aggressor and both are interested in maintaining the status quo. The incompatibility of the actors' interest is illusory and misperception is created.

The state-induced security dilemma posits that uncertainty is primarily caused by a hegemon state's need for the other states' acknowledgement. This need leads to the hegemon causing other states' insecurity. However, in the state-induced security dilemma no single state intends to change the prevailing status quo. According to Snyder, the hegemon state, in fact, intends to enhance its position during the status quo and the targets of the hegemon state do not aim to challenge the status quo either.

Collins argues that the state-induced security dilemma is synonymous with Wheeler and Booth's deliberate security dilemma.[71] However, there are some differences between the two. The state-induced security dilemma implies that the initiative that leads to insecurity is taken by a hegemon state, while in the deliberate security dilemma, it is not stated that the actor which takes the initiative is a hegemon or not. In addition, the aim of the hegemon in the state-induced security dilemma is to strengthen its hegemonic position, while the aim of the initiating state in the deliberate security dilemma is deterrence.

However, any attempt to categorise the security dilemma rests on shaky ground as these somehow contradict the foundations of the security dilemma set out above: uncertainty, lack of malign intention, and paradoxical policy. There are some points that need to be made to identify the logical fallacies in the above-mentioned attempts to categorise security dilemmas.

First, there is inconsistency with the principle of lack of malign intention. The security dilemma operates only among states which lack malign intention. Malign intentions could be aggression, invasion, or expansionist ambition, irrespective of the motives. Roe's second type of security dilemma, that is, the regular security dilemma which involves at least one state with expansionist ambition (although it is security motivated), is therefore unfounded as the security dilemma always operates among states with no expansionist ambition.

Some states may interpret their need for security to involve measures which are offensive; that is to say, they may perceive that their security can only be attained by harming another state's security. This interpretation by itself goes against the principle of lack of malign intention and makes the security dilemma irrelevant. It is true that defensive realist states have a certain level of assertiveness. However, to be assertive is not to be offensive and their assertiveness is only for a defensive purpose. Being assertive means being confident in articulating a state's national interest.[72] It is by no means harmful or aggressive.

Second, there is a failure to differentiate between the main constitutive elements and the regulator of misperception. This is clearly perceived in Roe's tight security dilemma and Snyder's system-induced security dilemma. These variants of the security dilemma are differentiated according to the degree of misperception. Misperception can regulate the severity of a security dilemma but it cannot create a security dilemma. However, misperception does not always exist in a security dilemma; that is to say, it is not a constitutive element of the security dilemma. Glaser has demonstrated that a security dilemma can exist without misperception.[73]

To conclude, Snyder's typology of security dilemma is irrelevant. The identification of a security dilemma is based on three principles: uncertainty, lack of malign intention, and paradoxical policy. One cannot drop any of these or include other elements (such as regulators) in the definition.

2.7 Security Dilemma and Conflict of Interest

Tang defines conflict of interest as "divergence between two states' interest—that is, they want different things, or they cannot have the same thing at the same time".[74] In correspondence with the anarchic state of international society, realism contends that international politics is essentially conflictual and that the security dilemma operates under conditions of anarchy. In the anarchic world, international politics is experiencing a social evolution from offensive realism to defensive realism.[75] Yet, according to Tang, the era of offensive realism has gone because the system is "self-destructive".[76] In other words, we have now reached an era of defensive realism where conquest is no longer easy. States are constrained by international law, norms, and long-term interest. Expansion will be regarded as a miscalculation, since those which appear to be aggressors are most likely to face a balancing coalition that eventually will decrease rather increase their chance of survival.[77] Based on this condition, there are two premises that need to be underscored regarding conflict of interest in contemporary international politics.

The first is that in contemporary international relations—in the era of defensive realism—a conflict of interest generally precedes a security dilemma, that is, it does not become an inherent part of it. The era of offensive realism was marked by a struggle for *lebensraum* and a state's only option was to conquer or be conquered. A security dilemma in the offensive realism era could arise between two status quo states which have improved their security defensively yet feel uncertain of one another's intention. In this case, the conflict of interest would be the territorial integrity of these states. Each state fears that its adversaries harbour expansionist ambitions and threaten their territorial sovereignty. This threat against territorial sovereignty becomes a conflict of interest that comes along with the security dilemma.

In the case of contemporary politics, where defensive realism has become the norm, states will not usually pursue their interests by taking other states' territory. However, genuine conflicts of interest—such as territorial, ideological, and trade disputes—are pervasive. This conflict of interest precedes the security dilemma instead of arising along with it. In other words, a conflict of interest stimulates the generation of a security dilemma although it does not necessarily lead to it.

One example of this is the rise of China. As China's military forces become more advanced, some but not all of its neighbours have started to feel uneasy. Countries such as Russia, Myanmar, North Korea, Mongolia, and Pakistan do not feel threatened by China's rise and a security dilemma between China and any one of these countries is unlikely to arise. This is simply because there is no significant conflict of interest between China and any of these countries. However, the situation is different with regard to countries such as India, Japan, Malaysia, South Korea, the Philippines, Vietnam, and especially the US (Table 2.2).

These are the countries with which China has a conflict of interest which precedes, but is not a prerequisite for, a security dilemma between

Table 2.2 Countries with which China has a security dilemma

Country	*Conflict of interest*
India	Regional prominence
Japan	Regional prominence, territorial disputes in East China Sea
Malaysia	Territorial disputes in South China Sea
South Korea	Territorial disputes in East China Sea
Philippines	Territorial disputes in South China Sea
Vietnam	Territorial disputes in South China Sea
US	Regional dominion

China and these countries. A conflict of interest has to be acute and play a significant role in bilateral relations to generate a security dilemma. For instance, China has a territorial dispute with North Korea in Mount Paektu and conflicts of interest with countries which maintain diplomatic relations with Taiwan (El Salvador, Guatemala, Paraguay, Honduras, Nicaragua, Panama, etc.) but a security dilemma does not apply to China and any of these countries, because these conflicts of interest are not acute. In contemporary international relations and the current defensive realism era, it is rare for a security dilemma to occur without an initial acute conflict of interest.

The second premise is that a conflict of interest—as understood by defensive realism—incorporates both objective and subjective aspects.[78] This means that a situation could be characterised in one of four ways: (1) objectively and subjectively reconcilable; (2) objectively reconcilable and subjectively irreconcilable; (3) objectively irreconcilable and subjectively reconcilable; and (4) both objectively and subjectively irreconcilable.

Tang contends that a security dilemma most likely applies in the situation where it is objectively reconcilable and subjectively irreconcilable[79] arguing that any misperception must be quite severe for this situation to lead to actual conflict. Nonetheless, the gap between objective and subjective aspects is not caused merely by misperception but also by severe subjectivity manifested in a narrow nationalist sentiment. Subjectivity here means the attitude that hinders states from perceiving an issue objectively for the common good.

For instance, the proper way to solve any dispute (e.g. trade or territorial) is through international legal mechanisms. Through such impartial legal mechanisms, any party in dispute with another should put aside its subjective views and attempt to solve the dispute with goodwill.

However, subjectivity makes a state perceive its national interest to be sacrosanct, making it reluctant to allow the dispute to be resolved by legal mechanisms. Although a state understands that there is a mechanism to solve the dispute, due to its narrow-mindedness, the dispute becomes tedious.

In this case, there is no misperception, since it is severe subjectivity that perceives an objectively reconcilable dispute as irreconcilable. Such subjectivity does not necessarily mean the state has an expansionist ambition, it could be defensively motivated, that is, it has a subjective interpretation of how to defend the state's interests.

2.8 The Continuum of the Security Dilemma

The security dilemma should be understood as a process, beginning with the activation of what can be described as a dormant or latent security dilemma that exists between defensive realist states, due to the anarchic nature of the international system and a conflict of interest. (As explained above, in the era of defensive realism, an initial acute conflict of interest is needed for a security dilemma to operate.) A dormant security dilemma is activated into an actual security dilemma by an accumulation of power that leads to paradoxical policy. This process continues with material and psychological regulators to become a spiral.

When the situation keeps worsening, as one (or more) state begins to harbour malign intentions, it (or they) moves to defection. Kydd defines a defection as an attempt to alter the status quo in a state's favour.[80] In other words, defection is a stage when one or both states' intentions change from defensive to offensive. The defection by one or more states can deteriorate and lead to an expansionist threat, a deadlock or a war. Tang describes the continuum of the security dilemma as a reversible process.[81] Figure 2.1 presents a schematic representation of the security dilemma process.

Figure 2.1 shows that the role of the regulators—both material and psychological—is very important in the security dilemma process. Although the function of the regulators is not to generate the security dilemma, the reversibility of the security dilemma process relies on these regulators' function. Jervis classifies material regulators as geography, polarity, military technology, and the distinguishability of offensive and defensive weapons.[82] Tang adds asymmetric power, external allies, and the concentration of ethnic groups.[83]

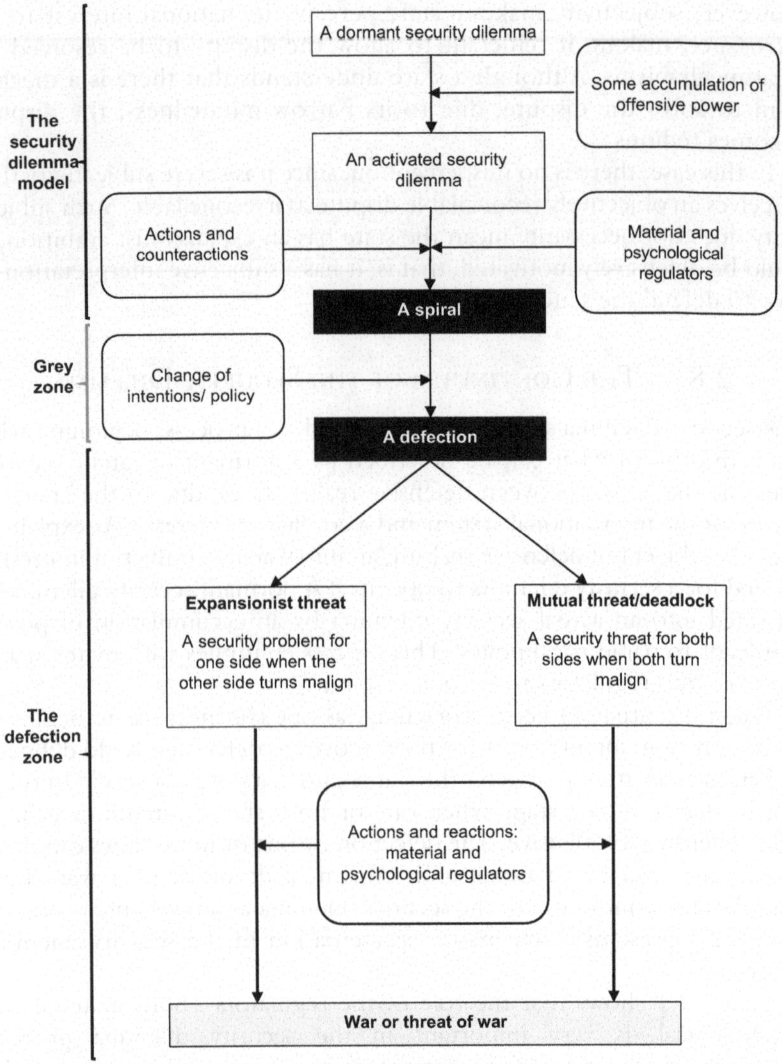

Fig. 2.1 The continuum of the security dilemma process (modified from Tang, *A Theory of Security Strategies for Our Time: Defensive Realism*, 2010, p. 65)

From Jervis' and Tang's category of material regulator, geography and concentration of ethnic groups are not adjustable. This means that their role in regulating the security dilemma process is static, while all other regulators are adjustable by the security dilemma actors.

For instance, power asymmetry, the relationship between asymmetric actors, renders the weaker party more sensitive and fearful. In the case of the SCS, the Philippines' behaviour vis-à-vis China can be described as "schizophrenic".[84] This certainly leads to the exacerbation of the security dilemma. The inability to distinguish between offensive and defensive armaments is also a factor that regulates the severity of the security dilemma.

China's projection of naval power recently definitely alerted other claimants to areas or resources under the SCS. China's actions were balanced by the Philippines' enhancing its defence cooperation with an extra regional ally, that is, the US. Here, we can see that although China's southeast neighbour is relatively weak and incapable of checking China militarily, it can still balance China's actions by diplomatic means.[85]

It is not straightforward to distinguish between offensive and defensive weapons as most weapons are for dual use although some can be categorised as purely offensive or defensive. However, the categorisation of weapons into either offensive or defensive—although possible—is relative and insignificant.[86] The meaningful way to assess a state's intention is by observing its military posture, military strategies, and military doctrines—rather than by assessing its military technology—because these do play a role in regulating the dynamic of the security dilemma.[87] For instance, China's accession to the Treaty of Amity and Cooperation in Southeast Asia in 2003 played a significant role in reducing tensions and ameliorating the security dilemma between China and other claimant states in the SCS.

The psychological regulator of the security dilemma is primarily fear which is one of the main themes in realism theories. The severity of fear can lead to a significant deterioration of the security dilemma, defection, and even conflict. Tang differentiates between two fundamental positions for states to cope with fear.[88] The first argues that states should assume the worst about another state's intentions. This is known as the offensive realist position. The second contends that states should not assume the worst about another state's intentions and therefore states need to take measures to reduce fear and uncertainty about other states. This is known as the non-offensive realist position.

As a regulator, fear can both exacerbate and ameliorate the security dilemma. Fear that is overwhelming and leads to a state assuming the worst about its adversaries will certainly worsen the security dilemma and even lead to conflict. However, defensive realism suggests engagement (which consists of reassurance and deterrence) to reduce fear and the severity of the security dilemma.[89]

Another psychological regulator of the security dilemma is belief and trust. In his ground-breaking study, Kydd provided an important explanation of how belief and trust drive states' behaviour in the security dilemma process.[90] Kydd shows how states in an anarchic world lose trust in each other and defect. In correspondence with Butterfield, he argues that trustworthy states presume that other states know them well. In other words, defensive realist states believe that other states know they are defensively motivated. Therefore, when a defensive realist state encounters what it considers as enmity from another state, it tends to interpret this as the other state's aggression or predatory ambition.[91]

According to Kydd, states' beliefs about others depend on two variables: first, the information received and second the likelihood of error in reports. States will modify their beliefs after receiving information; if a positive report is received, states will be more trusting, but on the other hand, if the report is negative, states will become more suspicious. Security-seeking states are therefore likely to believe that other states are trustworthy, while expansionist states are likely to believe that other states are fearful.[92]

Furthermore, Kydd described this as a spiral game, which consists of a non-cooperative equilibrium, a cooperative equilibrium, and a spiral equilibrium. In the spiral game, there are two categories of actors, that is, security-seeking and expansionist ones, and two behaviours, that is, trusting and fearful ones. The combination of the categories and behaviours makes up four types: security seeking and trusting, security seeking and fearful, expansionist and trusting, and expansionist and fearful. In the non-cooperative equilibrium, both actors and all four types defect, that is, they opt out of the game; in the cooperative equilibrium the security-seeking types cooperate and the expansionist types defect; and in the spiral equilibrium, only the security-seeking and trusting types cooperate, whereas the others choose to defect.[93]

The defection of a state causes uncertainty in its adversary, whether it is an expansionist state or a fearful security-seeking state. This uncertainty is the fundamental condition of the security dilemma and the spiral model.

The whole argument of the spiral model is that security-seeking states become more fearful of each other, knowing that the other side defects. This has an impact on the declining level of trust. Any defection—whether it is unilateral or mutual—causes the level of trust to decline (Fig. 2.2).

2.9 Can a Security Dilemma Be Mitigated?

To answer the above question, Booth and Wheeler offer a framework of the logics of insecurity,[94] a paradigm for perceiving the security issue in international politics. These logics are either fatalistic, mitigating, or transcending. Fatalistic logic maintains that in the anarchic situation, security is a zero-sum game and scarce. This logic contends that in the anarchic situation states' interests are conflicting and conflict is inevitable or predetermined. Further, the scarcity of security leads to states always dealing with security problems, including the security dilemma. According to the fatalistic view, Wheeler and Booth state, the security dilemma is inescapable due to the structure of the international system. This fatalistic thinking is inferred from works by Thucydides, Hobbes, and Bull, whose perspectives resemble that of offensive realism.

However, the notion of the predetermination of conflict is inconsistent with the security dilemma since the dilemma occurs due to uncertainty in

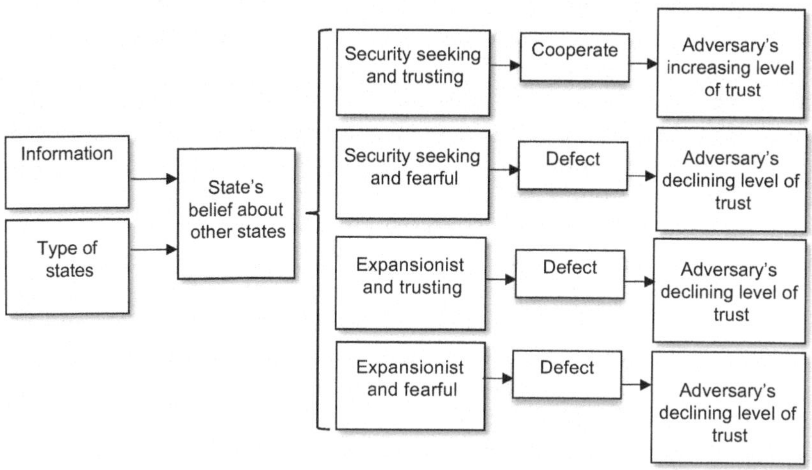

Fig. 2.2 Kydd's (2005) spiral equilibrium

international relations. Anarchy, as understood by security dilemma theorists—especially those subscribing to the notion of defensive realism—does not always lead to a security dilemma. In other words, it is not inevitable that the outcome of anarchy is a security dilemma.

The constitutive elements of the security dilemma are uncertainty, lack of malign intention, and paradoxical policy. So, fatalistic logic (with its predetermination) cannot answer the question of whether the security dilemma can be mitigated, and thus is effectively inconsistent with the concept of the security dilemma as such.

The second logic of insecurity, mitigation, contends that a certain development of behaviour could mitigate the security dilemma. Basically, this approach holds that the security dilemma cannot be eliminated, although it can be alleviated. Within this logic there are two streams. The first provides an explanation inferred from the anarchic nature of the international system. Accordingly, the security dilemma is inherent in anarchy and pervasive in the international system. The easing of the security dilemma therefore implies moderation of the anarchic nature of the international system. The proponents of this idea prescribe the improvement of anarchy towards a more mature version of itself as a remedy to the security dilemma.

An example of such mature anarchy, according to Buzan, is a society made up of large, politically reliable, relatively independent, tolerant agents that are somewhat evenly balanced in their power.[95] Such logic maintains that anarchy itself cannot be escaped, since human beings are fundamentally flawed and conflict of interest is inherent, but the manifestation of these, such as arms races and tensions, can be mitigated. States can modify their behaviour by complying with international law so that anarchy does not always lead to devastating outcomes. States must acknowledge their rights and duties in their relations in order to provide common security. In this sense, international law is a reflection of natural law which best serves the interests of all states.[96]

The logic of mitigation's second stream argues that although the security dilemma is a product of anarchy, it is conditional and not pervasive.[97] The logic extends this point by stating that actors involved in a security dilemma should have no expansionist ambition, while in fact many conflicts or wars are based on states' greed. It follows then that since the security dilemma operates between two or more states with a lack of malign intention, both of which are uncertain about each other's motives, a feasible strategy to lessen the tension would be one of reassurance. Kydd claims that any study on the security dilemma will be lacking if it does not address the role of reassurance; in Kydd's words, "reassurance is the flip side of the security dilemma coin".[98]

A strategy of reassurance is an attempt to reveal the lack of malign intention of a state to its adversaries. It is also a strategy to restore the trust between defensive realist states. Jervis advocates for the transparency of arms procurement, that is, since the security dilemma is caused by the inability to distinguish between offensive and defensive weapons, it is possible to mitigate it by the procurement of discernibly defensive weapons.[99] According to Tang, Jervis' idea is less meaningful since it is difficult to distinguish between offensive and defensive weapons.[100] Furthermore, to be effective, Kydd argues that reassurance must be adequate. For instance, the strategy of reducing troops on the border, as was done by the Soviet Union and China, and by India and China during their respective rapprochement, is considered by Tang to be merely a "small gesture".[101]

The defensive realist state must be willing to take greater risks when initiating reassurance, which can only happen if such a state values mutual cooperation and avoids "the sucker's payoff for unilateral action", as described in the stag-hunt model.[102] To sum up, the keyword for the first type of mitigation logic is "compliance" and for the second type it is "reassurance".

The third logic of insecurity, transcendence, maintains that the security dilemma can be escaped. According to this approach, anarchy is by no means inherent in the international system—states might have inherited anarchy from history, but this need not remain unchanged.

This view holds that states can construct an international system of harmony and security, an idea heavily influenced by Kant's *Perpetual Peace*. In this work, Kant argues that states can escape the horrors of the past by a moral cognitive process; that states have no reason to keep harbouring fear and distrust towards each other; that a peaceful world can be built by trade and socialisation among states; and that by doing so, they enhance a sense of community. It follows that the integration into a security community—which abates fear and mistrust—means the elimination of the security dilemma.[103]

Notes

1. Shiping Tang, *A Theory of Security Strategies for Our Time: Defensive Realism* (New York: Palgrave Macmillan, 2010), 33.

2. Jeffrey W. Taliaferro, "Security Seeking under Anarchy: Defensive Realism Revisited," *International Security*, 25, no. 3 (2000): 128–61; Tang, *A Theory of Security Strategies for Our Time: Defensive Realism*, 118.
3. *A Theory of Security Strategies for Our Time: Defensive Realism*, 34.
4. Herbert Butterfield, *History and Human Relations* (London: Collins, 1951), 19–20.
5. John H. Herz, "Idealist Internationalism and the Security Dilemma," *World Politics*, 2, no. 2 (1950): 157–80.
6. Alan Collins, "State-Induced Security Dilemma: Maintaining the Tragedy," *Cooperation and Conflict*, 39, no. 1 (2004): 27–44; Taliaferro, "Security Seeking under Anarchy: Defensive Realism Revisited," 128–61; Robert Jervis, "Was the Cold War a Security Dilemma?," *Journal of Cold War Studies*, 3, no. 1 (2001): 36–60.
7. "Cooperation under the Security Dilemma," *World Politics*, 30, no. 2 (1978): 167–214.
8. Barry R. Posen, "The Security Dilemma and Ethnic Conflict," *Survival*, 35, no. 1 (1993): 27–47; Wagner in Randall L. Schweller, "The Logic and Illogic of the Security Dilemma and Contemporary Realism: A Response to Wagner's Critique," *International Theory*, 2, no. 2 (2010): 288–305; Glenn H. Snyder, "The Security Dilemma in Alliance Politics," *World Politics*, 36, no. 4 (1984): 461–95; Paul Roe, "Actors' Responsibility in 'Tight', 'Regular' or 'Loose' Security Dilemmas," *Security Dialogue*, 32, no. 1 (2001): 103–16; Andrew Kydd, *Trust and Mistrust in International Relations* (Princeton, NJ: Princeton University Press, 2005), 13; Evan Braden Montgomery, "Breaking Out of the Security Dilemma: Realism, Reassurance, and the Problem of Uncertainty," *International Security*, 31, no. 2 (2006): 151–85; Kenneth N. Waltz, *Theory of International Politics* (Reading, MA: Addison-Wesley Pub. Co., 1979), 186–87.
9. Ken Booth and Nicholas J. Wheeler, *The Security Dilemma: Fear, Cooperation and Trust in World Politics* (Basingstoke: Palgrave Macmillan, 2008), 9.
10. Ibid., 4.
11. Tang, *A Theory of Security Strategies for Our Time: Defensive Realism*, 39.
12. Ibid., 40.
13. "Social Evolution of International Politics: From Mearsheimer to Jervis," *European Journal of International Relations*, 16, no. 1 (2010): 31–55.
14. Barry Buzan, *People, States, and Fear: An Agenda for International Security Studies in the Post-Cold War Era* (Boulder, CO: L. Rienner, 1991).
15. Butterfield, *History and Human Relations*, 22.
16. Reinhold Niebuhr, *Beyond Tragedy: Essays on the Christian Interpretation of History* (London: Nisbet, 1938), 103.

17. Ibid., 105.
18. Brian Schwertley, "Man's Need of Salvation: Total Depravity and Man's Inability," (Cambridge University Press, 2008).
19. Tang, *A Theory of Security Strategies for Our Time: Defensive Realism*, 35.
20. John H. Herz, *Political Realism and Political Idealism: A Study in Theories and Realities* (Chicago: University of Chicago Press, 1951), 3–4.
21. Alan Collins, *The Security Dilemmas of Southeast Asia* (New York: St. Martin's Press, 2000).
22. *The Catechism of the Catholic Church* (Strathfield, NSW: St. Pauls, 2000), second ed., n. 405.
23. Jeremy Cohen, "Original Sin as the Evil Inclination—A Polemicist's Appreciation of Human Nature," *Harvard Theological Review*, 73, no. 3–4 (1980): 495–520.
24. Ibid.
25. E. J. Hamilton and B. C. Rathbun, "Scarce Differences: Toward a Material and Systemic Foundation for Offensive and Defensive Realism," *Security Studies*, 22, no. 3 (2013): 436–65.
26. Ibid., 447.
27. Christoph Bluth, "The Security Dilemma Revisited: A Paradigm for International Security in the Twenty-First Century?," *The International Journal of Human Rights*, 15, no. 8 (2011): 1362–77.
28. Swaine, "China's Assertive Behavior—Part One: On 'Core Interests'".
29. Tang, "Social Evolution of International Politics: From Mearsheimer to Jervis," 31–55.
30. Butterfield, *History and Human Relations*, 20–22; Jervis, "Was the Cold War a Security Dilemma?," 36–60; Schweller, "The Logic and Illogic of the Security Dilemma and Contemporary Realism: A Response to Wagner's Critique," 288–305; Taliaferro, "Security Seeking under Anarchy: Defensive Realism Revisited," 128–61; Kydd, *Trust and Mistrust in International Relations*, 13; Collins, "State-Induced Security Dilemma: Maintaining the Tragedy," 27–44.
31. Tang, *A Theory of Security Strategies for Our Time: Defensive Realism*, 49–54.
32. Ibid., 31.
33. John J. Mearsheimer, "Can China Rise Peacefully?," *The National Interest*, 25 October 2014, http://nationalinterest.org/commentary/can-china-rise-peacefully-10204 (accessed 28 October 2016).
34. Robert Jervis, *Perception and Misperception in International Politics* (Princeton, NJ: Princeton University Press, 1976), 65.
35. Charles L. Glaser, "The Security Dilemma Revisited," *World Politics*, 50, no. 1 (1997): 171–201.
36. Robert Jervis, "Cooperation under the Security Dilemma," Ibid. 30, no. 2 (1978): 167–214.

37. Randall L. Schweller, "Neorealism's Status-Quo Bias: What Security Dilemma?," *Security Studies*, 5, no. 3 (1996): 90–121.
38. Shiping Tang, "A Systemic Theory of the Security Environment," *The Journal of Strategic Studies*, 27, no. 1 (2004): 1–34.
39. Charles L. Glaser, "Political Consequences of Military Strategy: Expanding and Refining the Spiral and Deterrence Models," *World Politics*, 44, no. 4 (1992): 497–538; Andrew Kydd, "Game Theory and the Spiral Model," Ibid. 49, no. 3 (1997): 371–400.
40. Tang, *A Theory of Security Strategies for Our Time: Defensive Realism*, 118–19.
41. Ibid., 31.
42. Hamilton and Rathbun, "Scarce Differences: Toward a Material and Systemic Foundation for Offensive and Defensive Realism," 436–65.
43. Ibid.
44. Kenneth N. Waltz, "The Origins of War in Neorealist Theory," *The Journal of Interdisciplinary History*, 18, no. 4 (1988): 615–28.
45. John J. Mearsheimer, "The False Promise of International Institutions," *International Security*, 19, no. 3 (1994): 5–49.
46. Hamilton and Rathbun, "Scarce Differences: Toward a Material and Systemic Foundation for Offensive and Defensive Realism," 436–65.
47. Ibid.
48. Ibid.; Waltz, *Theory of International Politics*, 126.
49. Kydd, *Trust and Mistrust in International Relations.*
50. Waltz, *Theory of International Politics*, 126.
51. Hamilton and Rathbun, "Scarce Differences: Toward a Material and Systemic Foundation for Offensive and Defensive Realism," 436–65.
52. John Fraher, "Arms Spending Spree in Southeast Asia Has Singapore Worried," *Bloomberg*, 24 March 2016, http://www.bloomberg.com/news/articles/2016-03-24/arms-spending-spree-in-southeast-asia-has-singapore-worried (accessed 1 November 2016).
53. Jervis, "Cooperation under the Security Dilemma," 167–214.
54. "Was the Cold War a Security Dilemma?," 36–60.
55. "Dilemmas About Security Dilemmas," *Security Studies*, 20, no. 3 (2011): 416–23.
56. Shiping Tang, "From Offensive to Defensive Realism: A Social Evolutionary Interpretation of China's Security Strategy," *China's Ascent: Power, Security, and the Future of International Politics*, (2008): 141–62.
57. Yves-Heng Lim, "A Tale of Two Realisms in Chinese Foreign Policy," *China: An International Journal*, 9, no. 2 (2011): 299–312.
58. Jervis, "Was the Cold War a Security Dilemma?," 36–60.
59. Booth and Wheeler, *The Security Dilemma: Fear, Cooperation and Trust in World Politics*, 45–46.

60. Schweller, "The Logic and Illogic of the Security Dilemma and Contemporary Realism: A Response to Wagner's Critique," 288–305.
61. Tang, *A Theory of Security Strategies for Our Time: Defensive Realism*, 41.
62. Kydd, *Trust and Mistrust in International Relations*, 73–74.
63. Ibid., 18–19.
64. Collins, *The Security Dilemmas of Southeast Asia*, 6–7; Glaser, "The Security Dilemma Revisited," 171–201; Booth and Wheeler, *The Security Dilemma: Fear, Cooperation and Trust in World Politics*, 45–47; Schweller, "The Logic and Illogic of the Security Dilemma and Contemporary Realism: A Response to Wagner's Critique," 288–305.
65. Tang, *A Theory of Security Strategies for Our Time: Defensive Realism*, 62–64.
66. Roe, "Actors' Responsibility in 'Tight', 'Regular' or 'Loose' Security Dilemmas," 103–16.
67. John Baylis and N. J. Rengger, *Dilemmas of World Politics: International Issues in a Changing World* (New York: Clarendon Press, 1992).
68. Roe, "Actors' Responsibility in 'Tight', 'Regular' or 'Loose' Security Dilemmas," 103–16.
69. Snyder, "The Security Dilemma in Alliance Politics," 461–95.
70. Collins, "State-Induced Security Dilemma: Maintaining the Tragedy," 27–44.
71. *The Security Dilemmas of Southeast Asia*, 135.
72. Walter Lee, "China's Unassertive Rise: What Is Assertiveness and How We have Misunderstood It?," *International Journal of China Studies*, 4, no. 3 (2013): 35.
73. Glaser, "The Security Dilemma Revisited," 171–201.
74. Tang, *A Theory of Security Strategies for Our Time: Defensive Realism*, 43.
75. "Social Evolution of International Politics: From Mearsheimer to Jervis," 31–55.
76. Ibid., 32.
77. Waltz, "The Origins of War in Neorealist Theory," 615–28.
78. Tang, *A Theory of Security Strategies for Our Time: Defensive Realism*, 43.
79. Ibid., 44.
80. Kydd, *Trust and Mistrust in International Relations*, 30.
81. Tang, *A Theory of Security Strategies for Our Time: Defensive Realism*, 64.
82. Ibid., 206.
83. Ibid., 66.
84. Schofield and Storey, *The South China Sea Dispute: Increasing Stakes and Rising Tensions*, 27.
85. Collins, *The Security Dilemmas of Southeast Asia*, 154.
86. Shiping Tang, "Offence-Defence Theory: Towards a Definitive Understanding," *Chinese Journal of International Politics*, 3, no. 2 (2010): 213–60.

87. Ibid., 259.
88. "Fear in International Politics: Two Positions," *International Studies Review*, 10, no. 3 (2008): 451–71.
89. *A Theory of Security Strategies for Our Time: Defensive Realism*, 102.
90. Kydd, *Trust and Mistrust in International Relations.*
91. Ibid., 50.
92. Ibid., 58.
93. Ibid., 61–63.
94. Booth and Wheeler, *The Security Dilemma: Fear, Cooperation and Trust in World Politics*, 10–18.
95. Buzan, *People, States, and Fear: An Agenda for International Security Studies in the Post-Cold War Era*, 208.
96. Booth and Wheeler, *The Security Dilemma: Fear, Cooperation and Trust in World Politics*, 16.
97. Tang, *A Theory of Security Strategies for Our Time: Defensive Realism*, 47; Schweller, "Neorealism's Status-Quo Bias: What Security Dilemma?," 90–121; Collins, *The Security Dilemmas of Southeast Asia*, 174.
98. Andrew Kydd, "Trust, Reassurance, and Cooperation," *International Organization*, 54, no. 2 (2000): 325–57.
99. Jervis, "Cooperation under the Security Dilemma," 167–214.
100. Tang, "Offence-Defence Theory: Towards a Definitive Understanding," 213–60.
101. Kydd, "Trust, Reassurance, and Cooperation," 325–57; Tang, *A Theory of Security Strategies for Our Time: Defensive Realism*, 153.
102. Kydd, "Trust, Reassurance, and Cooperation," 325–57.
103. Wheeler and Bluth in Baylis and Rengger, *Dilemmas of World Politics: International Issues in a Changing World*, 54.

CHAPTER 3

China's Claim in the South China Sea

China's behaviour in the South China Sea (SCS), which it asserts has always been defence motivated, is inseparable from its claim over the area. This chapter examines China's claim in the SCS from the international law perspective. In doing so, it explores the steps taken by China and other states in their exercise of territoriality and access to resources in the SCS. This is followed by a discussion of the United Nations Convention on the Law of the Sea (UNCLOS) Tribunal ruling and an evaluation of China's response to it.

3.1 China's Claim in the SCS

Since the founding of the People's Republic of China (PRC) in 1949, China was involved in a series of ongoing negotiations of various types to resolve the land border disputes with its neighbouring countries. However, there was no clear and definitive statement by China of its maritime border claim in the area, particularly in the SCS, until 9 September 1958, when the PRC made a Declaration on China's Territorial Sea. This marked its first official claim over the SCS.[1] In this 1958 declaration, it asserts:

> The breadth of the territorial sea of the People's Republic of China shall be twelve nautical miles (nm). This provision applies to all territories of the People's Republic of China including the Chinese mainland and its coastal islands, as well as Taiwan and its surrounding islands, the Penghu Islands,

K. H. Raditio, *Understanding China's Behaviour in the South China Sea*, https://doi.org/10.1007/978-981-13-1283-0_3

the Dongsha Islands, the Xisha Islands, the Zhongsha Islands, the Nansha Islands and all other islands belonging to China which are separated from the mainland and its coastal islands by the high seas.[2]

This claim was reasserted on 25 February 1992 when China promulgated its Law on the Territorial Sea and the Contiguous Zone. Article 2 provides that:

The land territory of the People's Republic of China includes the mainland of the People's Republic of China and its coastal islands: Taiwan and all islands appertaining thereto including the Diaoyu Islands; the Penghu Islands; the Dongsha Islands; the Xisha Islands; the Zhongsha Islands and the Nansha Islands; as well as the other islands belonging to the People's Republic of China.[3]

The statement above neither elaborates on nor clarifies China's claim in the 1958 declaration. When China ratified the UNCLOS on 7 June 1996, it reaffirmed the "sovereignty over all its archipelagos and islands" by making a reference to Article 2 of the 1992 law, but it did not support the claim based on the provision of the Convention.[4]

On 26 June 1998, China promulgated China's Exclusive Economic Zone and Continental Shelf Act.[5] This was the first time for China to make an official reference to "historic rights".[6] Although this Act is not a statement of China's claim over the SCS, it is an effort to support its assertion of what it perceives as its maritime domain. The term "historic rights" is recognised in international law. However, to be entitled to these "rights", a state should meet some specific requirements. China neither indicated the area for which it claims the "historic rights" nor expanded on what form of historic rights it enjoys.

Internationally, China made its claim known in the SCS through diplomatic correspondence in a series of events. On 7 May 2009, China sent a *note verbale* (no. CML/17/2009) to the UN Secretary General. This was a reaction to a joint submission by Malaysia and Vietnam to the UN Commission on the Limits of the Continental Shelf. In this *note verbale*, China asserts that:

China has indisputable sovereignty over the islands in the South China Sea and the adjacent waters and enjoys sovereign rights and jurisdiction over the relevant waters as well as the seabed and subsoil thereof (see attached map). The above position is consistently held by the Chinese Government and is widely known by the international community.[7]

In this document, China made the nine-dash line map known internationally (see Appendix A). Although it did not necessarily mean to support its claim according to international law by presenting the map, it attempted to indicate the area over which it enjoys sovereign rights and jurisdiction.

Another piece of diplomatic correspondence in which China asserts its claim in the SCS was dated 14 April 2011. This further *note verbale* was made as a response to the Philippines' protest against China's note in 2011. Its wording was similar to its earlier *note verbale* (no. CML/17/2009), with the added sentence: "China's sovereignty and related rights and jurisdiction in the SCS are supported by abundant historical and legal evidence."[8] This assertion became a pronouncement frequently made by Chinese governmental institutions when dealing with China's claim in the SCS.

In the aftermath of the 2012 Scarborough Shoal incident, the Philippines initiated arbitral proceedings against the PRC to challenge its claims in the SCS according to UNCLOS. In response, on 7 December 2014, China issued the Position Paper of the Government of the PRC on the Matter of Jurisdiction in the South China Sea Arbitration initiated by the Republic of the Philippines. In it, China argues that the subject matter of the arbitration is territorial sovereignty which is beyond the jurisdiction of UNCLOS. Since Annex VII of the UNCLOS states that the Convention does not have jurisdiction over sovereignty issues, China refused to accept and participate in the arbitration initiated by the Philippines. It additionally asserted that:

> China has indisputable sovereignty over the South China Sea Islands (the Dongsha Islands, the Xisha Islands, the Zhongsha Islands and the Nansha Islands) and the adjacent waters. Chinese activities in the South China Sea dates back to over 2,000 years ago. China was the first country to discover, name, explore and exploit the resources of the South China Sea islands and the first to continuously exercise sovereign powers over them.[9]

Notably, this position paper insists that sovereignty over the SCS islands should be ascertained before determining maritime rights. It also made explicit that China considers itself to have sovereignty over all features in the SCS and that becoming a party to and ratifying UNCLOS does not negate its claim.

In brief, China's claim in the SCS can be summarised as follows: (1) China claims all land features in the SCS, which are traditionally divided into four groups: the Dongsha Islands, the Xisha Islands, the Zhongsha

Islands, and the Nansha Islands; (2) China claims all islands in the SCS and its adjacent waters on the basis of historic rights.

3.2 China's Claim and Its Compatibility with International Law

3.2.1 *Land Claims*

The principle of international maritime law is "land governs the sea" and China has attempted to reconcile with it in its official documents concerning the SCS claim. China's official position is iterated as "China has indisputable sovereignty over the islands in the SCS and the adjacent waters, and enjoys sovereign rights and jurisdiction over the relevant waters as well as the seabed and subsoil thereof."[10]

In its White Paper published in response to the July 2016 Tribunal ruling, China asserts that its claim over the Paracel and Spratly Islands in the SCS dates back to the Western Han Dynasty in the second century BC.[11] It is undeniable that China has strong links with the Paracels and Spratlys, but in terms of exercising sovereignty according to international law, its claim is not indisputable.[12] According to international law, there are various specific ways to acquire sovereignty over territory: (1) occupation of *terra nullius* (no man's land); (2) prescription or maintaining effective administration for a considerable period; (3) cession, or transfer by treaty; (4) accession, or growth of territory naturally.[13] Conquest and subjugation is dismissed by Article 2 of the UN Charter.[14] This section examines whether China's activities throughout history are sufficient to establish its claim over islands in the SCS.

In this chapter, the claims over the Paracel and Spratly Islands will be considered separately. Both China and Vietnam have claimed the whole of these island groups, while the Philippines, Malaysia, and Brunei have claimed only some land features in the Spratlys. The dispute over the Paracel Islands involves China and Vietnam alone.

China argued that the French recognised China's sovereignty over the Paracels Islands in the Sino-French Treaty in 1887.[15] However, this assertion is not unequivocal, since France continued to seek hegemony over the Paracel Islands, which implies that the country did not consider the Paracel Islands were included in the 1887 Treaty.[16] In 1908, China established a physical presence on some of the Paracel Islands.[17] Between 1908 and 1921, China conducted official inspections and incorporated the Paracel Islands into Guangdong Province.[18]

From the 1920s to the 1930s, there were two centres of gravity in the Paracels. In the north-east, Woody Island became a centre for Chinese activities, while Pattle Island in the south-west acted as the base for French interests. The distance between these two centres is merely 100 km although they had different destinations for their traffic: Woody Island was linked with mainland China and Taiwan, and Pattle Island was connected to Vietnam and French Indochina. The route between Woody Island and Pattle Island was established by Japanese phosphate companies, making the Paracels a unified island group[19] (Fig. 3.1).

In December 1931, after the Japanese invasion of China, the French protested to China over the Paracel Islands. France asserted that the Paracel Islands were a part of Indochinese dominions as a result of King Gia Long's incorporation in 1816 and some activities conducted by King Minh Mang in 1835, that is, the construction of a stone tablet and a pagoda on one of the islands.[20] In 1932, the Paracel Islands were incorporated as an administrative delegation of French Indochina.

This act of exercising sovereignty over the Paracel Islands by France is dubious for two reasons. First, France's claim to the inheritance of King Gia Long is questionable because according to French writers, in 1837, the Vietnamese Kingdom did not consider the Paracel Islands to be Vietnamese territory.[21] Second, from 1908 to 1921, well before France's annexation in the 1930s, China had performed several operations and

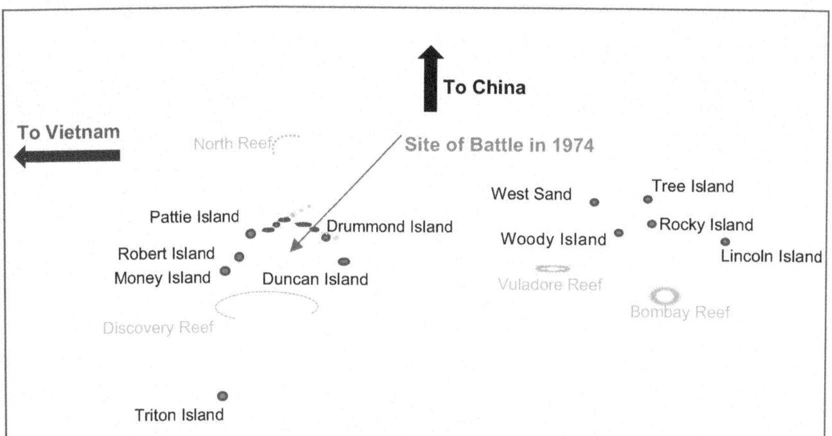

Fig. 3.1 The Paracel Islands—depicted by M. Glinoga

incorporations of the Paracel Islands into its territory, a fact which made French occupation of the islands disputable.

In 1947, the Republic of China (ROC) through its embassy in Paris announced a formal occupation of the Paracels in a communiqué.[22] In May 1950, ROC troops were withdrawn to Taiwan, making the islands unoccupied.[23] The existence of two Vietnamese states, that is, the Democratic Republic of Vietnam (DRV—North Vietnam) and the Republic of Vietnam (RVN—South Vietnam), after World War II further complicated the dispute.

In October 1950, France officially ceded control of the Paracel Islands to the RVN, South Vietnam, despite the fact that French troops still maintained a physical presence until 1956.[24] This act does not necessarily mean that today's Vietnam (Socialist Republic of Vietnam—SRV) inherited the claim from the RVN, since the SRV was not a union of the DRV and the RVN, but a union of the DRV and the Provisional Revolutionary Government of South Vietnam following the fall of Saigon in 1976.[25] It this sense, the SRV is a continuation of the DRV which absorbed the collapsed RVN.

As can be seen, the situation became even more complicated following the fall of Saigon and the establishment of the SRV. The Vietnamese claim is to some extent problematic. According to historical records of Chinese scholars, the DRV government unambiguously acknowledged China's sovereignty over the Paracels and Spratlys in the 1950s.

On 15 June 1956, DRV Vice Foreign Minister Ung Van Khiem acknowledged the Paracel and the Spratly Islands as Chinese territory to the Chinese *Charge d'Affaires*, Li Zhimin by publicly stating: "According to Vietnamese data, the Xisha (Paracel) and Nansha (Spratly) Islands are historically part of Chinese territory."[26] Chinese scholars also suggest that a similar statement was repeated on 14 September 1958 by DRV Premier Pham Van Dong, affirming that Vietnam "recognises and supports" China's declaration of its territorial waters, made on 4 September, which applied to the Spratly Islands.[27] However, a careful examination of the diplomatic note (see Appendix B), reveals the recognition of the 12 mile territorial waters, but the note does not state anything about the islands in the SCS.

In addition to that, under the Geneva Agreement, Vietnam was divided into the DRV and the RVN. When the DRV sent the note, the Paracels and Spratlys were under the administration of the RVN which consistently maintained its claim of sovereignty over these islands and protested against the sovereignty claims of other states.[28]

Nonetheless, when China launched a battle to seize the Paracel Islands from the RVN in 1974, the DRV kept silent about China's action. After 1976, Hanoi protested China's occupation of the Paracels in the midst of deteriorating relations, making its claim a political rather than a legal one.[29] This historical fact demonstrates that neither China nor Vietnam has a superior claim over the Paracels.

Like the Paracel Islands, the dispute over the Spratly Islands is also complex. China and Vietnam claim the whole of the Spratly Islands, while the Philippines, Malaysia, and Brunei claim only some land features of the island group. As with the Paracel Islands, China's claim over the whole Spratly Islands dates back to the Han Dynasty in the second century BC.

However, this claim is dubious for at least four reasons. First, according to a 1928 Chinese government report on the Paracels, the Paracel Islands were China's southernmost territory.[30] Second, a map produced in the 1930s on Qing-controlled territory included the Paracels, but not the Spratlys.[31] Thirdly, China did not lodge any protest over the French occupation of one land feature in the Spratly Islands in 1930, which was in stark contrast to its strong protests in 1932 and 1934 to France's incorporation of the Paracel Islands into Indochina.[32] Finally, the ROC did not officially lodge a protest when France occupied several land features of the Spratly Islands in 1933.

It was said that the government in Nanjing decided not to issue any protest after it understood that French activities were not conducted in the Paracel Islands. Furthermore, the minutes of the meeting of the Military Council on 1 September 1933, reveal the ROC stated that Triton Island in the Paracels is the southernmost island of Chinese territory.[33] No available historical record can demonstrate whether China or Vietnam performed any act of sovereignty over the Spratly Islands before the Japanese occupation in 1939.[34]

In 1877, the UK occupied the Spratly Islands without any protest by any state.[35] In 1930, France declared sovereignty over the Spratly Islands.[36] Initially, this French action was met with protest from the UK; however, later on, the UK abandoned its claim.[37] Eight years later in 1938, Japan occupied the Paracel and Spratly Islands, which France protested against.[38] After World War II, Japan relinquished its title over the Spratlys, but it was not clear whether any state would inherit the claim. In December 1946, the ROC sent its naval force to occupy the Spratly Islands.

The ROC considered this an act of sovereignty that would be recognised by international law.[39] If 1946 is a critical date to assess the strength of disputants' claims in the Spratlys, then China is probably the state that established the earliest claim there according to international law. The ROC troops withdrew from the Spratlys in 1950, although it did not relinquish its claim.

In 1956, a Philippine national, Thomas Cloma, occupied some of the Spratly Islands and called them the Kalayaan Island Group.[40] This action raised tension in the SCS and provoked protests by the PRC and the ROC. In the same year, ROC reoccupied Itu Aba, the largest island in the Spratlys and the RVN force hoisted a flag and erected a sovereignty marker on one of the Spratly Islands.[41] In 1956, Saigon authorities incorporated the Spratly Islands into Phuoc Tuy Province.[42]

Two years later, the PRC issued its territorial sea declaration, including the Paracel Islands and the Spratly Islands as its territory.[43] Until then, the PRC claim over the Spratly Islands was merely one on paper. The country had vociferously protested every action by other claimants that was perceived as a sovereignty violation, but it was simply unable to implement its claims physically.[44]

On the other hand, other claimants, that is, Vietnam (before and after the SRV) and the Philippines, continuously seized islands in the Spratlys and maintained their forces in their occupied land. The Philippines started to deploy its troops in the Spratly Islands in 1971; Malaysia joined the dispute in 1979, and China (PRC) entered the Spratlys in 1988, facing a clash with Vietnamese troops on Johnson South Reef.

Ultimately, it can be seen that China's action in the SCS has been sporadic and not uninterrupted. Its claim that the country is "the first to continuously exercise sovereign powers over them" is highly contestable. Also, according to UNCLOS—to which China is a party—not all offshore features are subject to a claim of sovereignty.

UNCLOS differentiates the offshore geographical features into (1) islands; (2) rocks/high-tide elevations; (3) low-tide elevations; (4) artificial islands, installations, and structures; and (5) submerged features. Islands are the only offshore features that are subject to a claim of sovereignty. Article 2 of UNCLOS rules that islands are entitled to a territorial sea, a contiguous zone, an exclusive economic zone (EEZ), and a continental shelf, while rocks that cannot sustain human habitation are only entitled to a territorial sea and a contiguous zone. To be qualified as an island, a land feature should be a naturally formed area of land, surrounded by water and above water at high tide.[45]

A question thus arises since no claimant state has clarified the geographical features of the SCS and it is likely that the majority of the offshore features are not above water at high tide, which means they are not the subject of sovereignty claim.[46] Therefore, the important next step to deal with sovereignty and maritime rights in the SCS is to define its geographical features.

3.2.2 Maritime Claims

Unlike its land claims, China's maritime claims are unclear. The ground for its maritime claims, therefore, is shaky. As presented above, China's statements of sovereignty in the SCS have always begun with a claim over islands, followed by a claim over "adjacent waters" and/or "relevant waters". These suggest that China is attempting to make its SCS claim compatible with UNCLOS.

However, the extent of this maritime claim remains uncertain, as is its nature. When China presented the nine-dash line map to the United Nations in 2009, its maritime claims were made even more ambiguously. What does the dashed line represent? How does China measure its maritime claims based on land features (even if we assume all SCS features belong to China)? If China claims the waters within the nine-dash line, then what exactly is the status of these waters? Do they constitute territorial seas, areas of jurisdiction rights or EEZs? These questions have never been elaborated on by China and answers cannot be found in any official Chinese document. The Chinese government seems to deliberately maintain this ambiguity as part of its strategy to further its maritime claims in the SCS.[47]

Despite this limited clarification from the Chinese government, it does provide some insight into China's maritime claim. First, the nine-dash line map that was presented in 2009 was originally published in 1947 by the Nationalist government of the ROC. However, the 1947 version and the 2009 version differ, since the earlier version shows 11 dashes due to a deal made between the PRC and DRV in 1950s. However, it is clear that the 2009 map appears to follow the 1947 version.[48]

The 1947 version is titled "Map of the South China Sea Islands" (*Nanhai Zhudao Weizhi Tu*). This indicates that the map was not meant to delimit China's maritime boundary, but to locate the islands in the SCS. Using the map—either the 1947 version or the 2009 version—to claim sovereignty over the maritime area and depict a unilateral maritime boundary are at odds with international law and the international practice of "the land governs the sea". China is unlikely to promote this interpretation as this would tarnish its image as a law-abiding state.

Second, if we examine it closely, the dashes in the nine-dash line map seem to have been drawn arbitrarily. These dashes are predominantly closer to the coasts of other SCS littoral states than they are to the land features of the SCS.[49] The length of every dash in both versions is also different from each other. Cartographically, the nine-dash line presented by China in 2009 is inconsistent with other Chinese maps, for instance, maps published by *Ditu Chubanshe* (1984) and Sinomaps (2013–2014).[50] Given the imprecise and vague nature of any version of these dash line maps which purport to relate to a Chinese claim over the SCS, the extent of China's maritime claims in the SCS is uncertain.

Even though China has not clarified the extent of its maritime claims in the SCS, it has provided a vague claim on the basis of historic rights. This is expressed in the Exclusive Economic Zone and the Continental Shelf Act on 26 June 1998. In Article 14, China states that "the provisions of this Law shall not affect the historic rights enjoyed by the People's Republic of China."[51] In other words, the term "historic rights" has never applied directly to China's maritime claim in the SCS in the official documents.[52] One of the statements from the Chinese government which shows the phrasing of this application of historic rights to the SCS is that by Foreign Ministry Spokesperson Jiang Yu during Regular Press Conference on 15 September 2011:

> China's sovereignty, rights and relevant claims over the South China Sea have been formed in the long course of history and upheld by the Chinese government. Our sovereignty over the islands in the South China Sea is based on discovery, occupation as well as long-term, sustained and effective management. The UN Convention on the Law of the Sea does not entitle any country to extend its exclusive economic zone or continental shelf on the territory of another country, and it does not restrain or deny a country's right which is formed in history and abidingly upheld.[53]

Moreover, the term "historic rights" has been widely used to support China's maritime claim in the SCS in media and academic forums. To cite some examples, Zhiguo Gao and Bing Bing Jia argued that China can affirm historic rights within the nine-dash line on the basis of the 1998 EEZ and Continental Shelf Act[54]; Colonel Shi Xiaoqin contended that

China's claim in the SCS is based on historic rights "under a regime independent of UNCLOS"[55]; Wu Shicun the President of National Institute for South China Sea Studies (a research institute affiliated with the Chinese Ministry of Foreign Affairs) argued that China is entitled to historic rights, inclusive of fishing rights and exploitation of resources within the nine-dash line.[56]

Similar to China's position on the extent of its maritime claims, the nature of its maritime claims in the SCS is vague. Problematically, in international law, the concept of historic rights is also ambiguous and this is not governed by UNCLOS. The concept of historic rights has evolved from the concept of historic bays and historic waters and has a broader meaning than the latter two.[57] The term "historic rights" also confers various extraordinary rights without reference to any sovereignty claim, such as fishing rights in high seas. The application of historic rights varies from one coastal state to another since international law does not specify any single regime for them. In one case, a state may be recognised only as having exclusive fishing rights, whereas in another case a coastal state may exercise full sovereignty.[58]

In international law, some historic rights claims are accepted, for instance, the Norwegian Fisheries case in 1951 and the Gulf of Fonseca case in 1992, while in some cases historic rights claims are contested, for instance, the Soviet's claim over the Peter the Great Bay which is contested by Western countries led by the US, and Tunisia's historic rights claim which is disputed by Libya.[59]

It is worth noting that China's practice in supporting other states' historic rights is primarily based on political considerations. In 1957, when China and the Soviet Union were still close allies, China supported the Soviet claim to Peter the Great Bay, on the other hand China refused to recognise Vietnam's claim over the Gulf of Tonkin in 1982.[60]

The problem with China' historic rights claim in the SCS is that it does not clarify the specific rights that the country claims. Zou Keyuan argues that China's claim of historic rights refers to EEZ and continental shelf regimes which incorporate jurisdiction and sovereign rights, but not full sovereignty.[61] In addition, Zou describes this claim as "historic rights with tempered sovereignty", which is not limited to fishery rights but includes exclusive rights to develop the resources and jurisdiction with regard to protection of the marine environment, conducting scientific research and establishing artificial islands in the sea areas.[62]

This "historic claim with Chinese characteristics" could be considered as a new kind of claim affecting the development of the concept of historic rights in international law. This interpretation is also in line with other Chinese scholars who argue that the waters within the nine-dash line should not be regarded as historic waters—which are treated as internal or territorial waters—and cannot be incorporated into an EEZ and continental shelves.[63]

However, it is disputable if China's historic claim is founded in the context of international law. Even though China has asserted that its historic rights claim over the SCS is based on international law independent of UNCLOS,[64] its claim, however, remains unconvincing.

First, a historic rights claim requires an open, widely recognised, and effective exercise of authority over the SCS and it is highly contentious if China has met this requirement. As mentioned earlier, there are many inconsistencies and a lack of precision in Chinese maps concerning its claim in the SCS. This fact demonstrates China's failure in meeting the open and widely recognised condition needed by international law.[65]

Second, China has not maintained an uninterrupted exercise of authority in the SCS as demanded by international law. In fact, the exercise of authority by China over the claimed area has been sporadic and rare.[66] Many features in the SCS are controlled by other littoral states such as Vietnam and the Philippines.

Thirdly, international law requires acquiescence by foreign states about a historic rights claim, while actually several countries do not give any consent concerning China's historic claim over the SCS. For instance, Vietnam has been consistent in protesting against China's claim in the SCS from as early as 1932.[67] Given the above-mentioned facts, China's historic rights claim in the SCS can be considered as standing on shaky ground.

3.3 The UNCLOS Tribunal Ruling

3.3.1 The Arbitration Process

On 22 January 2013, the Philippine government initiated arbitration proceedings to challenge China's maritime claim in the SCS. Manila aimed to "clearly establish the sovereign rights and jurisdiction of the Philippines over its maritime entitlements in the West Philippine Sea (the SCS)."[68] In August 2013, the Permanent Court of Arbitration (PCA) issued a press release stating that an Arbitral Tribunal had been established under Annex VII to the UNCLOS. The tribunal will be referred to in this research as "the UNCLOS Tribunal" or "the Tribunal".

The UNCLOS Tribunal conducted the arbitral proceedings according to the UNCLOS to which the Philippines and PRC are parties. To no one's surprise, China rejected this arbitration process. It insisted on three points. First, the Tribunal had no jurisdiction on the dispute, since the subject matter of the arbitration is the territorial sovereignty over features in the SCS. Second, the initiation of the arbitration constituted a breach by the Philippines of the 2002 Declaration on the Conduct of Parties in the SCS (the 2002 DoC), in which all parties commit to settle the relevant disputes through negotiation. Third, China had exempted itself from compulsory arbitration and other compulsory dispute settlement procedures.[69] These form China's justification for its refusal to participate in the arbitral proceedings.

On 12 July 2016, the UNCLOS Tribunal issued its ruling which dismissed China's maritime claim in the SCS. In its press release, the Tribunal asserted that it has jurisdiction on the subject matter of the arbitration. It admitted that UNCLOS does not rule on sovereignty and neither does the Tribunal. However, it stated the subject matter of the arbitration is the source of maritime entitlement, which falls within the UNCLOS' jurisdiction. It added that, according to Annex VII of the UNCLOS, China's absence from the arbitration does not affect the proceedings.

The Tribunal also rejected China's argument that the 2002 DoC prevents the Philippines from initiating arbitration. The 2002 DoC is a political declaration which is not legally binding. Furthermore, the Tribunal noted that the Philippines and China are parties to UNCLOS, which does not permit a state to exempt itself from the mechanism for the resolution of disputes set out in the UNCLOS.

3.3.2 *The Award of the Tribunal*

On China's historic rights and the "nine-dash line", the Tribunal ruled that the presence and activities of Chinese fishermen and navigators in the SCS was never meant to indicate sovereignty over its features. Rather, it represented the exercise of high seas freedom rather than historic rights. Furthermore, the ruling continued, there is no evidence that China had historically exercised exclusive control over the waters of the SCS. In addition to that, supposing that China ever exercises historic rights exclusively over the water within the nine-dash line, these excessive rights are incompatible with the UNCLOS and should be ceased by entry into force of the UNCLOS. In brief, the Tribunal concluded that it is unlawful to claim historic rights to resources within the nine-dash line.

The Tribunal also ruled that no feature of the Spratly Islands qualifies to be an island. Therefore, those features cannot generate an (EEZ). They are either high-tide elevations which cannot sustain human habitation for which they are only entitled to 12 nautical miles of territorial sea or low-tide elevations which have no maritime entitlement. Scarborough Shoal is ruled as a rock/high-tide elevation; Mischief Reef and Second Thomas Shoal are low-tide elevations and parts of the Philippine EEZ (see Appendix C). The Tribunal stated that the features of Spratly Islands cannot generate extended maritime zones as individuals or as a total unit.

In addition, the Tribunal ruled on the lawfulness China's actions in the SCS. Three actions are considered to be in violation of the Philippines' sovereign rights in its EEZ. First, China interferes with the Philippines' fishing and exploration activities. Second, China constructs artificial islands. Third, China fails to prevent its fishermen from fishing in the Philippines' EEZ. With regard to the Scarborough Shoal, the Tribunal ruled that both China and the Philippines have fishing rights to it. However, China's action in blocking the access for the Philippine fishermen to enter the shoal is unlawful.

The UNCLOS Tribunal gave substantial clarity on maritime rights in the SCS. This research argues that the ruling should be taken into account in assessing China's SCS behaviour for the following reasons. First, since China has failed to clarify its claim's ambiguity, the ruling serves as a guide to assess China's claim as well as the other disputant's claim. Second, China is a party to UNCLOS and so is bound by its provisions and dispute mechanisms.

After the ruling from the UNCLOS Tribunal on 13 July 2016, Beijing attempted to make its claim more agreeable to the UNCLOS. It separated China's sovereignty claim over the SCS islands (*Nanhai Zhudao*); their maritime entitlement (territorial sea and EEZ); and the historic rights—with no mention of nine-dash line.[70] The wording *Nanhai Zhudao* (the SCS islands) signifies a new development, given that in the previous official documents, that is, the Diplomatic Note to the UN Secretary General in 2011[71] and the 2014 Position Paper,[72] China asserted that *Nansha Qundao* (Spratly Islands) instead of *Nanhai Zhudao* are fully entitled to an EEZ and continental shelf. Tribunal ruled that all features in the *Nansha*

(Spratly) Islands cannot generate more than 12 nm territorial sea and it did not rule on *Xisha* (Paracel) and *Dongsha* (Pratas) Islands (which both might qualify as "islands" and be entitled to an EEZ). Therefore, Beijing's use of the wording *Nanhai Zhudao* (SCS islands) makes its claim more agreeable to the UNCLOS.[73] Even though China's attitude is still far from reconciliatory and compromising, this step after the UNCLOS Tribunal ruling signifies a slight change towards a more moderate and progressive orientation towards reconcile itself with the UNCLOS.

3.4 Conclusion

This chapter highlighted the importance of a territorial or jurisdictional claim (or both) in deciding whether a country is an expansionist or not. If a country, because of its growing power, harbours an ambition to conquer a territory for which this has no historical or legal basis, then it should be considered expansionist. This chapter finds that China's SCS claim precedes the founding of the PRC and thus is not directly due to its rising power. China has strong links with the SCS and has grounds to dispute its rights in it. Even though China has the right to dispute its rights in the SCS, in terms of exercising sovereignty according to international law, its claim is not indisputable. Its activities, as well as those of other claimants, have been sporadic and inconsistent.

Theoretically, the above points show that China is not an offensive realist nor expansionist. An offensive realist seeks to maximise its power by conquest and expansion.[74] This position resembles that of Nazi Germany. However, the behaviour of China in the SCS is a far cry from that of Nazi Germany.[75] Germany had no right to dispute the territory it invaded in the World War II and its claim over the newly occupied territory was purely based on military conquest. Furthermore, Germany had no strong historical presence to the invaded territory. In contrast, China has had a strong historical presence in the SCS and has inherited the territorial claim from the previous regime. As such, a country like PRC—which has had a strong historical presence in the SCS and has inherited the claim from the previous regime—cannot be characterised as that of an offensive realist or expansionist.

However, the UNCLOS Tribunal ruling eliminated the uncertainty of maritime rights disputes in the SCS to a great extent. China's historic rights and the nine-dash line ruled invalid and unlawful from the perspective of UNCLOS. China's response to the ruling is a barometer for whether China's future behaviour in the SCS is likely to be defensive or offensive. China's slight adjustment in reiterating its claim after the ruling gives hope that it may heed international law in guiding its future behaviours.

Notes

1. F. Dupuy and P. M. Dupuy, "A Legal Analysis of China's Historical Rights Claim in the South China Sea," *American Journal of International Law*, 107, no. 1 (2013): 124–41.
2. China Focus, *Declaration of the Government of the People's Republic of China on China's Territorial Sea*, 4 September 1958, Beijing, 2014, http://www.chinausfocus.com/upload/file/2014/Annex1-4.pdf (accessed 2 January 2017).
3. Shicun Wu, "Joint Development: An Ad Hoc Solution to the South China Sea Dispute," *China Oceans Law Review*, (2007): 1.
4. Xiaoqin Shi, "UNCLOS and China's Claim in the South China Sea," (2015).
5. D. P. O'Connell and I. A. Shearer, *The International Law of the Sea* (Oxford: Clarendon Press, 1982).
6. Dupuy and Dupuy, "A Legal Analysis of China's Historical Rights Claim in the South China Sea," 124–41.
7. United Nations, *Chinese Note Verbale to the United Nations Secretary General No. CML/8/2011*, 2011, http://www.un.org/Depts/los/clcs_new/submissions_files/mysvnm33_09/chn_2011_re_phl_e.pdf (accessed 12 February 2015).
8. Yun Sun, "Studying the South China Sea: The Chinese Perspective," *East and South China Seas Bulletin*, 9, (2012).
9. Foreign Ministry of the People's Republic of China, *Position Paper of the Government of the People's Republic of China on the Matter of Jurisdiction in the South China Sea Arbitration Initiated by the Republic of the Philippines*, Beijing, 2014, http://www.fmprc.gov.cn/mfa_eng/zxxx_662805/t1217147.shtml (accessed 8 December 2014).
10. United Nations, China's Diplomatic Note to the United Nations CML/8/2011, http://www.un.org/depts/los/clcs_new/submissions_files/mysvnm33_09/chn_2011_re_phl_e.pdf
11. *China Adheres to the Position of Settling Through Negotiation the Relevant Disputes Between China and the Philippines in the South China Sea (People's Republic of China Response to the 12 July 2016 ruling on the South China Sea territorial claims by the UNCLOS Tribunal)*, Beijing, 2016, http://usa.chinadaily.com.cn/epaper/2016-07/14/content_26088896.htm (accessed 15 July 2016).

12. Ian Storey, "China's Bilateral and Multilateral Diplomacy in the South China Sea," *Cooperation from Strength*, 56, (2012).
13. R. Y. Jennings, *The Acquisition of Territory in International Law*, vol. 1963 (Manchester: Manchester University Press, 1963), 6–7.
14. Melda Malek, "A Legal Assessment of China's Historic Claims in the South China Sea," *Australian Journal of Maritime and Ocean Affairs*, 5, no. 1 (2013): 28–36.
15. Greg Austin, *China's Ocean Frontier: International Law, Military Force and National Development*, vol. 17 (St Leonards, N.S.W: Allen & Unwin in Association with the Dept. of International Relations and the Northeast Asia Program, Research School of Pacific and Asian Studies, Australian National University, 1998), 110; Marwyn S. Samuels, *Contest for the South China Sea* (New York: Methuen, 1982), 52–53.
16. Austin, *China's Ocean Frontier: International Law, Military Force and National Development*, 17, 111–12; Samuels, *Contest for the South China Sea*, 53.
17. Austin, *China's Ocean Frontier: International Law, Military Force and National Development*, 17, 112.
18. Samuels, *Contest for the South China Sea*, 67.
19. Ibid., 63.
20. Austin, *China's Ocean Frontier: International Law, Military Force and National Development*, 17, 114–15.
21. Ibid., 104.
22. Ibid., 120.
23. Dieter Heinzig, *Disputed Islands in the South China Sea: Paracels, Spratlys, Pratas, Macclesfield Bank* (Wiesbaden: Harrassowitz, 1976), 22–23.
24. La souverainete sur les archipels Paracels et Spratleys, 110–111 in Austin, *China's Ocean Frontier: International Law, Military Force and National Development*, 17, 120.
25. Ibid., 126.
26. Han, Nianlong. *Diplomacy of Contemporary China*. Hong Kong: New Horizon Press, 1990 quoted in Junwu Pan, "Territorial Dispute between China and Vietnam in the South China Sea," *Journal of East Asia and International Law*, 5, no. 1 (2012): 213–34.
27. Ibid.
28. Interview with Centre of International Law, National University of Singapore (NUS) senior researcher, Hao Duy Phan SJD on 18 December 2015.
29. Austin, *China's Ocean Frontier: International Law, Military Force and National Development*, 17, 129.
30. Ibid., 136–37; Samuels, *Contest for the South China Sea*, 68.
31. Austin, *China's Ocean Frontier: International Law, Military Force and National Development*, 17, 137.

32. Ibid., 138; Bill Hayton, *The South China Sea: The Struggle for Power in Asia* (Yale University Press, 2014), 54; Samuels, *Contest for the South China Sea*, 61–62.
33. Bill Hayton, "Fact, Fiction and the South China Sea," *Asia Sentinel*, 25 May 2015, http://www.asiasentinel.com/politics/fact-fiction-south-china-sea/ (accessed 4 May 2016).
34. Austin, *China's Ocean Frontier: International Law, Military Force and National Development*, 17, 133.
35. Ibid., 133–34.
36. Samuels, *Contest for the South China Sea*, 64.
37. Austin, *China's Ocean Frontier: International Law, Military Force and National Development*, 17, 135.
38. Ning Lu, *Flashpoint Spratlys* (Singapore: Dolphin Trade Press, 1995), 25; Heinzig, *Disputed Islands in the South China Sea: Paracels, Spratlys, Pratas, Macclesfield Bank*, 30.
39. Hayton, *The South China Sea: The Struggle for Power in Asia*, 95.
40. Samuels, *Contest for the South China Sea*, 81–86.
41. Austin, *China's Ocean Frontier: International Law, Military Force and National Development*, 17, 145.
42. Ibid.
43. Ibid., 149.
44. Samuels, *Contest for the South China Sea*, 93.
45. Division for Ocean and the Law of the Sea, Office of Legal Affairs, United Nations, *United Nations Convention on the Law of the Sea*, http://www.un.org/depts/los/convention_agreements/texts/unclos/UNCLOS-TOC.htm (accessed 12 March 2016).
46. Robert Beckman, "The UN Convention on the Law of the Sea and the Maritime Disputes in the South China Sea," *The American Journal of International Law*, 107, no. 1 (2013): 142–63.
47. Ibid., 156. According to the author's interview with a Chinese Academy of Social Sciences (CASS) Scholar on 5 November 2015 in Beijing, Chinese top leaders still have not reached an agreement on the meaning of the nine-dash line.
48. US Department of State, *Limits in the Seas: Maritime Claims in the South China Sea*, NO. 143, Washington, DC, 2014, https://www.state.gov/documents/organization/234936.pdf (accessed 3 February 2015).
49. Ibid., 5.
50. Ibid., 7.
51. United Nations, *Exclusive Economic Zone and Continental Self Act*, 26 June 1998, http://www.un.org/Depts/los/LEGISLATIONANDTREATIES/PDFFILES/chn_1998_eez_act.pdf (accessed 11 May 2016).
52. Beckman, "The UN Convention on the Law of the Sea and the Maritime Disputes in the South China Sea," 142–63.

53. Foreign Ministry of the People's Republic of China, *Foreign Ministry Spokesperson Jiang Yu's Regular Press Conference on 15 September 2011*, Washington, DC, http://www.china-embassy.org/eng/fyrth/t860126.htm (accessed 3 March 2016).
54. Zhiguo Gao and Bing Bing Jia, "The Nine-Dash Line in the South China Sea: History, Status, and Implications," *American Journal of International Law*, 107, no. 1 (2013): 98–124.
55. Shi, "UNCLOS and China's Claim in the South China Sea."
56. Wu, "Joint Development: An Ad Hoc Solution to the South China Sea Dispute," 1.
57. Keyuan Zou, "Historic Rights in International Law and in China's Practice," *Ocean Development & International Law*, 32, no. 2 (2001): 149–68.
58. R. R. Churchill and A. V. Lowe, *The Law of the Sea* (Yonkers, NY; Manchester: Manchester University Press, 1999), vol. 3, 43.
59. Zou, "Historic Rights in International Law and in China's Practice," 149–68.
60. Ibid., 157–58.
61. Ibid., 160.
62. Ibid.
63. L. I. Jinming and L. I. Dexia, "The Dotted Line on the Chinese Map of the South China Sea: A Note," Ibid. 34, no. 3–4 (2003): 287–95.
64. Shi, "UNCLOS and China's Claim in the South China Sea."
65. US Department of State, *Limits in the Seas: Maritime Claims in the South China Sea*, NO. 143, Washington, DC, 2014, https://www.state.gov/documents/organization/234936.pdf (accessed 3 February 2015).
66. Zou, "Historic Rights in International Law and in China's Practice," 149–68.
67. Dupuy and Dupuy, "A Legal Analysis of China's Historical Rights Claim in the South China Sea," 124–41.
68. Department of Foreign Affairs of the Republic of the Philippines, *Notification and Statement of Claim on West Philippine Sea*, 22 January 2013, Manila, https://www.dfa.gov.ph/index.php/2013-06-27-21-50-36/unclos (accessed 8 March 2015).
69. Foreign Ministry of the People's Republic of China, *Position Paper of the Government of the People's Republic of China on the Matter of Jurisdiction in the South China Sea Arbitration Initiated by the Republic of the Philippines*, Beijing, 2014, http://www.fmprc.gov.cn/mfa_eng/zxxx_662805/t1217147.shtml (accessed 8 December 2014).
70. "Full Text of Chinese Government Statement on China's Territorial Sovereignty and Maritime Rights and Interests in South China Sea," *Xinhuanet*, 12 July 2016, http://news.xinhuanet.com/english/2016-07/12/c_135507754.htm (accessed 15 July 2016).

71. United Nations, *Chinese Note Verbale to the United Nations Secretary General No. CML/8/2011*, 2011, http://www.un.org/Depts/los/clcs_new/submissions_files/mysvnm33_09/chn_2011_re_phl_e.pdf (accessed 12 February 2015).
72. Foreign Ministry of the People's Republic of China, *Position Paper of the Government of the People's Republic of China on the Matter of Jurisdiction in the South China Sea Arbitration Initiated by the Republic of the Philippines*, Beijing, 2014, http://www.fmprc.gov.cn/mfa_eng/zxxx_662805/t1217147.shtml (accessed 8 December 2014).
73. Andrew Chubb, "South China Sea: Did China Just Clarify the Nine-Dash Line?," *East Asia Forum*, 14 July 2016, http://www.eastasiaforum.org/2016/07/14/did-china-just-clarify-the-nine-dash-line/ (accessed 16 August 2016).
74. Taliaferro, "Security Seeking under Anarchy: Defensive Realism Revisited," 128–61; Tang, *A Theory of Security Strategies for Our Time: Defensive Realism*, 108.
75. "China behaving like Nazi Germany in South China Sea, says Benigno Aquino," *The Guardian*, 3 June 2015, https://www.theguardian.com/world/2015/jun/03/china-nazi-germany-south-china-sea-philippine-president-benigno-aquino (accessed 13 June 2015).

CHAPTER 4

China's Interests in the South China Sea

4.1 China's Growing Interests in the SCS

China has multiple stakes in its near seas, particularly the South China Sea (SCS). As the country has been growing enormously in the past decades in almost every aspect, so are its interests. This chapter discusses the significance of the SCS to China's economy, geopolitics, security, national integrity, and the regime's legitimacy, and if any offensive or defensive motivation exists in those interests.

4.1.1 Resources

The presence of natural resources, primarily hydrocarbons and fisheries, is undoubtedly a factor, contributing to the strategic importance of the SCS. However, the strategic value of these resources depends on their exact extent, their ease of recovery, and their direct significance to China's (or any other proximal nation's) needs.

In China, coal is the primary energy source, accounting for about 70% of total energy consumption. However, oil and gas are also important. In 1993, China became a net oil importer when its crude oil imports exceeded its export. By 1996, China was experiencing a decrease in oil production and the demand growth was 5.8% annually, compared to output growth of 2.8%.[1] The International Energy Agency predicted that by 2030, China would supersede the US as the biggest consumer of oil, and its gas market

K. H. Raditio, *Understanding China's Behaviour in the South China Sea*, https://doi.org/10.1007/978-981-13-1283-0_4

would be bigger than the countries of the European Union combined.[2] China became a net importer of natural gas in 2007, and the demand for such imports is expected to rise significantly after 2020.[3] The growth of its population and its modernisation agenda will render energy and food resources (including fish and seafood) as important for China's sustainable development.

The US Energy Information Administration estimates that within the SCS there can be found 11 billion barrels (1.7 billion tonnes) of oil and 190 trillion cubic feet (5.4 trillion cubic metres) of natural gas hydrocarbon reserves.[4] China's Ministry of Land and Resources has more optimistic data, calculating 23–30 billion tonnes of petroleum resources and 16 trillion cubic metres of natural gas deposits within the nine-dash line. This latter estimate would mean the total hydrocarbon deposits in the SCS comprise one-third of China's total oil and gas resources and account for 12% of global hydrocarbon resources.[5] In brief, there is a considerable gap regarding the estimation of the hydrocarbon resources between China and other countries.

Accordingly, the SCS should not be considered simply as having the potential to provide a panacea for China's energy security problem for at least two reasons. First, it is important to distinguish between resources and reserves. A resource estimate indicates the whole quantity of hydrocarbons on site. Reserves are an element of the resources that may be extractable at the actual market price. It has been suggested that the recovery factor for the SCS is 10%—which is lower than the conventional rate of 35%—while the recovery factor for natural gas is assessed to be about 75%.[6] The hydrocarbon resources in the SCS can only help to alleviate China's energy security problem if it is assessed in terms of production, instead of the quantity of resources on site. Second, China's energy security challenge should focus more on managing domestic demand, that is, increasing its efficiency and encouraging energy conservation.[7] The capacity of the SCS reserves in compensating for the gap between expected demand and supply is insignificant. It is misleading to posit that the hydrocarbon reserves in the SCS could alleviate energy security issues in China or any claimant state.[8]

In terms of fishery resources, the SCS represents 12% of the world's fish catch, and this resource keeps depleting.[9] China's fish consumption grew annually at 6% from 1990 to 2010, and its population consumes 34% of the world's fish food supply—almost three times that of Central Asia and Europe combined and over five times that of North America.[10]

According to the World Bank's estimation, China's fish consumption per capita will reach 41 kg by 2030—which is more than double world's average.[11] The majority of maritime fishing activities (78%) take place in China's disputed waters, including the SCS.[12] Moreover, about 15 million people work in the Chinese fishery industry.[13] This makes China's effort to secure its purported "traditional fishing ground" for its fishermen extremely urgent.

In brief, the hydrocarbon and fishery resources add strategic value to the SCS, particularly in the context of China's development and modernisation. Since China has been fishing in the SCS since ancient times, its interest in defending the access to the SCS resources is not offensive. However, action taken to monopolise these resources in the SCS, such as expelling Philippine fishermen from the Scarborough Shoal, is an offensive realist action.

4.1.2 Security

Regarding security in the SCS, China faces two challenges: the first is the security of its territory—especially in its eastern coastal provinces—from enemy invasion; the second is security for its trade route. Historically, China was invaded several times from the sea by Japan and European powers during the rule of the Qing Dynasty. The Republic of China (ROC)—which was marred by civil war and the Sino-Japanese War—did not have a chance to fortify its maritime border by developing its navy. Regrettably, China did not learn from this historical experience during the reign of Mao Zedong. Even though the country was successful in launching its atomic bomb in 1964, it still overlooked the development of its navy during this period.

Chinese scholars suggest that China was a great maritime power during the Ming Dynasty, in which the famous voyage of Zheng He to the Southeast Asian region took place. However, after the Ming Dynasty, China ignored its navy, which resulted in the country's humiliation due to the intrusion of the eight-nation alliance in 1900 and the Japanese invasion in the 1930s. Chinese scholars attribute China's defeat in this latter instance to its weak navy.[14]

After entering an era of reform and modernisation, the country began to realise the importance of a strong navy to safeguard its maritime border. One scholar argued that "neglecting the sea is a historical failure; today and in the future, we have to bear the burden."[15]

Despite the fact that China's weak navy was responsible for not preventing the invasions of the early twentieth century, China has never perceived itself as a maritime power in the last 500 years.[16] Historically, China's main threats came from Mongols from the steppes, which propelled it to build the Great Wall. The idea that an enemy will invade from the sea was unthinkable at the time for the Chinese. China has the deep-rooted mindset of being a continental power, instead of a maritime power regardless of the fact that great sailors in coastal areas like the Hokkien of Fujian Province were instrumental to its continental authority. This authority system did not contribute sufficiently for China to develop its maritime power.[17]

Similarly, Zheng He's expedition to Southeast Asia cannot be accepted as evidence for China's status as a great maritime power since extensive sea trade lasted only during the Ming Dynasty. Thus, the longstanding mindset of China as a continental power remained unchanged. Even after China was defeated by the Japanese at the end of the nineteenth century, the country did not pay significant attention to the development of its naval strength. Therefore, the problem with Chinese naval development is not a matter of policy failure; it is rather the result of its deep-rooted mindset as a continental power—constructed by China's experiences in ensuring security throughout its history.

After the end of the tumultuous Mao era, China underwent modernisation and economic development under Deng Xiaoping's leadership. Unlike his predecessor who was guided by radical leftist ideology, Deng embraced the market economy and permitted some of the Chinese provinces to prosper ahead of others. These provinces, such as Guangdong, Zhejiang, and Fujian are located in Chinese coastal areas. In fact, most Chinese also inhabit China's eastern regions, making them the most populated in the country. This adds more vulnerability for China's security.

The seas adjacent to China's prosperous areas from north to south comprise the Bohai Sea, the Yellow Sea, the East China Sea, and the SCS; these are known as "the near seas" and are China's frontier. They form a "maritime strategic belt" to protect China's population and flourishing economy.[18] It has been suggested by Zhang Wenmu, a Chinese strategist, that if China does not have absolute control over Taiwan and other islands in the SCS, it will not be able to guarantee the security of Chinese commercial hubs such as Shenzhen, Shanghai, and Guangzhou.[19]

The security of sea routes, which is related to China's survival and economic development, is also a significant issue. This security concern reaches beyond Chinese geographical territory to China's interest in the global economy. China is aware that the post-war system after 1945 is based on maritime transportation instead of continental traffic. In this global system, a country does not fight another country to grab new territory for survival. The great challenge is control over the sea itself and competition for trade, technology, and mobility. Sea traffic supports international trade and the global economy. It has even been claimed that whoever controls the sea, controls the global economy.[20]

As China becomes an economic giant, it demands an uninterrupted access to resources to fuel its economic engine. Zhang has argued that China considers equal sharing of the resources as an "international democratic right", a demand which seems very urgent since China is experiencing an "absolute dependence" on energy resources.[21] He goes on to suggest the Chinese concept of sea power and sea right. According to him, sea power is the capability of a state to sail through the sea and maintain the security of the sailing expedition. Sea right is a right endowed by international law to sovereign states to use the sea for their national interest. Zhang continues by stating that sea power is the means to achieving sea right.[22] He implies that if a state does not have sea power, it cannot exercise its sea right. By developing its navy, China aims to exercise the rights as enjoyed equally by other great powers.

China's interests are not confined to its territory but expand beyond its boundaries. Moreover, as the economy becomes the country's main priority, the national defence serves where China's economic interests lie. In the sea, China's interests lie along the sea lanes of its trade routes. China's oil imports account for 10% of its total energy consumption and transportation, with some manufacturing sectors relying heavily on them. It is projected that its dependence on oil imports will reach 75% by 2030.[23]

Half of China's oil consumption is from imports and 80%-90% of that oil is imported across the SCS. Moreover, the SCS is the passage for 80% of oil imports to Japan, South Korea, and Taiwan respectively.[24] Given that the SCS is the shipping route for nearly all China's oil imports, the SCS becomes crucial for China's development. The SCS is one of the region's most important trade routes, since goods accounting for USD 5 trillion are carried by ships through these waters annually.[25]

Sea trade, directly and indirectly, also impacts one-seventh or about 180 million members of the Chinese labour force.[26] The fact that the US dominates global maritime security gives a sense of insecurity to China; it seems that its development is in the hands of others.[27] China insists that its maritime vein lies along the SCS—from the Malacca Strait to the Gulf of Aden, and it claims rights to secure this sea lane.[28] One significant difference between China and a hegemonic power like the US is that it only needs to secure the sea lane that is crucial to its development instead of dominating the sea lanes globally.

Without a strong navy, China will not be able to secure its sea lanes and develop sustainably. As China's dependency on international trade and energy importation is growing deeper, it feels more pressure to secure its interests at sea. China is facing traditional security threats and non-traditional security threats due to piracy.

In 2012, 60% of China's oil was imported from overseas; based on conservative estimates this number will keep rising to 75% in 2030.[29] China imports its oil mainly from the Persian Gulf, Africa, Russia, and Central Asia.[30] Half of its oil imports pass the Gulf of Aden which is known as a den of pirates.[31]

In December 2008, China launched its navy to join the global anti-piracy operation off the coast of Somalia in the Gulf of Aden. This was the first time that China participated in the global initiative to combat the piracy. Admiral Wu Shengli, commander of the Chinese Navy, stated that the operation aimed to protect the nation's "strategic interest" and play a role in peacekeeping in the region.[32] In this operation, China deployed 800 crew members including 70 soldiers from the PLAN, 2 destroyers (DDG-169 Wuhan and DDG-171 Haikou), and the supply ship *Weishanhu*.

Despite China's heavy reliance on resource imports since it became a net oil importer in 1990s, it only deployed its navy at the end of 2008. There are at least two reasons that have propelled China to deploy its frigates to join the anti-piracy operation. The first is the hijacking of the Chinese ship Zhenhua-4 in the Gulf of Aden on December 2008. To rescue the ship and its 30 crew members, China needed to ask a smaller country, Malaysia, for help. A Malaysian naval ship and helicopter successfully countered the Somali pirates. This was not the first time that year that a Chinese ship had been hijacked; according to the Chinese Foreign Ministry, previously there were seven hijacking cases within 2008 involving Chinese ships or Chinese crew members.[33]

The second reason for China's naval deployment is due to the initiatives from India and Pakistan to join the anti-piracy operation in October 2008.[34] China was the last of the permanent members of the Security Council to join the operation. If China had not joined the operation, it would have been seen as a free rider in the international community, due its heavy dependence on sea transportation yet minimal contribution in maintaining its security.

The traditional security threat which endangers China's sea lane of communication comes from other states that China considers aim to contain its growth. The 2010–2011 Obama pivot to Asia has been regarded by many in Beijing as targeting China. However, many years before this, in 1993, China experienced the unpleasant Yinhe incident, in which a Chinese ship was interrupted by US naval forces. The Yinhe sailed from Tianjin to its final destination, Kuwait and transited in Shanghai, Hong Kong, Singapore, Jakarta, Dubai, and Dammam. The US Navy blockaded the ship near the Gulf of Aden because of the suspicion that the ship carried chemical weapons for Iran.[35] This stranded it for 12 days near the entrance to the Strait of Hormuz.

The Yinhe incident pinpointed China's vulnerability in securing a route valuable to its economic interest in high seas. Together with other incidents vis-à-vis the US, such as the 1999 bombing of the Chinese Embassy in Belgrade, the 2001 EP-3 reconnaissance incident in Hainan, and the 2009 *Impeccable* incident, the Yinhe incident demonstrates that without a powerful military, China can never secure its interest beyond its borders or deal with a great power's infringement. Given the many threats faced on its sea route, China has acted with urgency to secure the closest sea lanes to its territory, that is, the SCS. The Chinese leadership has also been concerned about terrorism activities in the Malacca Strait which potentially endanger the safety of its shipping and the US' "economic neo-containment" by disrupting its sea lanes of communication.[36]

In terms of defence capacity building, China has secretly built the Yulin submarine base in Hainan Island as a home for China's nuclear-propelled submarines as early as 2008. This base is close to the SCS which China is determined to dominate. The security threat in the Asia-Pacific is sensed not primarily from construction of this base—which has been characterised by concealment and stealth—but from its increased capacity in nuclear-propelled submarines.[37] It is estimated that by 2025, China will possess 10–15 nuclear-propelled attack submarines (SSN) and 6–8 nuclear-propelled ballistic missile submarines (SSBN).[38]

This inevitably prompts US suspicion over China's military build-up. The US intelligence activities in the SCS and China's near seas were conducted in the early 2000s. One of the prominent events was the 2001 EP-3 Reconnaissance incident on Hainan Island. It is difficult to ascertain who first militarised the SCS. Were the US activities triggered by China's military build-up in the region or was China provoked by the US moves—making the militarisation of the SCS a self-fulfilling prophecy?

Both China and the US, as well as other claimants, have militarised the SCS since they deployed their military personnel to seize land features or conduct offensive military activities. In the case of the 2009 *Impeccable* incident, the US cast sophisticated eyes on the Yulin submarine base. Since China did not have the capability to retaliate against the US' intelligence activities, this was seen by the Chinese as unveiling China's vulnerability.[39] The incidents in the SCS between the US and China underscore the lack of trust and transparency between these two states. On one side China keeps expanding its military capability and on the other the US intensifies its monitoring on China's growing power.[40]

Apart from its nuclear submarine base in Hainan, China also harbours an ambition to build its aircraft carriers. This has been envisioned by Liu Huaqing, in his outlined two stages of naval development. Liu believes that the Chinese Navy should become a green water power dominating the seas adjacent to its territory. The primary goals of this strategy are controlling the SCS and reclaiming Taiwan.[41] The next stage would be building a blue water navy which operates in the Indian and Pacific Oceans and beyond.[42]

According to Liu, the development of each stage will require aircraft carriers. For instance, operations in the SCS which is a hundred miles away from China's mainland needs air power backed up by aircraft carriers, given the short reach of Chinese fighter planes.[43] Liu claims that China also has no choice but keep up with the development of the Indian and Japanese navies.[44]

In brief, the interest in securing the SCS for defence and economic development is not an offensive realist attitude. History has shown that the sea is China's weak point. Moreover, securing the trade route is also an inevitable choice for rising China. From this point of view, China harbours no malign intention in defending its interest in the SCS.

4.1.3 Geopolitics

China's geopolitical claim in the SCS has become relevant, given the speed of its economic development. Since the practice of international law does not allow a country to claim sovereignty over an exclusive body of water, establishing a claim over land features in the SCS becomes decisive to dominating the waters of the SCS. Historically, China had no interest over the Paracels and Spratlys, as revealed by one author: "until the Second World War, the islands in the SCS were only worth their weight in guano."[45] The land features in the SCS indeed do not have significant value in themselves; they serve as the legal basis to control the surrounding waters and manage the resources within them.

Strategically, the SCS also provides the shortest access to connect the Indian Ocean and the western Pacific. For instance, the US Pacific Command made use of the SCS to reach the Indian Ocean during its military operation in Afghanistan in 2001 and 2002 by transiting its assets and supplies in its bases in Pearl Harbour, Guam, and Japan. This route has been accessed by other regional navies as well.[46]

The strategic importance of the SCS for China's development propels Beijing to develop its navy southward instead of eastward. Even though China is not comfortable with the US containment, building its navy eastward to contest the US prominence in the Pacific is less urgent than dominating the southern sea. By controlling the SCS, China can establish a sea denial zone, which means its rivals are denied access to use the waters and general area adjacent to mainland China for a certain time.[47] Dominion in the SCS benefits Beijing not only in securing its development but also in consolidating its centrality in Asia.[48]

If China rules the SCS and has a strong presence there, it will become a de facto "Southeast Asian nation"; correspondingly Russia is both a European and Far Eastern nation and the US is both an Atlantic and Pacific nation.[49] With its active diplomacy in Six-Party Talks through the Shanghai Cooperation Organization, China has already become an East Asian and Central Asian nation simultaneously. The control of the SCS will give Beijing a role in participating or even dominating in Southeast Asian affairs and this role for China as a Southeast Asian nation would undoubtedly boost its leverage in international diplomacy.

Strategically, China's interpretation of the Mahan Doctrine influences the way China perceives the geopolitical meaning of the SCS. Chinese navy officers have been interested in Mahan since the earliest day of the Communist rule, and it gained significance in the 1980s thanks to Admiral Liu Huaqing.[50] According to the Mahan Doctrine, to possess sea power, a country must secure each of "three pillars": global trade, naval and commercial fleets, and distributed naval bases along the sea routes to meet warships' need for fuel.[51] Mahan also pointed out that a country's sea power lies in its capability to secure and dominate the sea route of its warships and merchant shipping.

He referred to this as the "command of the sea" which is defined as that "overbearing power on the sea which drives the enemy's flag from it, or allows it to appear only as a fugitive; and through which commerce moves to and fro from the enemy's shores. This overbearing power can only be exercised by great navies."[52]

In accordance with Mahan's theory on sea control, Liu Huaqing projected that the Chinese navy should be able to control the near seas, within two island chains. The first island chain stretches from Japan to the Liuqi Islands, then to Taiwan and the Philippines. The seas within the first island chain include the Yellow Sea, the East China Sea, and the SCS. The second island chain stretches from Japan's Ogaswara-gunto Islands to the Northern Mariana Islands, which includes Guam. The projection of Chinese navy control over the seas within these two island chains reveals China's realist attitude which perceives all these islands as "archipelagic extensions of the Chinese landmass."[53]

China also considers that these island chains are the traditional frontiers of US containment against the country.[54] Therefore, these island chains strategically mean two things for China. First, they are a demarcation of China's denial of other countries' access to this part of the sea, which is meant as a no-go zone area for US military activities. Second, they comprise the boundaries of the containment that needs to be broken to fulfil China's ambition to be a sea power (Fig. 4.1).

The Mahanian view resonates very well in this era of Chin's strong economic focus. Therefore, China sees its main sea lanes, that is, the SCS, as subject to its control. China sees its near seas, especially the SCS, as its property with which it can channel its ambition to become a great power. Historically, great powers gained their domination by controlling the seas adjacent to their territory. The US sought control over the Caribbean, Italy over the Mediterranean, and Greece over the Aegean.[55]

Major General Jiang Shiliang, director of the Military Communications and Transportation Department of the People's Liberation Army (PLA) General Logistics Department in his publication on Chinese Military Science interprets the Mahan Doctrine in this way:

> In modern times, securing the absolute control of communications is turning with each passing day into an indispensable essential factor in ensuring the realization of national interests. Economic development, the top priority of China's leadership, depends on the command of communications on the sea, which is vital for the future and destiny of the nation.[56]

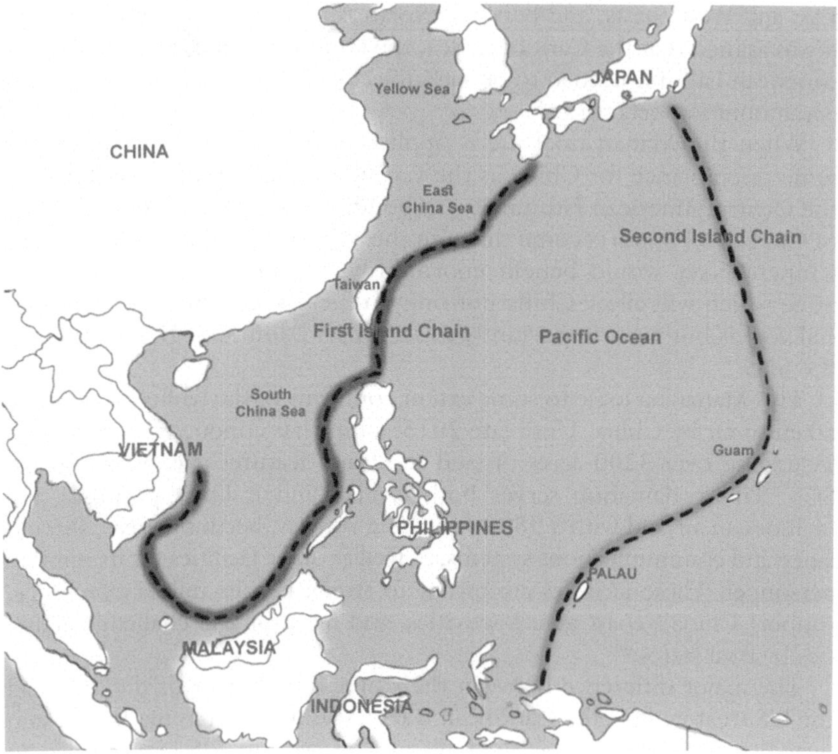

Fig. 4.1 The first and second island chains as depicted by A.B. Maramis

Strategically, Jiang describes the Mahan doctrine of "command of communications" as comprising four essential points. The first is the strategic importance of the access or passageway to support the flow of resources and information during battle. The second is the control over vital locations such as seaports, islands, and bases to ensure the command of communication. The third is the capability to exercise power over seas. Finally, the fourth is the system of support facilities to ensure naval operations.[57]

Mahan guided the US policy in the nineteenth century towards a perception of the importance of the Caribbean Sea and especially the Central American Isthmus. This isthmus holds considerable strategic importance for the US since it may channel trade interest in the Far East and support the free movement of the US Navy and commercial shipping between the

East and West coasts, and between North America and Asia.[58] Therefore, it was argued that the Caribbean Sea, the Gulf of Mexico, and the Central American Isthmus needed to be the subject to US domination, given their paramount importance.

When the Mahan doctrine is applied to China, the SCS bears the same resemblance for China as the Caribbean Sea does for the US, and the Central American Isthmus corresponds to the Malacca Strait.[59] Most of China's oil imports come through the SCS via the Malacca Strait. The Chinese Navy would benefit enormously if it can install bases in the SCS, which will allow China not only to fuel its warships and commercial vessels but most importantly to secure and dominate the sea lanes in the SCS.

This Mahanian logic to some extent conforms to the reality of the steps taken so far by China. Until late 2015, China has conducted reclamation by adding over 3200 acres of land to 7 land features it controls on the SCS. This reclamation serves both civilian and military purposes and includes an airfield with a 9800-foot-long runway, berthing areas, surveillance and communications systems, as well as other facilities for its military personnel. These facilities are meant to strengthen its military presence, support China's coast guard activities, and monitor and challenge activities by rival states.[60]

The major difference between the Chinese treatment of the SCS and the US treatment of the Caribbean is that Washington has made no claim over the Caribbean Sea or the Gulf of Mexico. The US strategy was to prevent any European navy from establishing bases along the sea lanes leading to the isthmus.[61] In the nineteenth century, the US enjoyed the privilege of being the most powerful navy in the region; there was no significant challenge from other powers. However, for China, to apply Mahanian logic in the SCS is not an easy task. China has overlooked the development of its navy during the Mao era. In addition, many of the geographical features in the SCS are occupied by other rival claimants, that is, Vietnam and the Philippines.

There are strong indications that China's naval strategists are interested in the Mahan Doctrine and are trying to apply it to the Chinese context. The massive construction of artificial islands in 2014 and 2015 also supports the argument that China adopts the Mahan doctrine to some extent. This could be seen as an offensive realist move. However, practically, there is no compelling evidence that China has ever denied access for a US military ship to enter its first island chain, let alone its second island chain, even though it has been involved in several skirmishes with US naval vessels in the vicinity of China's controlled features in the SCS.

China has enjoyed great opportunities in the aftermath of the Cold War. Since the 1990s, the military balance began to shift to Asia—in favour of China. Hugh White suggests three factors for this shift. First, China's growing economy has boosted its defence budget. Second, there has been trade of military weaponry and technology from Russia and the former Soviet states to China. Third, the collapse of the Soviet Union dispelled China's primary continental menace and made it prioritise its naval development.[62]

However, China's ambition to dominate the SCS is restrained by the activities of other claimants, including their occupation of SCS areas. Each claimant state keeps condemning other claimants' activities for violations of sovereignty such as detaining other claimant countries' fishermen and sabotaging research activities. Therefore, China perceives controlling sea lanes in the SCS as difficult to carry out in practice without maintaining its territorial claim over all SCS features.

Despite its limited development, the Vietnamese Navy cannot be underestimated since it is the only navy in the region which dared to directly fight the Chinese Navy in the 1974 Paracel incident and the 1988 Johnson Reef incident. Additionally, even though the Philippine Navy is very weak, probably the weakest in Southeast Asia, Manila is a staunch ally of Washington in the region.[63] This creates a hurdle for China to pursue its interest in the SCS.

4.1.4 Taiwan

Taiwan is of great significance to China in many aspects. General Douglas MacArthur perceived Taiwan as "an unsinkable aircraft carrier" from which external powers can project their forces along China's maritime boundary.[64] Taiwan's strategic position also enables outside powers to execute a strategic containment against China. The island served the US intelligence operations against the People's Republic of China (PRC) during the Cold War, which underlines how insecure China can be if Taiwan is dominated by a rival power. The failure to control Taiwan will be detrimental to China's ambition of dominating its near seas and becoming a global sea power.[65]

Beijing has asserted that Taiwan is one of its core interests—which means it will not tolerate its independence from the PRC. Beijing is unsatisfied with the status quo and is trying to change it in its favour. To accomplish this, China must dominate the SCS. The relationship between Taiwan and the SCS is like two sides of a coin—China needs to control Taiwan to break the containment in the first island chain. Concomitantly, China also needs to dominate the SCS to ensure Taiwan's return to the mainland.

Securing of the first island chain, which is demarcated by an imaginary line stretching from southernmost Japan, Taiwan, and the Philippines is China's priority. If China cannot control Taiwan than it cannot realise its ambition to rule the seas within the first island chain, which are the Yellow Sea, the East China Sea, and the SCS. According to Lin Sixing, a professor at Jinan University, the fall of Taiwan to external forces means two things: first, there is no security for the southeastern Chinese coastal region; second, China is denied access to the Pacific.[66] China will be permanently restrained within the first island chain, and it will lose the opportunity to realise its ambition to be a sea power.[67]

The first island chain serves both as a defensive stronghold and as an offensive projection of China's power, a posture which is meant to tackle two main challenges.[68] The first is resisting invasion from the maritime boundary with an advanced maritime defence system, including nuclear arsenals. The second is securing the maritime routes and maritime interest in far seas. To cope with the latter, China's strategy should include "offshore defence", "near seas defence", and "far seas defence" simultaneously.[69]

In other words, China's maritime strategy cannot be properly executed as long as Taiwan is not under Beijing's full control. Moreover, since Taiwan is a core interest, China cannot exert its control over it if Beijing does not have significant power in the SCS. The strategy in the SCS that China needs to apply to prevent Taiwan's independence is sea denial. Sea denial is a strategy to create the SCS as a no-go zone for external powers, especially the US.

China is uneasy with the US military operations in the SCS for various reasons. First, it sees the US military activities as an intelligence operation to collect data on China's nuclear submarine base in Yulin, Hainan. Second, China also sees these US activities as a means of containment. Third, since the US is bound by the Taiwan Relations Act to resist any form of coercion that threatens Taiwan security, the US military activity in the SCS is seen by Beijing as an impediment to realising its unification with the mainland. Thus, China perceives that limiting access to US military activity in the SCS is crucial to distance Taiwan from the US and therefore increase the possibility for the mainland to reunify the island.[70]

China perceives Taiwan as its legitimate territory and this position is shared by most states including the US. Taiwanese reunification is also a priority in China's defence and diplomatic agenda. From this point of view, securing the SCS and Taiwanese reunification are inseparable. If China dominates the SCS, it will be one step ahead in bringing back Taiwan. On the other hand, if Taiwan is reunified with China, this also helps China to gain control of the SCS. Hence, from this perspective China's interest in the SCS is not offensive.

4.1.5 The Legitimacy of the Chinese Communist Party

Beijing undoubtedly sees the SCS from the perspective of supporting the Chinese Communist Party's (CCP) legitimacy. There is a two-way relationship between domestic legitimacy and foreign policy in that Chinese domestic politics shapes foreign policy and Beijing's foreign behaviour has a deep impact on the Communist Party's standing. Historically, the CCP gained legitimacy from its staunch position against a foreign invader who brought great humiliation to the Chinese people, especially during the Sino-Japanese War.[71] Since the SCS dispute is seen mainly as a sovereignty issue, the CCP's policy to defend China's territorial integrity becomes spotlighted in the Chinese politics.

The SCS issue is undoubtedly related to Chinese nationalism. The Chinese government and its people believe that features in the SCS have been parts of China since "time immemorial". The nine-dash line was drawn during the rule of the Kuomintang in 1947, and the Communist Party perceives it inherited all the territory of the ROC. In particular, since President Ma Ying-Jeou has asserted that all the features in the SCS belong to the ROC,[72] the SCS no longer becomes a PRC issue, but China's issue. Failure to defend sovereignty over the inherited territory would damage the reputation of the Communist regime.

Foreign diplomats were frequently told by Chinese government officials that Beijing receives great pressure from the people to adopt tougher measures in the SCS.[73] The patriotic sentiment in the Chinese media and among ordinary citizens regarding the SCS issue is extremely strong. Based on the survey conducted by the *People's Daily*, a Communist regime media organ, in January 2011, 97% of 4300 respondents considered that the SCS should be upgraded as a core interest.[74] According to two national surveys conducted by Cornell University's Jessica Wells and Yale University's Allan Dafoe between October 2015 and March 2016, Chinese netizens support government actions in the SCS, even though they think the actions are not as tough as the talk.[75] The surveys also found that the approval of Chinese government's SCS policy is waning after "provocative" moves by the US, for example, the FONOP in the SCS. This demonstrates that Chinese people feel very strongly about the SCS and they urge the government to act resolutely.

However, to simply attribute Beijing's move in the SCS to popular nationalism seems a gross simplification. First, the SCS is not a top issue for the Chinese people. In fact, they are more concerned about social justice, welfare, and equality,[76] all of which have a big impact on CCP legitimacy. Yet the source of the Communist Party's legitimacy is its ideology and role in advancing Chinese aspirations.[77] Moreover, Chinese people care more about domestic problems and how the Communist Party addresses these determines the nature of its popular support.

If Beijing fails to meet the popular demand to behave more assertively in the SCS, it may damage the Party's reputation, but this will not lead to its collapse. Only if corruption and mismanagement mar the government and lead to the collapse of the economy, Chinese people can use their nationalism to stand against the Party, and this would be a great threat to its survival.[78]

Based on this argument, it is unlikely that adopting a conciliatory approach for the SCS issue will have an enormous impact on the CCP's legitimacy. It is likely that the government will adopt a tough stance and measures in the SCS issue to shore up its legitimacy.[79] On the other hand, it is widely accepted that Chinese people's opinions on the SCS issue—as well as other foreign policy matters—are constructed by the government for its benefit.[80] As mentioned above, several surveys have demonstrated that Chinese opinion favours government actions in the SCS.

Nevertheless, Beijing can soothe people's hawkish sentiment. In the case of the dispute in the East China Sea over Diaoyu (Senkaku) Islands vis-à-vis Japan, the government has shown its control over popular demonstrations. The Diaoyu dispute involves highly patriotic sentiment since the Chinese people suffered enormously from Japanese atrocities during the Sino-Japanese War. In the 1990s, Beijing and Tokyo underwent a crisis over Diaoyu which involved nationwide protest in China. The CCP demonstrated its competency by putting aside hyped nationalist sentiment and focusing on economic development.[81] Even in the 2000s, when China had already become a regional power, similar tensions involving strong patriotic sentiment from the Chinese public to take tougher measures against Tokyo did not make Beijing give into people's irredentist demand. Through diplomacy and consultations, Beijing has successfully avoided damaging its relations with Tokyo. The two countries signed a joint development agreement to make the East China Sea a "sea of peace, cooperation and friendship" in autumn 2006.[82] The value of deepened bilateral relations has largely contributed to a high degree of pragmatism between the two states.[83]

Yet Chinese nationalism is a double-edged sword. On one hand people will judge the Party based on its performance in upholding Chinese nationalism; on the other hand, such nationalism is a means to shore up the legitimacy of the CCP.[84] The CCP controls the media, information, and communication channels. The regime fosters the narrative of Chinese victimisation and asserts the role of the Communist Party in liberating the Chinese people from the shackle of foreign invaders. In the contemporary era, unlike other selfish and power hungry states, Beijing portrays China as a benign, upright, and selfless state which pursues nothing but peaceful development. This propaganda is carried out by the government and its affiliates and targeted primarily at domestic audiences. Consequently, Chinese mainstream opinion is uncritical of Beijing's foreign policy and sometimes biased against accepting foreign criticism. At worst, the public even demands the government adopt tougher measures. This makes the efforts to mitigate tensions and resolve the disputes in China's near seas Herculean tasks.[85]

To sum up, it is true that what matters in the SCS is the CCP's reputation among the Chinese population.[86] In the eyes of Beijing, Communist legitimacy on the SCS tramples over international objection. However, Chinese people are concerned more with domestic issues that have a direct impact on their livelihood. As long as the SCS is related to China's economic interest and future development, it has become a matter of concern for the people. Based on this premise, the SCS issues can pose a threat to the Communist regime's survival if they matter to China's economic development.[87] Whereas, as observed from the East China Sea tension, sovereignty—the direct link between the SCS and the CCP's legitimacy—can harm the CCP's reputation but not threaten its survival.

Unfortunately, the narrative of a century of humiliation is already popularly shared among Chinese people. Since this has been proven successful in boosting the CCP's legitimacy, the Party will still hold on it. Instead of seeing the SCS in the context of common global maritime interest, due to government-backed nationalist rhetoric, the Chinese public perceive it as

China's property since time immemorial. Furthermore, the SCS has created a smear on China's image internationally. This has made Beijing less popular and comfortable in the current international order. At worst, it may cause Beijing to have lower confidence in international cooperation to secure the sea as common property.

With the Tribunal ruling on July 2016 which is disadvantageous for China, Beijing looks odd diplomatically, and this could lead to higher irredentist sentiment or even a sense of insecurity for the CCP. To cope with this legitimacy issue, the CCP needs to create a balance between gaining support from its domestic audience by becoming assertive and restraining itself from receiving more diplomatic backlashes.

In short, the ruling CCP is very sensitive about its legitimacy. Since the population appears to demand tougher measures, the government needs to follow public opinion to some extent. However, this is sometimes only a pretext for the government to adopt tougher measures in order to boost its legitimacy. This striving by the Chinese government to action in its own interests is domestically driven and not necessarily offensive.

4.2 Conclusion: In Defence of China's Interest in SCS

This chapter aimed to present some points on the nature of China's interest in the SCS. As discussed, China's SCS interests (resources, security, Taiwan issue, the Communist Party's reputation) are not inherently offensive realist. This can be seen from the fact that (1) Chinese people has been fishing and using the SCS for economic activities since ancient times, (2) China needs to secure its economic hubs along its eastern coast and maritime routes that are vital to its development, (3) China perceives the SCS as the realm to prevent Taiwan from independence, (4) defending the SCS is one of the main tasks to protect the reputation of the CCP before the Chinese population.

However, it could become a source of concern if China's geopolitical strategy follows the Mahan Doctrine. The Doctrine—which is hegemonic in nature—suggests that the expulsion of a rival power from the near seas serves a state's security. In the context of China, this means pushing out the US from the first and second island chains to prevent it from gathering intelligence information and/or intervene in a potential future cross-Strait conflict and launch containment against China. Even though there is a strong indication that China's top military leaders interest in the Mahan

Doctrine has grown, the only evidence that indicates China behaves according to this doctrine is the massive building of artificial islands in the SCS in 2014–2015.

The growing interests of China in its near seas have led the country to find an appropriate position in the international system. China's growing interests do not necessarily induce the country to harbour hegemonic ambition in the region. There is the possibility that China might shift its behaviour to being offensive and hegemonic during this adaptation process. However, its initial stated motives do not show the country behaving in an offensive or hegemonic way.

It is undeniable that China's growing power has led to these growing interests. The world needs to accept the fact that today's China is not the same China as that of the past. As a rising power with a huge population, China has the right to access the high seas where its future prosperity lies. It has the right to defend its security and survival by developing its navy and securing its maritime access.

China's growing interests in the SCS also expose its vulnerability which fuels its anxiety. Inadvertently, its growing interests sharpen China's rivalry with Japan and the US. Therefore, China does not perceive that the security of its sea lanes is a common problem for all sea lane users. Securing sea lanes through "international cooperation" to some extent equals relying on the US.[88] On the other hand, Japan and the US are also anxious about China's move in securing its interests in the SCS. If China exerts full control over the SCS, it will create great anxiety for Japan, since it can threaten the sea lanes without having a direct military confrontation.[89]

Japan is concerned that China will not stop in the SCS, but it will advance to the Indian and Pacific Oceans.[90] The US is also uneasy with China's vision to dominate the SCS. The control over all land features in the SCS is an attempt to make the SCS akin to a Chinese lake, and its recent posturing has shown the credibility of the US concern about a lack of freedom of navigation in this lake. Even with the limited features that China occupies, activities such as its land reclamation are seen by the US as a grave threat to the freedom of navigation.[91]

The above points demonstrate that overall, its interests in the SCS are fundamentally not offensive realist in the sense of open military confrontation or expansionism. Regardless of its leadership's concern for its purported vulnerability, it is attempting to achieve its security by pursuing a moderate policy. After the 1995 Mischief Reef incident, there has not been any military conflict in the SCS, and China has never opened fire to pursue its interests in the SCS. The next chapter discusses China's behaviour throughout the history of the PRC and describes the changing nature of China's SCS behaviour from defensive realist to offensive realist.

Notes

1. Haijiang Henry Wang, "The Perplexing Dispute over Oil," *Resources Policy*, 23, no. 4 (1997): 173–78.
2. International Energy Agency, "World Energy Outlook 2015," https://www.iea.org/Textbase/npsum/WEO2015SUM.pdf.
3. IEA, "World Energy Outlook 2010" cited in Nick A. Owen and Clive H. Schofield, "Disputed South China Sea Hydrocarbons in Perspective," *Marine Policy*, 36, no. 3 (2012): 809–22.
4. PBS Newshour, "5 Things You Should Know About the SCS Conflict," 16 May 2015, http://www.pbs.org/newshour/updates/5-things-didnt-know-south-china-sea-conflict/ (accessed 1 August 2016).
5. Li Guoqiang, "China Sea Oil and Gas Resources," China Institute of International Studies, 11 May 2015, http://www.ciis.org.cn/english/2015-05/11/content_7894391.htm (accessed 4 August 2016).
6. Owen and Schofield, "Disputed South China Sea Hydrocarbons in Perspective," 809–22.
7. Daojiong Zha, "China's Energy Security: Domestic and International Issues," *Survival: Global Politics and Strategy*, 48, no. 1 (2006): 179–90.
8. Owen and Schofield, "Disputed South China Sea Hydrocarbons in Perspective," 809–22.
9. Adam Greer, "The South China Sea Is Really a Fishery Dispute," *The Diplomat*, 20 July 2016, http://thediplomat.com/2016/07/the-south-china-sea-is-really-a-fishery-dispute/ (accessed 3 August 2016).
10. Ibid.
11. Ibid.
12. Ibid.
13. Simon Denyer, "China's Fishermen on the Front Line in the South China Sea," *The Sydney Morning Herald*, 16 April 2016, http://www.smh.com.au/world/chinas-fishermen-on-the-front-line-in-the-south-china-sea-20160413-go52bp.html (accessed 16 July 2016).
14. 李昌新 曹云华, "美国崛起中的海权因素初探," *当代亚太*, [Cao Yunhua, Li Changxin, "The Initial Thoughts of Maritime Factors in America's Rising," *Jinri Guoshi*], 5 (2006): 23–29.
15. 杨勇, "发挥海陆兼备优势是大型海陆复合国家的必然选择," *黑龙江社会科学*, [Yang Yong, "Capitalizing the Consolidated Land and Maritime Advantage Is the Inevitable Path of Big Powers," *Heilongjiang Shehui Kexue*], no. 3 (2004): 26–29.

16. "Continental Power: Wang Gungwu Interview," *Global ARC Quarterly*, Fall 2012, http://www.cwaholt.com/wp-content/uploads/2014/10/Wang-Gungwu.pdf (accessed 8 August 2016).
17. Ibid.
18. Dutton, "Three Disputes and Three Objectives: China and the South China Sea," 42.
19. Wenmu Zhang, "Sea Power and China's Strategic Choices," *China Security*, 2, no. 2 (2006): 17–31.
20. "Continental Power: Wang Gungwu Interview," *Global ARC Quarterly*, Fall 2012.
21. "Sea Power and China's Strategic Choices," 17–31.
22. Ibid., 24.
23. Michael A. Glosny, Phillip C. Saunders, and Robert S. Ross, "Correspondence: Debating China's Naval Nationalism," *International Security*, 35, no. 2 (2010): 161–69.
24. Chris Rahman and Martin Tsamenyi, "A Strategic Perspective on Security and Naval Issues in the South China Sea," *Ocean Development & International Law*, 41, no. 4 (2010): 315–33.
25. "SCS: Expert Clash over China Threat to Commercial Trade," *The Sydney Morning Herald*, 13 January 2016, http://www.smh.com.au/world/south-china-sea-experts-clash-over-china-threat-to-commercial-trade-20160113-gm4s9c.html (accessed 10 August 2016)
26. 倪乐雄, "中国"海上生命线"问题凸显," *同舟共进*, [Ni Lexiong, "The Emerging of China's 'Maritime Life Line' Problem" *Tongzhou Gongjin*], 11 (2009): 16–17; "海权即生命," *今日国土*, [Ni Lexiong, "Maritime Rights Is Vital," *Jinri Guotu*], no. 7 (2010): 16–17.
27. Zhang, "Sea Power and China's Strategic Choices," 17–31; James R Holmes and Toshi Yoshihara, " 'China's Caribbean' in the South China Sea," *SAIS REVIEW*, 26, no. 1 (2006): 79.
28. 倪乐雄, "中国"海上生命线"问题凸显,"[Ni Lexiong, "The Emerging of China's 'Maritime Life Line' Problem," *Tongzhou Gongjin*], 16–17.
29. US Department of Defense, *Annual Report to Congress: Military and Security Developments Involving the People's Republic of China 2014*, Washington, DC, 2014, http://www.defense.gov/Portals/1/Documents/pubs/2014_DoD_China_Report.pdf (accessed 26 September 2016).
30. Ibid.
31. "Explaining China's Participation in Anti-Piracy Operations in the Gulf of Aden," (Department of Political Science, Massachusetts Institute of Technology, 2009), 5.
32. "Chinese Navy Sets Sail for Anti-Piracy Mission off Somalia," *Xinhuanet*, 26 December 2008, http://news.xinhuanet.com/english/2008-12/26/content_10562510.htm (accessed 25 September 2016).

33. "China Thanks Malaysia for Pirate Rescue," *The Star Online*, 23 December 2008, http://www.thestar.com.my/news/nation/2008/12/23/china-thanks-malaysia-for-pirate-rescue/ (accessed 28 September 2016).
34. "Explaining China's Participation in Anti-Piracy Operations in the Gulf of Aden," 12.
35. " 'Blockade' Ship's Cash Call," *South China Morning Post*, 15 August 1993, http://www.scmp.com/article/40507/blockade-ships-cash-call (accessed 20 September 2016).
36. Marc Lanteigne, "China's Maritime Security and the 'Malacca Dilemma'," *Asian Security*, 4, no. 2 (2008): 143–61.
37. Gurpreet S. Khurana, "China's New Submarine Base at Hainan: Analyses of Recent Media Reports," (2008).
38. Ibid.
39. Mark Valencia, "The Impeccable Incident: Truth and Consequences," *China Security*, 5, no. 2 (2009): 22–28.
40. Ibid., 24.
41. Ian Storey and You Ji, "China's Aircraft Carrier Ambitions: Seeking Truth from Rumors," (DTIC Document, 2004), 78.
42. Ibid.; Hugh White, *The China Choice: Why America Should Share Power* (Victoria: Black Inc., 2013), 67–68.
43. Storey and Ji, "China's Aircraft Carrier Ambitions: Seeking Truth from Rumors," 86.
44. Ibid., 78; 倪乐雄, "海权即生命," [Ni Lexiong, "Maritime Rights is Vital," *Jinri Guotu*], 16–17.
45. Joshua P. Rowan, "The US-Japan Security Alliance, ASEAN, and the South China Sea Dispute," *Asian Survey*, 45, no. 3 (2005): 414–36.
46. Rahman and Tsamenyi, "A Strategic Perspective on Security and Naval Issues in the South China Sea," 315–33.
47. Rowan, "The US-Japan Security Alliance, ASEAN, and the South China Sea Dispute," 414–36.
48. Holmes and Yoshihara, " 'China's Caribbean' in the South China Sea," 79.
49. John W. Garver, "China's Push Through the South China Sea: The Interaction of Bureaucratic and National Interests," *The China Quarterly*, 132 (1992): 999–1028.
50. Toshi Yoshihara and James R. Holmes, "Command of the Sea with Chinese Characteristics," *Orbis*, 49, no. 4 (2005): 677–94. Liu Huaqing, the Chinese Admiral who served as commander of the People's Liberation Army Navy (PLAN) from 1982–1988 and became a member of the Politburo Standing Committee afterwards until 1997 was known as the father of the modern Chinese Navy as well as the "Chinese Mahan".
51. Ibid.

52. Alfred Thayer Mahan, *The Influence of Sea Power upon History, 1660–1783* (Boston: Little Brown, and Company, 1890; reprint, New York: Dover Publications, 1987), 71 cited in Holmes and Yoshihara, " 'China's Caribbean' in the South China Sea," 79.
53. Robert D. Kaplan, "The Geography of Chinese Power," *Foreign Affairs*, 89, no. 3 (2010): 22–41.
54. Storey and Ji, "China's Aircraft Carrier Ambitions: Seeking Truth from Rumors," 86.
55. Kaplan, "The Geography of Chinese Power," 22–41.
56. Jiang Shiliang, "The Command of Communications," *China Military Science*, 2 October 2002, cited in Holmes and Yoshihara, "'China's Caribbean' in the South China Sea," 79.
57. Toshi Yoshihara and James R. Holmes, *Chinese Naval Strategy in the Twenty-First Century: The Turn to Mahan* (London: Routledge, 2008), 74.
58. "Can China Defend a 'Core Interest' in the South China Sea?" *The Washington Quarterly*, 34, no. 2 (2011): 45–59.
59. Ibid., 48.
60. US Department of Defense, *Annual Report to Congress: Military and Security Developments Involving the People's Republic of China 2016*, 2016, http://www.defense.gov/Portals/1/Documents/pubs/2016%20China%20Military%20Power%20Report.pdf (accessed 2 January 2017).
61. "Can China Defend a 'Core Interest' in the South China Sea?" 45–59.
62. White, *The China Choice: Why America Should Share Power*, 67.
63. It is too early to assess the direction of the US-Philippines Defence Cooperation under President Duterte. He might distance himself from Washington, but he might not touch the defense cooperation between two countries. See Prashanth Parameswaran, "Recalibrating US-Philippine Alliance under Duterte," *Rappler*, 1 October 2016, http://www.rappler.com/thought-leaders/147840-recalibrating-us-philippine-alliance-duterte (accessed 15 October 2016).
64. Yoshihara and Holmes, "Command of the Sea with Chinese Characteristics," 677–94.
65. Zhang, "Sea Power and China's Strategic Choices," 17–31; Yoshihara and Holmes, "Command of the Sea with Chinese Characteristics," 677–94.
66. *Red Star over the Pacific: China's Rise and the Challenge to US Maritime Strategy* (Naval Institute Press, 2011), 53.
67. Ibid., 21.
68. 倪乐雄, "国家海权战略的当代转型与威慑作用," *国际观察*, [Ni Lexiong, "The Modern Transformation and Deterrence Function of Maritime Strategy," *Guoji Guancha*], (2012).

69. Ibid.
70. Kaplan, "The Geography of Chinese Power," 22–41; Yoshihara and Holmes, *Red Star over the Pacific: China's Rise and the Challenge to US Maritime Strategy*, 6–7.
71. Erica Strecker Downs and Phillip C. Saunders, "Legitimacy and the Limits of Nationalism," *International Security*, 23, no. 3 (1998): 114.
72. "Outgoing Taiwan President Ma Ying-jeou Visits Remote and Disputed Islands to 'Assert Taipei's Sovereignty'," *South China Morning Post*, 9 April 2016, http://www.scmp.com/news/china/article/1934938/outgoing-taiwan-president-ma-ying-jeou-visits-remote-and-disputed-islands (accessed 19 October 2016).
73. Interview with an Indonesian diplomat in Beijing, November 2015.
74. Edward Wong, "China Hedges over Whether South China Sea Is a "Core Interest" Worth War," *The New York Times*, 30 March 2011, http://www.nytimes.com/2011/03/31/world/asia/31beijing.html?_r=0 (accessed 5 April 2016).
75. Jessica Chen Welss, "Here's What China's People Really Think About the South China Sea," *The Washington Post*, 14 July 2016, https://www.washingtonpost.com/news/monkey-cage/wp/2016/07/14/heres-what-chinas-people-really-think-about-the-south-china-sea/ (accessed 19 July 2016).
76. Bruce Gilley and Heike Holbig, "The Debate on Party Legitimacy in China: A Mixed Quantitative/Qualitative Analysis," *Journal of Contemporary China*, 18, no. 59 (2009): 339–58.
77. Ibid.
78. Erik Beukel, "Popular Nationalism in China and the Sino-Japanese Relationship," (Copenhagen: Danish Institute for International Studies, 2011), 24.
79. "Legality of China's Claims in SCS 'Not Weak': George Yeo," *The Strait Times*, 3 June 2016, http://www.straitstimes.com/asia/se-asia/legality-of-chinas-claims-in-south-china-sea-not-weak-george-yeo (accessed 19 October 2016).
80. Robert Sutter, "China's Self-Absorbed Nationalism," *The Diplomat*, 31 August 2012, http://thediplomat.com/2012/08/chinas-self-absorbed-nationalism/ (accessed 17 May 2016).
81. Downs and Saunders, "Legitimacy and the Limits of Nationalism," 114.
82. Beukel, "Popular Nationalism in China and the Sino-Japanese Relationship," 20.
83. Ibid., 22.
84. Suisheng Zhao, "Foreign Policy Implications of Chinese Nationalism Revisited: The Strident Turn," *Journal of Contemporary China*, 22, no. 82 (2013): 535–53.

85. Sutter, "China's Self-Absorbed Nationalism," *The Diplomat*, 31 August 2012.
86. Bilahari Kausikan, "Pavlovian Conditioning and 'Correct Thinking' on the SCS," *The Strait Times*, 1 April 2016, http://www.straitstimes.com/opinion/pavlovian-conditioning-and-correct-thinking-on-the-south-china-sea (accessed 28 September 2016).
87. Holmes and Yoshihara, "'China's Caribbean' in the South China Sea," 79; Jian Yang, "China's Security Challenges: Priorities and Policy Implications," *Asia Pacific Countries' Security Outlook and Its Implications for the Defense Sector*, (2010): 141–59.
88. Holmes and Yoshihara, "'China's Caribbean' in the South China Sea," 79.
89. Shigeo Hiramatsu, "China's Advances in the South China Sea: Strategies and Objectives," *Asia Pacific Review*, 8, no. 1 (2001): 40–50.
90. Ibid.
91. US Department of Defense, *IISS Shangri-La Dialogue "A Regional Security Architecture Where Everyone Rises" as delivered by Secretary of Defense Ash Carter*, 30 May 2015, https://www.defense.gov/News/Speeches/Article/606676 (accessed 9 November 2016).

CHAPTER 5

China's Defection in the South China Sea

Official statements from the Chinese government often iterate that China will not pursue a hegemonic ambition. Since Deng Xiaoping assumed leadership, China has also been portrayed by Chinese scholars like Tang Shiping as a defensive realist state that is willing to accept constraint in its behaviour. To some extent, this paradigm is manifested in China's foreign policy both regionally and globally, for example, by participating in many international forums such as the ASEAN Regional Forum (ARF) and the East Asia Summit to maintain peace and stability in the region.

However, without underemphasising the above-mentioned initiatives, this chapter argues that the test for China as a defensive realist state is in the South China Sea (SCS). China is a defensive realist state if the country sends appropriate signals in the SCS towards other claimants, that is, an open attitude to non-military solutions, self-restraint, and a reassurance policy. This chapter concludes that even though China was originally a defensive realist state, it defected to becoming an offensive realist state towards other SCS claimant states. Supporting evidence is produced and evaluated in this chapter by interpreting China's recent behaviour with reference to criteria of a defensive or offensive realist state.

5.1 China as a Defensive Realist State

The definition of the defensive realist state and its cousin—an offensive realist state is discussed in Chap. 2. From the perspective of defensive realism, if a state accumulates too much power it will consequently face

K. H. Raditio, *Understanding China's Behaviour in the South China Sea*, https://doi.org/10.1007/978-981-13-1283-0_5

balancing issues. This is because states wish to survive, but this will ultimately hamper the rise of those other states that might achieve prominent power.[1] A state will not bandwagon other rising states simply because a state always fears other states' intentions with regard to its survival.

The motives for balancing behaviour are rooted in uncertainty and fear. States never know other states' intentions in the present or the future. A state may be satisfied with the territory and the resources it possesses, yet when it witnesses other states' military build-ups, its leaders become concerned that its adversaries or competitors are inherently more dangerous than it had previously believed.[2] This can create distrust and suspicion, and it leads to a security dilemma.

Jervis defines a security dilemma as a situation in which "the means by which a state tries to increase its security decreases the security of others".[3] It is a dilemma for every security-seeking state because in an international system of anarchy, each state has to empower its self-help capability. On the other hand, it is not easy to ascertain an "appropriate amount" of power that will not provoke other states' suspicions. However, arguing that a particular state is defensive realist emphasises the relatively small degree of threat that it poses to other states, because a defensive realist state will pursue neither the maximisation of power nor hegemony to guarantee its security. It is therefore not surprising that this theory is used by some Chinese scholars to counter the China threat theory.[4]

Tang Shiping provides two criteria for a defensive realist state. First, it acknowledges the existence of security dilemmas; second, it exercises self-restraint.[5] A defensive realist state recognises that accumulating power provokes other states' anxiety in the same way as its uneasiness rises from others' advancement of power. A defensive realist state will keep developing its power, but it reassures other states of its defensive nature. This is pursued by engaging in cooperation, not merely in terms of security but also of other realms. A defensive realist state also exercises self-restraint and accepts other states' constraints. It believes that the need to exercise security is common to all states.

Since a defensive realist state does not have an expansionist ambition, it expresses its non-expansionist intention through reassurance strategy, manifested in a cooperative attitude that initiates chains of mutually rewarding behaviour and eventually fosters trust.[6] This will lead to the alleviation of security dilemmas between states, or even alliances of states.

Tang argues that under Deng's leadership, China has undergone a transition from offensive to defensive realism. There are four points in support of his argument.[7] The first is that China has adopted non-interference in other states' domestic affairs. Unlike in the Mao era, China no longer exports its revolution nor does it support communist elements in foreign countries. The second is that China is aware of neighbouring countries' anxiety towards its behaviour. Therefore, Deng has reassured regional countries of its benign intentions to alleviate neighbouring countries' suspicions. According to Tang, this reflects China's recognition of the major aspects of the security dilemma. The third is China's ascendency to international organisations and treaties that are essentially rule-based, and require compliance from their members and/or signatories. This reflects China's willingness to be constrained by others. Finally, China has made a breakthrough in security cooperation, especially in its surrounding regions. The country has adopted a "good neighbour policy" towards its southeast neighbours. Moreover, China actively participates in regional security forums such as ASEAN and it even initiated the establishment of the Shanghai Cooperation Organization (SCO). Tang points to these behaviours as proof of a panacea to the security dilemmas between China and its neighbouring countries. Tang argues that overall, China's adopted policies since Deng Xiaoping are solidly rooted in defensive realism[8] and he further suggests that this tendency means China is unlikely to revert to its former offensive realism.[9]

Contrary to Tang, Mearsheimer argues that China aspires to be a regional hegemon because it is the best option to ensure its security. Particularly, in the SCS and China's territorial dispute, becoming a regional hegemon serves the resolution favourably.[10] Therefore, the SCS, in which China has so much at stake, becomes a litmus test for China to show if it is a genuine defensive realist state.

5.2 The SCS as a Litmus Test for China's Defensive Realist Behaviour

This chapter suggests whether China is a defensive realist state should be assessed by using more rigorous concepts. The criteria for China as a defensive realist state is as follows: whether the country is willing to reassure other claimants, beyond simple assertions, by sending a signal bearing political cost.[11]

Signals sent need to have some value to be reassuring. An offensive realist state can send a signal indicating a cheap negotiation point with the intention of luring other states into a false sense of security or reassurance.

However, signals should not be too costly either, since that can put a defensive realist state at risk and make it prone to exploitation.[12] Hence, a defensive realist state bears political cost in signalling to other states to ameliorate their anxiety. In the SCS, China has a lot of opportunity to send costly signals to other claimant states such as maintaining an open attitude to non-military dispute solutions, conducting self-restraint, and adopting a reassurance policy.

First, being open to non-military solutions for the dispute bears political cost in that China has the biggest military power among the claimants in the SCS. The country has the capability to "recapture" all land features in the SCS such as they did in recapturing the Paracel Islands from South Vietnam in 1974. However, in the aftermath of the 1995 Mischief Reef incident, China and other claimant states have maintained their positions to pursue peaceful means to resolve territorial disputes in the SCS as declared in the DoC.

Regionally, this legal mechanism has been a peaceful and legitimate means to resolve territorial disputes in Southeast Asia. For instance, Indonesia and Malaysia submitted a case to the International Court of Justice (ICJ) for the resolution of territorial disputes over the Sipadan and Ligitan Islands in 2002. Likewise, Thailand and Cambodia also submitted a case to the ICJ for the resolution of the territorial dispute over the Preah Vihear temple and its surrounding area in 2011. Seeking resolution through a legal mechanism has been a commonly accepted practice in the Southeast Asian region. Nevertheless, China perceives legal mechanisms as too costly—as it showed in the dismissal of the United Nations Convention on the Law of the Sea (UNCLOS) Tribunal initiated by the Philippines. To resolve the SCS dispute, it only favours negotiations with the parties directly concerned.

There are reasons why China prefers bilateral negotiations to international legal mechanisms. These reasons are (1) historically it has proven to be successful in winning other countries' favour, ameliorating the security dilemma and creating a favourable situation for itself[13]; (2) by making concessions through bilateral negotiations, Beijing displays its superiority as a country of considerable weight in the region,[14] something that cannot be done through international legal mechanisms; and (3) since China's claim in the SCS is not compelling according to international law, Chinese leaders cannot be confident of winning the case.[15]

Second, self-restraint bears a political cost. China is not satisfied with the status quo in the SCS. Even though it exerts full control over the

Paracel Islands, its physical presence in the Spratly Islands is limited. In the Spratlys, Vietnam occupies a total of 21 features, the Philippines occupies 9 features, and Malaysia 5. China itself only occupies 7, although it claims all features in the Spratly Islands.[16] China understands that the US and its allies, as well as other claimants demand that it does not change the status quo in the SCS. However, maintaining this status quo means China has to bear a situation where it cannot foster its claim over all the features in the SCS.

The Chinese public seems to be unsatisfied with the current situation in the SCS. According to research cited in Sect. 4.1.5, strong nationalist sentiment dominates public discussion among Chinese netizens—who urge the government to adopt harsher measures against other claimants in the SCS.[17] The Chinese government's effort in defending its territorial claim in the SCS will directly affect its legitimacy. Chinese people will strongly oppose any measure taken by the government that can be perceived as a sign of weakness. Therefore, whether China is a defensive realist state can be assessed from its behaviour in bearing this political cost.

Third, adopting a reassurance policy bears political cost as China has interests in having the SCS dispute managed between relevant parties bilaterally and is strongly opposed to internationalising the SCS issue. Therefore, China needs good relationships with other claimant states. Given that all claimant states except China are members of ASEAN, China adopted a reassurance strategy towards ASEAN states by actively participating in various ASEAN forums. This aimed to hinder ASEAN being used by external powers to constrain China in the SCS issues.

China will be in a very difficult position in the SCS if ASEAN states lean towards the position of the US and its allies. However, any reassurance policy cannot stop other claimant states from inclining towards external powers. Some claimant states could continue to advocate the so-called China threat while reaping the benefit from cooperation with China.[18] Even worse, China's reassurance policy could be misunderstood by other claimants as a sign of a wavering determination in asserting China's claim. They could fail to reciprocate China's reassurance and continue "encroaching" on the features in the SCS and internationalising the SCS issue.[19]

Overall, no matter how other claimant states blatantly accuse China of being aggressive and expansionist, no matter how the US and its allies have expressed grave reservation towards China's behaviour in the SCS, China is a defensive realist state if it sends the above-mentioned costly signals. This chapter attempts to assess whether China's behaviour in the

SCS conforms to defensive realism by evaluating its claims and behaviour throughout the history of the People's Republic of China (PRC).

5.3 Brief History of Conflict in the SCS

This section discusses four major incidents in the SCS: the 1974 Battle of Paracel Islands, the 1988 Johnson Reef incident, the 1995 Mischief Reef incident, and the 2012 Scarborough Shoal standoff. China was the main actor in these events. As shown in Chap. 4, in the SCS China has shown no offensive or expansionist interests. This argument is supported with reference to China's behaviour, especially in the SCS conflicts. This section attempts to demonstrate the defensive aspects of China's behaviour particularly in the first three incidents. By showing the defensive aspects of these three incidents, support is shown for the argument that China's initial motive is that of a defensive realist state—one which does not seek security by deliberately coming into conflict with others, except under extreme conditions.[20] This argument prepares the ground for the operation of the security dilemma which is the focus of the Chaps. 6 and 7.

Over time, in the SCS, China conducted many kinds of activities from military operations to signing a declaration of conduct, and from seizing new land features to making concessions. This range of behaviour needs to be seen in a historical as well as a dynamic global political context. Every claimant in the SCS sees itself as a victim of the others' encroachments. Vietnam and the Philippines see themselves as victims of China's bullying, but on the other hand China sees other claimants as ungrateful and abusing its patience.[21]

China's first military operation in the SCS was launched in 1974 to "recapture" the Paracel Islands (Crescent Group) from the Republic of Vietnam (RVN).[22] This action was taken by China in the midst of the deterioration of its relations with the DRV and the anticipation of the fall of Saigon in 1975. The poor relationship between China and the DRV has its origins in the sour relationship between China and the Soviet Union. The conflict between Beijing and Moscow led the Soviets to adopt an encirclement strategy towards China by offering ideological bonds and material aid to its allies in Asia and proposing a collective security system for both communist and non-communist Asian countries.[23] The Soviet Union also gradually increased its naval presence in Asia since the early 1970s.[24] On the other hand, since the early 1970s, China's main foreign policy was to tackle Soviet expansionism and this influenced the Chinese perception of strategic relations between Hanoi and Moscow.[25] China believed that gaining some measure of control in the SCS would enable it to break the Soviet Union's encirclement.[26]

Furthermore, China also believed that the US would not defend the RVN, since the Sino-US relationship had undergone rapprochement that culminated in the visit of President Nixon in 1972. Although prior to 1974 the Paracel Islands were occupied by the RVN, China had anticipated the fall of Saigon and the complexity of the issues after the reunification of Vietnam.[27] Beijing predicted that after the fall of Saigon, Hanoi would occupy the Paracel archipelago.[28] This would create a serious threat to China, since Beijing-Hanoi relations continued to worsen and, as Moscow's ally, Hanoi could accommodate the Soviet Union in making a forward base of operation against China in the Paracel Islands.[29] Hanoi indeed kept silent at China's action in the battle of Paracel Islands; however, it asserted sovereignty over the Paracels in 1978.[30] In 1977, Beijing attempted to seek a de-escalation of tension with Hanoi through diplomacy.[31] These attempts seemed futile since the relationship between China and Vietnam continued to deteriorate until it culminated in the 1979 Sino-Vietnamese War.

China's decision to take over the Paracels reflects a shrewd strategic calculation in defending what it perceives as legitimate rights in the SCS. Overall, this action served as a deterrent against a Vietnam-Soviet Union coalition against China, because at the fall of Saigon, China became the only political entity claiming the islands. China anticipated the worst scenario from the close Soviet-Vietnam relationship, one which may threaten its security by using the land features in the SCS.

While China was successful in recovering the Paracel Islands, it did not have a physical presence in the Spratly Islands. It was not until 1988 that China launched an operation in the Spratly Islands that resulted in clashes with Vietnamese troops. During the 1970s and 1980s, the situation in the Spratlys continued to deteriorate as coastal states in the SCS laid claim to the islands. In 1978, the Philippine government officially declared sovereignty over several islands in the Spratlys and named the Kalayaan Island Group (KIG). In the same year, Hanoi publicly asserted its claim over the Paracels and the Spratlys by claiming the islands under its sovereignty rights. In 1979, Malaysia joined the dispute by claiming 12 islets in the Spratly group, including Swallow Reef and Amboyna Cay.[32] In 1986, according to Chinese sources, Vietnam occupied 29 islands in the Spratlys.[33] China felt frustrated that almost all high-tide elevations had been occupied by Vietnam, the Philippines, and Malaysia and because of the fact that China had no physical presence in those features.[34] Occupying some features in the Spratly Islands will strengthen China's position as one of the SCS claimants; otherwise China can never initiate dispute negotiation.

Since April 1987, China has conducted several patrols over the Spratly Islands with an intention to occupy some land features.[35] In November 1987, the Central Military Commission and the State Council approved a proposal and then immediately deployed the People's Liberation Army Navy (PLAN) and the State Oceanic Administration (SOA) to occupy nine reefs, including Fiery Cross.[36] A series of clashes took place between China and Vietnam from January to March 1988. One of the worst occurred on Johnson Reef on 14 March 1988, when the PLAN sank all Vietnamese vessels, and 74 Vietnamese soldiers died.[37]

In the aftermath of these incidents, the Chinese Ambassador in Manila told the Philippines that China was willing to put aside the dispute in the hope that it might be resolved through consultation when the conditions were ripe.[38] Furthermore, at a press conference in Singapore on 13 August 1990, Chinese Premier Li Peng announced China's readiness to shelve the dispute and engage in joint cooperation to develop the Spratlys, which was followed by a gradual reduction of Chinese naval exercises in the SCS since the mid-1990s.[39] This statement was reiterated by Chinese Foreign Minister Qian Qichen and Vice Foreign Minister Tang Jiaxuan in 1993.[40] In 1992, ASEAN countries (Brunei, Indonesia, Malaysia, the Philippines, Singapore, and Thailand) signed the ASEAN Declaration on the SCS, which emphasised peaceful means in resolving the sovereignty dispute in the SCS. This was meant to enhance ASEAN cohesiveness and prevent further tension in the region.

In 1995, another high-profile conflict took place in the Spratly Islands: at Mischief Reef. This time it was between China and the Philippines. Contrary to popular belief, the 1995 Mischief Reef dispute was not the first time China had seized features claimed by the Philippines. China occupied Spratlys' six atolls in the area claimed by the Philippines at the end of the 1980s, while US troops still maintained their presence in the country.[41] Even after 1987, *People's Daily*, the Chinese government mouthpiece, protested against the ASEAN countries of Malaysia and the Philippines, occupying the Spratly Islands. In the aftermath of the 1995 Mischief Reef incident, China occupied 7 features, Taiwan 1, Vietnam 27, the Philippines 8, and Malaysia 3.[42] The net result of the 1995 Mischief

Reef incident was that China stepped up its physical presence in the Spratlys by occupying the Mischief Reef area, while the Philippines drew the world's attention to China's behaviour in the SCS.[43]

After the 1995 Mischief Reef incident until the late 2000s, China's behaviour in the Southeast Asia region moderated. Ralf Emmers describes this period as one of de-escalation.[44] However, this period was not conflict-free. Despite some skirmishes between warships, vessels, and fishing boats from China and other claimants, overall the disputes did not destabilise the region.[45] From the late 1990s, the SCS tension was reduced and the parties concerned seemed content to keep the status quo.[46] China itself became more open to discussing the SCS issue in the context of ASEAN.[47]

The situation became heated again in between 2007 and 2009. Particularly in May 2009, China delivered a *nota verbale* in response to the two submissions by Vietnam and Vietnam and Malaysia combined to the UN Commission on the Limits of the Continental Shelf (CLCS). In this *nota verbale*, China attached the so-called nine-dash line map that demarcates its territorial claim in the SCS. This was the first time that China had asserted its maritime territorial claim in the SCS by using the nine-dash line map in an international forum. However, China included the map without any clarification according to international law.

It was not until April 2012 that another high-profile incident took place in the SCS, this time in Scarborough Shoal—about 123 miles west of the Philippine's Subic Bay—within the Philippine EEZ (Exclusive Economic Zone). Prior to April 2012, neither the Philippines nor China had maintained a permanent presence at the disputed shoal. The situation worsened when the Philippine Navy attempted to arrest eight Chinese fishing boats that were operating in the shoal's lagoon in April 2012. This attempt was disrupted by China Marine Surveillance (CMS), resulting in a one-month standoff between the two sides. By the end of May, China had dispatched seven CMS and Bureau of Fisheries Administration ships.

In early June 2012, according to Manila, an agreement was reached with China to end the standoff in the Scarborough Shoal in the middle of June. However, after both parties withdrew from the disputed territory, Chinese ships returned and have maintained their presence in the Scarborough Shoal ever since. Furthermore, China blocks the access for Philippine fishermen to conduct activities in the vicinity of the shoal. The occupation of Scarborough Shoal was undoubtedly a breach of the 2002 DoC.[48] The incident is a shift in China's maritime strategy from a low profile during the period of de-escalation to a more "proactive" one.[49]

In the aftermath of China's seizure of Scarborough Shoal, Beijing continued to exert pressure against its southeast neighbour by banning the importation of Philippine bananas and other fruits, affecting a $75 million market that supported 200,000 jobs.[50] The Philippine economy was severely impaired by this embargo, given that 30% of the country's banana exports and other tropical fruits go to China.

In addition to the Scarborough Shoal incident, China also became involved in months of a standoff with Vietnam when China laid the oil rig Haiyang Shiyou (HSY) 981 into the Vietnamese-claimed EEZ. China claimed that the oil rig was placed adjacent to the Paracels' Woody Island of which it asserts de facto control. This move is clearly geopolitically motivated and aimed at asserting China's claim in the SCS. Chinese top national oil companies (NOC) leaders like China National Offshore Oil Corporation's (CNOOC) Wang Yilin and Sinopec's Fu Chengyu described HSY 981 as "mobile national territory".[51]

From the above-mentioned incidents, China seems very skilful in deploying non-military statecraft like the maritime militia and the NOC to assert its SCS claim. This deployment aims to substantiate China's historic rights claim which emphasises the use of the SCS by Chinese civilians. It is also an attempt to avoid the image of being aggressive militarily. The maritime militia is one of its three sea forces, the others being the Chinese Coast Guard and Chinese Navy. This militia consists of civilians (fishermen) with special training, salary, and financial and logistic subsidies from the government and it operates under a direct military chain of command.[52] The maritime militia played a significant role in provoking the Philippine Navy in the beginning of the 2012 Scarborough Shoal standoff and the repulsion of Vietnamese vessels to secure the oil rig in the 2014 HSY 981 incident. The maritime militia and the Chinese NOC as instruments of non-military statecraft demonstrate China's sophistication in asserting its SCS claim.

Chinese officials frequently describe the country's behaviour as exercising considerable constraint. Moreover, Beijing also often defends its behaviour as responses to activities by other claimants. It is true that in most cases Beijing's behaviour depends on other claimants' positions.[53] But in this sense, the behaviour of China is in no way comparable to that of Vietnam or the Philippines. The massive construction of artificial islands, for instance, does show the asymmetrical nature of the power of China compared with other claimants. While Vietnam has expanded its occupied features of West London Reef and Sand by 65,000 and 21,000 square metres respectively since 2010, China's area of "reclamation" on its controlled features is more than 50 times that of Vietnam's.[54] The use of non-military statecraft also demonstrates China's overwhelming advantage in asserting its claim *vis-à-vis* other claimants, this in no way masks China's aggressive behaviour.

5.4 Does China's Behaviour in the SCS Reflect that of a Defensive Realist State?

Given the above-mentioned history of China's behaviour in the SCS, three questions can be posed to analyse China's behaviour according to the defensive realist code. These are discussed in the following three sections.

5.4.1 Is China Open to Non-military Solutions for the SCS Dispute?

China is open to non-military solutions, but it is limited to direct negotiation with the parties concerned—which means rival claimant states. China is reluctant to resort to international legal mechanisms because it refuses to accept the political cost of this, as explained in Sect. 5.2.

In the aftermath of the 2012 Scarborough Shoal incident, the Philippines initiated arbitration proceedings which undoubtedly exerted a diplomatic pressure for China. It also created an impression that China is opposed to peaceful means to resolve the territorial dispute in the SCS. The Philippines has the right to be upset with China's seizure in 2012 of the Scarborough Shoal—a land feature that lies within its EEZ, known to the Philippines as Panatag and to the Chinese as the Huangyan Island. By conducting this action, China breached the 2002 DoC whereby any party has committed not to occupying any additional features in the SCS.[55]

On 7 December 2014, a week before the Permanent Court of Arbitration's (PCA) six-month deadline for a response, China issued its position paper in regard to the arbitral proceedings instituted by the Philippines. The Chinese government iterated its refusal to accept or participate in the arbitration process.

There are some points that need to be highlighted in China's position paper: (1) China considers the core issue of the arbitration is the territorial sovereignty, which is not the domain of the UNCLOS, a convention that the arbitration is based on; (2) China accused the Philippines of breaching international law by bringing the case to the PCA, since the two parties had agreed to resolve the matter through bilateral negotiation; (3) China stated that it filed a declaration in 2006 to be exempted from compulsory arbitration and other compulsory dispute settlement procedures; (4) China announced that its rejection of the process of arbitration is in accordance with international law. China maintained this position after the Tribunal ruling concluded on 12 July 2016.

In response to the UNCLOS Tribunal ruling, the official statement from the Chinese government states:

> China stands ready to continue to resolve the relevant disputes peacefully through negotiation and consultation with the states directly concerned on the basis of respecting historical facts and in accordance with international law. Pending final statement, China is also ready to make every effort with states directly concerned to enter into provisional arrangements of a practical nature, including joint development in relevant maritime areas, in order to achieve win-win results and jointly maintain peace and stability in the SCS.[56]

The rejection of the UNCLOS Tribunal is at odds with the defensive realist code, since China is bound by the dispute resolution mechanism. However, historically, China has peacefully settled its disputes with its neighbours. In many cases, China has shown its willingness to settle disputes through peaceful bilateral negotiations, and even to compromise and relinquish its territory to its neighbours.[57] This has happened to smaller neighbours such as Afghanistan, Pakistan, Nepal, and Myanmar.[58] In the case of the SCS, China has proposed joint development in the Spratlys with other claimants. Further, prior to the ARF meeting in August 1995, the then Chinese Foreign Minister Qian Qichen made a concession to the ASEAN members by affirming that China was prepared to hold multilateral talks on the Spratly issues based on the 1982 UNCLOS.[59] It is unclear why this signal was not followed up by China and other ASEAN members, particularly the claimant states in the SCS.

Although China's commitment to peaceful resolution needs to be respected, it remains political rhetoric and lacks concreteness. The idea of involving only "states directly concerned" is also odd, since the SCS is a regional issue. China failed to resolve its dispute in the Tribunal and formulate the Code of Conduct in the SCS. China insists that discussions on the Code of Conduct which it considers to be more legally binding than the Tribunal's decision can be held when "the time is ripe". This has created a deadlock in the dispute settlement process and has resulted in more uncertainty. Therefore, these points illustrate that China's commitment in resolving the SCS dispute is limited to a declaration only and is characterised by a lack of concreteness.

5.4.2 *Does China Show Self-restraint in the SCS?*

This research argues that China's behaviour in the SCS throughout the history of the PRC does show some qualities of self-restraint, although they have become scarcer in recent years. When China recaptured the Paracel Islands from the RVN in 1974, it could also have done the same with Saigon's occupied features in the Spratly Islands. China has a more powerful navy and the RVN's collapse was imminent. Moreover, China had resumed its relations with the US, which made it less likely to defend the RVN in the SCS. However, China decided not to extend further south and demonstrated restraint concerning the Paracel Islands.

There are some explanations for China's behaviour. First, the Paracel Islands are geographically closer to China, thus they were easier to control than the farther Spratly Islands; China would need more resources and power to seize the Spratlys. Second, Chinese operations in the Paracel Islands were meant as a deterrence strategy against the Soviet Union. China perceived the Soviet Union and its ally, the DRV as the biggest threat to them. Control over the Paracel Islands was necessary for China as a bulwark, before it could be used as a forward base for operations against China.[60] Third, China did not want to arouse the anxiety of other coastal states, for example, the Philippines, which had occupied three of the Spratly Islands since 1971.[61] Confrontation with other coastal states would only create a setback in its diplomatic relations and create a more difficult situation for China.

Even though China perceived the Spratly Islands as its territory, it was not until 1988 that they took action to maintain its presence. Was this another demonstration of Chinese self-restraint, or simply a matter of limited capability? This research suggests that the delay was due to a combination of both. In terms of capability, the PLAN had been underdeveloped since the establishment of the PRC. Although it was relatively strong compared to other claimants' navies, the PLAN was weak compared to those of the US or the Soviet Union. China's top leaders realised the weakness of the PLAN and to address this and its unfavourable situation in the Spratlys, China's naval power started to develop in the 1970s, preparing for the launch of an operation there.[62]

In the 1970s and 1980s, Chinese leaders were preoccupied with countering Soviet encirclement of their nation. However, when Deng Xiaoping assumed power in 1978, he launched many reforms and encouraged openness to international exchanges and trade, thus changing the direction of China's foreign policy to become less confrontational. China was attempting to mend its sour relations with the Soviet Union and maintain regional stability. Eleven years later in May 1989, Deng and Gorbachev shook hands to end the hostility between the two countries. The two countries seemed to put a big effort into this rapprochement. Three years earlier in 1986, Gorbachev delivered his Vladivostok speech, saying that the Soviet Union would not back Vietnam if it decided to have a military confrontation with China.[63]

China seemed to perceive fewer obstacles to launching an operation in the Spratlys in 1988 due in part to the altered Soviet position. Furthermore, to create a favourable condition for China's reform and opening up, it attempted to minimise conflict with its neighbours. Hence, in September 1988 it asserted that no action would be taken against ASEAN countries, which obviously at the time did not include Vietnam.[64]

Overall, China has perceived the operation in the Spratly Islands as necessary on several fronts. From Beijing's point of view, other claimants had taken advantage of China's unfavourable situation including domestic chaos and superpowers' encirclement to encroach on China's territory in the SCS.[65] Due to the fact that most of the Spratlys had been occupied by Vietnam, the Philippines, and Malaysia, China considered it hardly possible to assert sovereignty in the area without maintaining a physical presence. As a PLAN official stated, China perceived its presence in the island group as necessary for gaining a favourable position for negotiation.[66]

In 1995, Chinese troops clashed with Philippine troops at the Mischief Reef. At this time, China seemed to expand its presence in the Spratly Islands, developing its naval capabilities to project its strategic interest in the Asia Pacific, especially in the area historically believed to be its territory.[67] In the late 1990s, China's navy was the most powerful compared with other claimant states and it could occupy a few more features in the Spratlys without major obstacles from other claimants. However, China chose to behave in a rational and careful manner, focusing mainly on diplomatic efforts.[68] This attitude was reflected in the signing of the DoC in November 2002 and the signing of the Treaty of Amity and Cooperation (TAC) in Southeast Asia in 2003.

Mearsheimer argues that self-restraint serves China's hegemonic interest because it makes little sense to enter into conflict with the US while its power is inferior.[69] It is logical to wait until China closes the capability gap with the US to realise its hegemonic ambition. He invokes Deng Xiaoping's dictum of *taoguang yanhui* as evidence of how China chooses to hide and grow its capability in order to achieve its ends at a more opportune time. In other words, Mearsheimer suggests that there is nothing defensive in adopting self-restraint; in fact, it serves China's hegemonic ambition.

Two points need to be made regarding Mearsheimer's suggestion. First, self-restraint in defensive realism has a different meaning from self-restraint in the context of offensive realism. In offensive realism, self-restraint serves an offensive strategy, because a state should advance its offence when its power is sufficient to overcome the rival. However, self-restraint in defensive realism means accepting the restraint from other states or external powers (e.g. international law, international regimes). It means giving up an expansionist or hegemonic ambition because an aspiring hegemon will face a balancing behaviour from other states and the net result of this would be counterproductive to the state's security. In brief, self-restraint in offensive realism is a strategy, while in defensive realism it is a mindset or paradigm.

Second, as mentioned in Sect. 5.3, China seized the Philippines-controlled features prior to the 1995 Mischief Reef incident, when the US troops were still stationed in the country. China did not wait for a closing of the power gap with the US, in order to then grab more land features in the SCS by military means, since it understands that the US role in sustaining Philippine control over the SCS features is limited. After the US military left the Philippines in 1992, China launched a military operation to seize the Mischief Reef in 1995, and it could have advanced to take control over more features. However, since the 1995 Mischief Reef incident, China realised the impact of the Philippines' and other claimant states' balancing powers and subsequently began to adopt a reassurance policy in the region. Despite its superior military strength, China has never fired a shot in the SCS since the 1988 Johnson Reef incident.

In the current decade, it seems that China is straying from its defensive realist strategy. The most notable recent event was the 2012 Scarborough Shoal incident when China exerted its power militarily, diplomatically, and economically against the Philippines. China's conduct was clearly a violation of the DoC, in which all parties are committed to "refraining from action of inhabiting on the presently uninhabited islands, reef, shoals, cays, and other features". China's move to quarantine imported Philippine fruits in the aftermath of the incident, aimed at consolidating its full control over the Scarborough Shoal was also incompatible with international norms.[70] The later building of artificial islands in 2014–2015 was also an aggressive move to strengthen China's presence in the SCS. The huge area reclaimed is another indicator of China's display of power. The UNCLOS Tribunal has ruled China's behaviour (building artificial islands, prohibiting other countries from conducting economic activities in their EEZ) unlawful.

5.4.3 *Does China Adopt Reassurance Policies in the SCS?*

China's policy of reassurance was the main cause of the period of de-escalation which started in the aftermath of the 1995 Mischief Reef incident. However, since between 2007 and 2009, China's behaviour is less reassuring.

According to Mearsheimer, a state that has a large power advantage over its rivals is likely to adopt aggressive behaviour, because it is supported by major resources that it possesses.[71] Great powers like Japan (1848–1945), Germany (1862–1945), and the Soviet Union (1917–1991) behaved aggressively to expand their territory as their power increased.[72] Tang Shiping summarises offensive realist logic as "when a states believes that it can do harm to you, it will—not just may."[73] Therefore, offensive realism assumes that a rising power like China cannot rise peacefully.[74]

China' behaviour is not expansionist, because it has not been hungry for new territory when its power has been rising. In fact, even though China has a capability to behave aggressively, it adopted a reassurance policy towards the Southeast neighbours, until recently.

After the 1988 Johnson Reef incident and the 1995 Mischief Reef incident, China established a limited presence in the Spratly Islands, which qualified it as an SCS claimant state. China would not have needed to launch its reassurance policy if it had not had any presence in the SCS, especially the Spratlys, despite the country's longstanding claim and strong public sentiment about the SCS. The series of incidents in the SCS made Southeast Asian countries realise that China's behaviour had the potential to destabilise the region, which led China to exert more efforts in balancing this by adopting a reassurance policy towards its ASEAN counterparts—while stressing the peaceful nature of its rise.[75] In addition to that, due to severe criticism of China's activities regarding Taiwan and the SCS issue in the mid-1990s, China was prompted to adopt a more moderate policy in dealing with its security.[76]

The most notable one was in the fallout from the 1995 Mischief Reef incident until between 2007 and 2009. In that period, the SCS tension was reduced, and the parties concerned seemed content to keep the status quo.[77] China itself became more open to discussing the SCS issue in the context of ASEAN.[78]China's behaviour in the Southeast Asian region, especially after the 1995 Mischief Reef incident until between 2007 and 2009 was described as relatively self-restrained, accommodating, and reassuring. Emmers describes this period as one period of de-escalation.[79]

China realised that without regional stability, development and modernisation of the country would be hard to attain. The reassurance policy towards ASEAN was adopted as the good neighbour (***mulin waijiao wending zhoubian***) guideline that gained prominence in Chinese foreign policy.[80] This situation was conducive to the signing of the Declaration on the Conduct of Parties in the South China Sea (DoC) in November 2002 and the TAC in Southeast Asia, which prevents the signatories from using a military approach in dealing with disputes in the region, in 2003. In the following years, these two agreements were effective in restraining the claimant states from making any provocative moves. In March 2005, China, the Philippines, and Vietnam signed an agreement entitled the Joint Marine Seismic Undertaking (JMSU) that was applauded as a breakthrough in the dispute, before it finally elapsed in 2008.[81] Despite China expanding its structures on Mischief Reef in 1998, no occupation of new features took place during this period.[82] Apart from security-related matters, China also provided generous economic, infrastructure, and commercial assistance to ASEAN countries.[83]

During the period of de-escalation, the situation in the SCS was not completely free of conflict. Some skirmishes between warships, vessels, and fishing boats from China and other claimants did take place, but overall, the disputes were low profile and no dramatic tension occurred.[84]

There are some qualities during the period of de-escalation that characterise China's behaviour, as well as other claimants in the SCS:

- Multilateral dialogue on SCS issues other than territorial dispute resolution[85]
- China's insistence on bilateral negotiation on the issue of the dispute settlement[86]

- China's statement that it is ready to work towards a peaceful solution of the dispute based on international law[87]
- The willingness to prevent further tension by all signing the 2002 DoC and TAC
- Shared self-restraint and accommodation[88]
- Despite China expanding its structures on Mischief Reef in 1998, since 1995 it has not occupied any new disputed features in the SCS[89]
- Generous economic, commercial, infrastructure and cultural programmes provided by China to ASEAN countries.[90]

However, the decade of de-escalation is now past. Since the mid-2000s, the tension in the SCS has continued to escalate until today. In 2009, China delivered a *nota verbale* to the UN with a nine-dash line map attached with it, without any explanation of the briefly sketched claim according to the UNCLOS—even though China was one of its signatories. This claim has been rejected by Vietnam and the Philippines. In July 2010, Indonesia, a country in the far southeast that was not a claimant state to the disputes in the SCS, became the first to officially request a clarification concerning China's nine-dash line claim through a diplomatic note to the UN.[91]

China's most worrisome behaviour is its blatant rejection of the UNCLOS Tribunal ruling. It stated that China will not accept, participate, acknowledge, or implement the ruling. The rejection of legal restraint is one of the qualities of both hegemonic and rogue states. As one of the regional superpowers, China's dismissal of the Tribunal ruling leaves a compelling question about how offensively the country can behave at the expense of the smaller states in the region.

5.5 China's Defection in the SCS

This research aims to explore China's defection in the SCS after the de-escalation period following the 1995 Mischief Reef incident. Based on Kydd's definition, Sect. 2.8 elaborated on defection as an attempt to alter the status quo in a state's favour.[92] In addition to that, defection is also a stage when one or both states' intentions change from defensive to offensive. The defection by one or more states can deteriorate and lead to an expansionist threat, a deadlock and/or war (as discussed in Chap. 2). This section attempts to define defection in the context of China's behaviour in the SCS. As indicated earlier, a defection should be differentiated from merely assertive moves which lead to deeper tension. Finding the point of defection is one of the main tasks of this research. Theoretically, it is more meaningful to see how far China can go as a rising power in adopting offensive measures.

In brief, a defection in the SCS should meet the following requirements. First, it must not be a one-off action; it must be a move that changes the status or the position in favour of the initiator. Second, it must be a breach of the agreed consensus among parties in the SCS. Concretely, the agreed consensus in the SCS is the 2002 DoC. Third, it must be a move that has not been made during the period of de-escalation. Contrary to the defensive realist qualities mentioned above, China in its defections demonstrates its offensive realist characteristics—such as displaying power (instead of advocating peaceful negotiation), norm violation (instead of self-restraint), and hegemonic behaviour (instead of reassuring other rival claimants).

Not all China's actions and reactions in the SCS are similar in tone. In a dispute where there had been no means of resolution (prior to the UNCLOS Tribunal), all states involved attempted to defend or substantiate their claims in the SCS. This made tension inevitable. Protests over joint exploration projects, incidents between fishermen and maritime law enforcement agencies from different states, standoffs with other states' military ships, and the installation of oil rigs all contributed to escalating the tension, but none can be seen individually as a point of defection. Those actions were not permanent, they did not change the situation or claimants' position in the long term and all took place in the period of de-escalation.

In contrast, the 2012 Scarborough Shoal incident is a defection on the part of the Chinese, because it established China as the new occupant of the feature, changing its former status. It breached the 2002 DoC in which it clearly agreed that all parties would not exert control over new features in the SCS. The blockade preventing Philippine fishermen from conducting activities in the vicinity of the shoal which is also unlawful based on the UNCLOS Tribunal ruling. Moreover, these actions did not occur during the period of de-escalation.

Another defection is China's construction of massive artificial islands which lasted from August 2014 and was claimed complete in June 2015.[93] According to Pentagon, the operation covered seven reefs in the Spratly Islands: Fiery Cross Reef, Mischief Reef, Cuarteron Reef, Subi Reef,

Gaven Reef, Johnson South Reef, and Hughes Reef—a total reclamation area of 3000 acres.[94] Such a size dwarfs the combined reclamation area of all the other claimants including Vietnam, Malaysia, the Philippines, and Taiwan which amounted to 100 acres over the past 45 years.[95] In the reclamation area, China has built three airstrips, constructed deep ports that are suitable for large warships and installed radar and communication equipment. This installation gives rise to a suspicion that China is militarising the SCS and planning to coerce other claimant states into accommodating its claim.[96] Peter Dutton argued that China's extensive island building in the Spratlys "fundamentally changed regional political and security dynamics".[97] This island fabrication is indeed an aggressive attempt to exert control over the SCS and increase the risk of military conflict. Through this means, China has strengthened its presence and control in the SCS in an unprecedented way and hampered the patrol activities of other claimant states in their own EEZs. It may also turn the SCS into China's "strategic strait".[98]

The UNCLOS Tribunal ruling has ruled China's massive building of artificial islands unlawful.[99] It also threatens stability in the region which the 2002 DoC attempts to maintain. More importantly, it has significantly bolstered China's presence and accommodated its assertiveness in an unprecedented way.

China's rejection of the Tribunal ruling is also an offensive action. As discussed in Sect. 5.4.1, compliance with international law is defensive realist behaviour. However, this research is cautious about labelling China's rejection of the Tribunal ruling as a defection. First, a defection should be a behaviour that is intended to change the status quo in the long term, instead of a mere position or statement which can be different with what happens in reality. Comparisons with the case of Russia versus the Netherlands and India against Bangladesh help us to understand why China deserves to be given the benefit of the doubt. In August 2015, Russia lost its case at the International Tribunal of the Law of the Sea (ITLOS) to the Netherlands over Greenpeace's ship, the Dutch-flagged *Arctic Sunrise*. The ITLOS ruled that Russia must compensate the Netherlands over the ship's seizure in 2013. Russia, which initially rejected the jurisdiction of ITLOS and dismissed the ruling, eventually found a face-saving solution and complied with most of the ruling by claiming that the measure was taken in accordance with its national law.[100] In 2014, India also lost its case to smaller Bangladesh over a maritime dispute in the

Bay of Bengal. In response to the ITLOS award, India behaved as a great power and accepted the decision, renewing negotiations with Bangladesh based on the ruling.[101]

Second, as discussed in Sect. 3.3.2, in its response to the UNCLOS Tribunal ruling, China iterated its claim in a way that is more agreeable to the content of the ruling. This subtle change demonstrates that China's rejection of the UNCLOS Tribunal ruling is not absolute. Time will show whether there could be some positive changes in the future.

Third, in the aftermath of Duterte's visit to China in October 2016, Beijing allowed Philippine fishermen access to the Scarborough Shoal. According to the Philippine Defence Secretary Delfin Lorenzana, Chinese patrol boats are no longer harassing or preventing Philippine fishermen from conducting activities in the nearby waters of the Scarborough Shoal.[102] This position was mentioned by Chinese President Xi Jinping to his Philippine counterpart, on the sidelines of the Asia Pacific Economic Cooperation summit in Lima, Peru, on 19 November 2016.[103] This demonstrates that China has adjusted itself to the Tribunal ruling to some extent.

On one hand, China's decision can be seen as a strategy to reconcile itself with the UNCLOS Tribunal ruling. The Scarborough Shoal access was given at the right time after President Duterte's visit to imply that it was a reward to Manila for taking a reconciliatory approach towards Beijing.[104] China's decision to grant access to the shoal seems to be a face-saving strategy after its diplomatic setback in the aftermath of the ruling in July 2016. Therefore, China's rejection of the ruling should not be seen prematurely as a defection.

However, regardless of the new development in the Scarborough Shoal after President Duterte's visit, this research argues that China's control over the shoal in 2012 is a defection since China still holds control today over the strategic reef in the Scarborough Shoal.[105] Giving access to Philippine fishermen does not mean giving up the control over the Shoal. The seizure of the Scarborough Shoal in 2012 was a strategic action for the long term. There are clear parallels between the 1974 Paracel incident and the 2012 Scarborough Shoal incident which suggest that the latter was premeditated.[106] China's seizure of the Scarborough Shoal has altered the status quo in favour of China and this control was intended to be permanent (Table 5.1).

Table 5.1 China's actions in the SCS and their significance

Categories	*Actions*
Assertive behaviours	China put pressure on US energy companies to end joint cooperation with Vietnam in the SCS. China imposed a unilateral fishing ban in the SCS. Chinese naval patrol vessels were involved in an incident with a Vietnamese fishing boat. China protested against a claim for extended continental shelves and renewed its claim, which covers 80% of the SCS. China passed new legislation entrusting the administration of the Paracel and Spratly Islands to Sansha city in Hainan Province. A standoff with US military ships took place. China placed the HSY 981 oil rig in the vicinity of the Paracel Islands.
Defection	China seized the Scarborough Shoal from the Philippines' control and blocked access to it for Philippine fishermen. China established a programme of building massive artificial islands.
Potential defection	China reacted against the UNCLOS Tribunal ruling (preventing the Philippines from conducting activities in its EEZ).

5.6 Conclusion

The chapter has argued that China's behaviour in the SCS is a litmus test for the country as a defensive realist state. A defensive realist state sends a signal that is neither too cheap nor too costly. In a nutshell, a costly signal in the SCS can be summarised as one which portrays an attitude of a state opening itself to non-military solutions in the SCS dispute, engaging in self-restraint and the adoption of a reassurance policy.

China and other clamant states in the SCS have issued a DoC to resolve the SCS dispute peacefully. However, China has blatantly rejected the UNCLOS Tribunal ruling on July 2013, though it has balanced the rejection with reiterating its commitment to peaceful means for resolving disputes. Since China dismisses all means of peaceful dispute resolution except negotiations with the rival claimants, which other claimants are reluctant to involve themselves in, the process towards dispute resolution appeared to have reached a deadlock. Therefore, it can be understood that China's readiness to resolve the SCS dispute for the time being is only limited to a declaration and exhibits a lack of concreteness.

In terms of self-restraint, China showed restraint during encirclement from the superpowers in the Cold War era. Even in the 1990s and 2000s, as China's power grew substantially, the country did not use excessive force to strengthen its claim in the SCS. Nevertheless, the 2012 Scarborough Shoal incident and the massive construction of artificial islands demonstrate China's lack of self-restraint.

In terms of reassurance policy, China has been involved in the region's treaties and has adopted a good neighbourhood policy in the aftermath of the 1995 Mischief Reef incident. However, no reassurance has been provided to clarify the SCS claim, which has created considerable anxiety among other claimant states.

From the three criteria mentioned above, China displays some qualities of a defensive realist state. China had exercised self-restraint and initiated reassurance strategy in the SCS which led to the de-escalation of tension in 1995 until between 2007 and 2009. However, China still needs to back up its commitment to peaceful dispute resolution with concrete actions instead of a mere rhetoric. Overall, during the period of de-escalation (1995 until between 2007 and 2009), China adopted defensive realist strategy in the SCS.

Nevertheless, China has defected from defensive realism to offensive realism in two of its behaviours: first, the seizure of the Scarborough Shoal in 2012 followed by the halt of access for Philippine fishermen to conduct activities in the vicinity of the Shoal; second, the monumental construction of artificial islands in 2014–2015. These activities are violations of the DoC and the UNCLOS—to which China is a party; they change the status quo in the field; and did not take place in the period of de-escalation.

The UNCLOS Tribunal ruling issued on 12 July 2016 clarifies the ambiguity over China's excessive claim and the legality of its activities in the SCS. China's rejection of the Tribunal ruling is a potential defection. It will be a defection if in reality China continues its activities which are against the Tribunal ruling. In response to the ruling, China did make an adjustment in its SCS claim as discussed in Chap. 3 Sect. 3.3. Moreover, China also gives Philippine fishermen access to the Scarborough Shoal after the visit of President Duterte to China on October 2016.

To conclude, the PRC's behaviour in the SCS was originally defensive realist. However, China's control over Scarborough Shoal incident in 2012 and the massive construction of artificial islands in 2014–2015 demonstrate China's defection from defensive realism to offensive realism. In the future, the UNCLOS Tribunal ruling should be a measurement to assess whether China defects from defensive realism.

Notes

1. Waltz, *Theory of International Politics*, 126.
2. Glaser, "The Security Dilemma Revisited," 171–201.
3. Robert Jervis, "Cooperation under the Security Dilemma," Ibid. 30, no. 2 (1978): 167–214.
4. The most notable scholar in promoting China as a defensive realist state is Tang Shiping. Alongside him are also some scholars, that is, Zhang Yunling and Yves-Heng Lim.
5. Tang, "From Offensive to Defensive Realism: A Social Evolutionary Interpretation of China's Security Strategy," 141–62.
6. Kydd, *Trust and Mistrust in International Relations*, 183.
7. Tang, "From Offensive to Defensive Realism: A Social Evolutionary Interpretation of China's Security Strategy," 141–62.
8. Ibid., 156.
9. Ibid., 141.
10. Mearsheimer, "Can China Rise Peacefully?" *The National Interest*, 25 October 2014.
11. Kydd, *Trust and Mistrust in International Relations*, 187.
12. Ibid., 188.
13. M. Taylor Fravel, *Strong Borders, Secure Nation: Cooperation and Conflict in China's Territorial Disputes* (Princeton: Princeton University Press, 2008), 314.
14. For China, resolving disputes through legal mechanism is unfavourable. First, China avoids the situation where it has to comply with external demands against its will. Second, before international law, all countries are seen equal. As a country with a big power mindset, China aspires to be treated as such. Giving concession to the smaller countries demonstrates its "magnanimity." See Eric Hyer, "The South China Sea Disputes: Implications of China's Earlier Territorial Settlements," *Pacific Affairs*, 68, no. 1 (1995): 34–54.
15. Austin, *China's Ocean Frontier: International Law, Military Force and National Development*, 17, 309–10; Storey, "China's Bilateral and Multilateral Diplomacy in the South China Sea."
16. Andrew Chubb, "The South China Sea: Defining the 'Status Quo'," *The Diplomat*, 11 June 2015, http://thediplomat.com/2015/06/the-south-china-sea-defining-the-status-quo/ (accessed 2 March 2016).
17. Linda Jakobson, "China's Unpredictable Maritime Security Actors," (Lowy Institute for International Policy, 2014), 26–27.
18. Lijun Sheng, *China's Policy Towards the Spratly Islands in the 1990s* (Canberra: Strategic and Defence Studies Centre, Australian National University, 1995), 287, 8–9, 21.

19. Ibid., 21–22.
20. Tang, *A Theory of Security Strategies for Our Time: Defensive Realism*, 31.
21. Zhang, "China's Growing Assertiveness in the South China Sea: A Strategic Shift?," 20–21.
22. Some of the Paracel Islands were seized by China in 1956, see Mark J. Valencia, *China and the South China Sea Disputes* (Oxford: Oxford University Press for the International Institute for Strategic Studies, 1995), vol. 298, 32.
23. King C. Chen, *China's War with Vietnam, 1979: Issues, Decisions, and Implications* (Stanford, CA: Hoover Institution Press, Stanford University, 1987), 22–23.
24. Fravel, *Strong Borders, Secure Nation: Cooperation and Conflict in China's Territorial Disputes*, 287.
25. Robert S. Ross, *The Indochina Tangle: China's Vietnam Policy, 1975–1979* (New York: Columbia University Press, 1988), 8.
26. Chi-Kin Lo, *China's Policy Towards Territorial Disputes: The Case of the South China Sea Islands*, vol. 10, 64 (Routledge, 1989).
27. 刘华清, *刘华清回忆录* (北京: 解放军出版社, 2004) [Liu Huaqing, *Liu Huaqings's Memoir* (Beijing: Jiefangjun Chubanshe, 2004)], 341–42.
28. Garver, "China's Push Through the South China Sea: The Interaction of Bureaucratic and National Interests," 999–1028; Lo, *China's Policy Towards Territorial Disputes: The Case of the South China Sea Islands*, 10, 68.
29. Fravel, *Strong Borders, Secure Nation: Cooperation and Conflict in China's Territorial Disputes*, 287.
30. Lo, *China's Policy Towards Territorial Disputes: The Case of the South China Sea Islands*, 10, 111.
31. Ibid., 109.
32. Austin, *China's Ocean Frontier: International Law, Military Force and National Development*, 17, 154–55.
33. Sheng, *China's Policy Towards the Spratly Islands in the 1990s*, no. 287, 8–9.
34. 刘华清, *刘华清回忆录*,[Liu Huaqing, *Liu Huaqings's Memoir* (Beijing: Jiefangjun Chubanshe, 2004)], 543–35.
35. Ibid., 494–96.
36. Xu, Tiemao in Fravel, *Strong Borders, Secure Nation: Cooperation and Conflict in China's Territorial Disputes*, 293.
37. Ibid., 287–88.
38. Sheng, *China's Policy Towards the Spratly Islands in the 1990s*, no. 287, 10.
39. Ibid.
40. Ibid., 10–11.

41. Austin, *China's Ocean Frontier: International Law, Military Force and National Development*, 17, 83.
42. Sheng, *China's Policy Towards the Spratly Islands in the 1990s*, no. 287, 26.
43. Daojiong Zha and Mark J. Valencia, "Mischief Reef: Geopolitics and Implications," *Journal of Contemporary Asia*, 31, no. 1 (2001): 86–103.
44. Emmers, "The De-escalation of the Spratly Dispute in Sino-Southeast Asian Relations."
45. Beukel, *China and the South China Sea: Two Faces of Power in the Rising China's Neighborhood Policy*, 13.
46. Ibid., 14.
47. "NIDS China Security Report 2011."
48. Ian Storey, "Can the South China Sea Dispute Be Resolved or Better Managed?" (Strategizing Change in Asia: The 27th Asia-Pacific Roundtable, 2013), 9.
49. 张洁, "黄岩岛模式与中国海洋维权政策的转向," *Southeast Asian Studies*, [Zhang Jie, "The Scarborough Shoal Model and the Shift in China's Maritime Rights Defence Strategy"] no. 4 (2013).
50. Dreyer, "Sansha: New City in the South China Sea."
51. Erica Downs, "Business and Politics in the South China Sea: Explaining HYSY 981's Foray into Disputed Waters," *China Brief*, XIV, no. 12 (2014): 6–8.
52. Andrew S. Erickson, "The South China Sea's Third Force: Understanding and Countering China's Maritime Militia," *Testimony Before the House Armed Service Committee Seapower and Projection Forces Subcommittee*, 21 September 2016, http://docs.house.gov/meetings/AS/AS28/20160921/105309/HHRG-114-AS28-Wstate-EricksonPhDA-20160921.pdf (accessed 21 November 2016).
53. Hyer, "The South China Sea Disputes: Implications of China's Earlier Territorial Settlements," 34–54.
54. Carlyle A. Thayer, "No, China Is Not Reclaiming Land in the South China Sea," *The Diplomat*, 7 June 2015, http://thediplomat.com/2015/06/no-china-is-not-reclaiming-land-in-the-south-china-sea/ (accessed 10 July 2016).
55. Fravel, *Strong Borders, Secure Nation: Cooperation and Conflict in China's Territorial Disputes*, 316; Bonnie S. Glaser, "Beijing as an Emerging Power in the South China Sea: Statement before the House Foreign Affairs Committee," *Center for Strategic and International Studies*, (2012).
56. "Full Text of Chinese Government Statement on China's Territorial Sovereignty and Maritime Rights and Interests in South China Sea," *Xinhuanet*, 12 July 2016.

57. Fravel, *Strong Borders, Secure Nation: Cooperation and Conflict in China's Territorial Disputes*, 300; Hyer, "The South China Sea Disputes: Implications of China's Earlier Territorial Settlements," 34–54.
58. "The South China Sea Disputes: Implications of China's Earlier Territorial Settlements," 34–54.
59. Sheldon W. Simon, "ASEAN Regional Forum," in William M. Carpenter and David G Wiencek (eds.), *Asian Security Handbook: An Assessment of Political Security Issues in the Asia Pacific Region* (New York: M.E. Sharpe, 1996), p. 47 quoted in Emmers, "The De-escalation of the Spratly Dispute in Sino-Southeast Asian Relations," 131.
60. Fravel, *Strong Borders, Secure Nation: Cooperation and Conflict in China's Territorial Disputes*, 287.
61. Austin, *China's Ocean Frontier: International Law, Military Force and National Development*, 17, 77.
62. Sheng, *China's Policy Towards the Spratly Islands in the 1990s*, no. 287, 15.
63. Ibid., 11.
64. Ibid., 12.
65. Shee Poon Kim, "The South China Sea in China's Strategic Thinking," *Contemporary Southeast Asia*, 19, no. 4 (1998): 369–87.
66. Ibid.
67. Ibid., 371.
68. Ibid., 378–79.
69. Mearsheimer, "Can China Rise Peacefully?" *The National Interest*, 25 October 2014.
70. Glaser, "Beijing as an Emerging Power in the South China Sea: Statement before the House Foreign Affairs Committee."
71. John J. Mearsheimer, *The Tragedy of Great Power Politics* (W. W. Norton, 2014), 37.
72. Ibid., 169–233.
73. Tang, "Fear in International Politics: Two Positions," 451–71.
74. Mearsheimer, "Can China Rise Peacefully?" *The National Interest*, 25 October 2014.
75. Glaser, "Tensions Flare in the South China Sea."
76. Robert Sutter and Chin-hao Huang, "China-Southeast Asia Relations: China's Toughness on the South China Sea," *Comparative Connections*, 15, no. 1 (2013).
77. Beukel, *China and the South China Sea: Two Faces of Power in the Rising China's Neighborhood Policy*, 14.
78. "NIDS China Security Report 2011."
79. Emmers, "The De-escalation of the Spratly Dispute in Sino-Southeast Asian Relations."

80. Zhang, "China's Growing Assertiveness in the South China Sea: A Strategic Shift?," 19.
81. Schofield and Storey, *The South China Sea Dispute: Increasing Stakes and Rising Tensions*, 24.
82. Emmers, "The De-escalation of the Spratly Dispute in Sino-Southeast Asian Relations," 135.
83. Dutton, "Three Disputes and Three Objectives: China and the South China Sea," 42.
84. Beukel, *China and the South China Sea: Two Faces of Power in the Rising China's Neighborhood Policy*, 13.
85. Emmers, "The De-escalation of the Spratly Dispute in Sino-Southeast Asian Relations," 131.
86. Beukel, *China and the South China Sea: Two Faces of Power in the Rising China's Neighborhood Policy*, 13.
87. Ibid.
88. Emmers, "The De-escalation of the Spratly Dispute in Sino-Southeast Asian Relations," 135.
89. Ibid.
90. Dutton, "Three Disputes and Three Objectives: China and the South China Sea," 42.
91. Ian Storey, "The South China Sea Dispute: How Geopolitics Impedes Dispute Resolution and Conflict Management," in *Global and Regional Powers in a Changing World* (Buenos Aires, Argentina, 2014), 6.
92. Kydd, *Trust and Mistrust in International Relations*, 30.
93. Ron Huisken, "What's Really Behind China's Island Building?" *The National Interest*, 14 January 2016, http://nationalinterest.org/blog/the-buzz/whats-really-behind-chinas-island-building-14900 (accessed 2 January 2017).
94. Katie Hunt, "Showdown in the South China Sea: How Did We Get Here?" *CNN*, 2 August 2016, http://edition.cnn.com/2015/10/28/asia/china-south-china-sea-disputes-explainer/ (accessed 1 January 2017).
95. Ibid.
96. Paul McLeary Dan De Luce, "In South China Sea, a Tougher US Stance," *Foreign Policy*, 2 October 2015, http://foreignpolicy.com/2015/10/02/in-south-china-sea-a-tougher-u-s-stance/ (accessed 2 December 2016).
97. Peter Dutton, "A Maritime or Continental Order for Southeast Asia and the South China Sea?" *Naval War College Review*, 69, no. 3 (2016): 5.
98. Ibid.
99. Permanent Court of Arbitration, "Press Release of the South China Sea Arbitration (The Republic of the Philippines vs The People's Republic of China)," news release, 2016.

100. Jerome A. Cohen, "Is There a Way for Beijing to Save Face After the South China Sea Arbitration Ruling?" *South China Morning Post*, 15 June 2016, http://www.scmp.com/comment/insight-opinion/article/1975070/there-way-beijing-save-face-after-south-china-sea (accessed 20 June 2016).
101. Ibid.
102. Katie Hunt and Kathy Quiano, "China Allows Philippines Fishermen Access to Disputed Shoal in South China Sea," *CNN*, 31 October 2016, http://edition.cnn.com/2016/10/31/asia/philippines-china-scarborough-shoal-fishermen/ (accessed 2 January 2017).
103. "Xi Tells Duterte that Scarborough Shoal Will Stay Open to Philippine Fishermen," *South China Morning Post*, 20 November 2016, http://www.scmp.com/news/china/diplomacy-defence/article/2047747/xi-tells-duterte-scarborough-shoal-will-stay-open (accessed 5 December 2016).
104. Ankit Panda, "South China Sea: Philippine Fishermen Gain Access to Scarborough Shoal After Duterte's China Trip," *The Diplomat*, 29 October 2016, http://thediplomat.com/2016/10/south-china-sea-philippine-fishermen-gain-access-to-scarborough-shoal-after-dutertes-china-trip/ (accessed 2 November 2016).
105. Hunt and Quiano, "China Allows Philippines Fishermen Access to Disputed Shoal in South China Sea," *CNN*, 31 October 2016.
106. Euan Graham, "South China Sea History Lesson: Parallels from the Paracels?" *The Interpreter*, 31 March 2016, http://www.lowyinterpreter.org/post/2016/03/31/South-China-Sea-History-Lesson-Parallels-from-the-Paracels.aspx (accessed 15 April 2016).

CHAPTER 6

Security Dilemma Between China and Other South China Sea Claimant States

6.1 Introduction

This chapter aims to discuss the operation of the security dilemma between China and other claimant states. There are six claimants in the South China Sea (SCS; five states and one entity): China, Vietnam, the Philippines, Malaysia, Brunei, and Taiwan. Their attitudes towards China's behaviour in the SCS are different, due to many factors. Brunei is obviously least vocal among these claimant states. The Philippines and Vietnam are probably the most anxious about China's SCS behaviour because of their geographical proximities and frequent skirmishes with China. Although there is no formal alliance among SCS claimant states against China, these countries share anxiety regarding China's behaviour in the region.

The dichotomy of China vis-à-vis other claimant states exists because of several reasons. First, the Southeast Asian claimant states share the same concern that China, as a newly emerging large power, would use military power to resolve the SCS dispute, resulting in regional instability that is severely harmful to their interests. On Chinese side, the primary concern is that the legitimacy of China's SCS claim is waning due to a limited physical presence and the involvement of external powers called upon by other claimant states in the SCS affairs.

Second, all Southeast Asian claimant states are ASEAN states and the 2002 Declaration on the Conduct of Parties in the South China Sea (the

K. H. Raditio, *Understanding China's Behaviour in the South China Sea*, https://doi.org/10.1007/978-981-13-1283-0_6

2002 DoC) was made between China and ASEAN. Regardless of the fact that ASEAN is fragmented, all members of ASEAN wish that either China or other claimant states do not make any moves that could threaten the stability in the region. The 2002 DoC is a political consensus to ameliorate both sides' worries.

Third, since the SCS tension has escalated in the second half of the 2000s, the skirmishes, protests, or even conflicts are mostly between China and any Southeast Asian claimant state (the Philippines, Vietnam, and Malaysia). There is no notorious incident recorded among the Southeast Asian claimant states themselves.

Fourth, in some of these incidents, there is a strong indication of support among fellow Southeast Asian claimant states. For instance, in the aftermath of the 2012 Scarborough Shoal incident, the Vietnamese Foreign Ministry issued a statement of concern urging all parties to practise restraint while invoke the United Nations Convention on the Law of the Sea (UNCLOS) and the 2002 DoC as the means to maintain peace and stability in the region.[1] Malaysian Prime Minister Najib Razak stated his country's support for the Philippines over the incident during a meeting in May 2012 with the then Philippine Vice President Jejomar Binay, proposing a peaceful resolution in accordance with international law.[2] The Philippines and Vietnam issued a joint statement on strategic partnership in November 2015[3] and Vietnam has strongly supported the Philippines in the UNCLOS Tribunal.[4] Malaysia, due to its grave unease for China's recent military exercises in the oil-rich James Shoal located only 80 km from its coast, seems to support the Philippines and Vietnam lately.[5] Even ASEAN's failure to express its concern over the situation in the SCS is primarily because of China's meddling.[6]

Overall, the security dilemma between China vis-à-vis other claimants is primarily about the anxiety. The Southeast Asian claimant states who share the anxiety towards China's behaviour in the SCS are considered as "other claimants" in this model. A claimant state does not have to be a direct victim, like the Philippines was in the 2012 Scarborough Shoal incident, to understand that China's offensive act has defected from a defensive realist position.

Regarding the operation of the security dilemma, the discussion in this chapter correlates significantly with that of the Theoretical Framework in Chap. 2. It begins with identifying the elements of the security dilemma (uncertainty, lack of malign intention, and paradoxical/self-defeating policy). Then, in Sect. 6.3, it explains the nature of the conflict of interest in the SCS in terms of subjectively and objectively reconcilable differences. Section 6.4 further discusses the operation of the security dilemma that culminated in China's defection from defensive realism in the 2012 Scarborough Shoal incident and the massive construction of artificial islands in 2014–2015. The last section discusses measures that can be adopted by China—as a defected state—to ameliorate the security dilemma in the region.

6.2 The Elements of the Security Dilemma in the SCS

Uncertainty is the one element that dominates the course of tension in the SCS. The SCS dispute is not something new in the region; it can be traced back to the aftermath of World War II. Historically, the tension in the SCS is unpredictable, and states are uncertain about other states' intention. The notion of offensive realism presumes that states know about the outcome of power maximisation, which is conflict, and that the uncertainty is only about the time such conflict will occur[7] is therefore not applicable in the context of the SCS. There was a period when tension de-escalated and the SCS claimant states, including China, alleviated distrust and suspicion.[8] In the aftermath of the 1995 Mischief Reef incident until the second half of the 2000s, China adopted a conciliatory approach towards Southeast Asian countries and this successfully stabilised the region. China's behaviour in the period of de-escalation is discussed in Sect. 5.4.3.

However, the tension began to rise since the second half of the 2000s. The uncertainty about the intentions of China's continuous military build-up creates anxiety among other claimants. Given the vast territory of the country and the size of its population, China considers its military build-up justifiable. Moreover, China has experienced tremendous economic growth since the 1980s, which has created suitable conditions to build up the country across all fields, including the military. The increase in the country's military budget is a reasonable outcome of its economic rise. As a percentage of GNP, the military budget has declined from 2.2% in 2009 to 2% in 2012, according to the World Bank.[9] The US, which has a smaller population than China, spends about four times as much as China on its military (according to the official exchange rate). Due to the difficulty in assessing the appropriate amount of military power necessary to gain security, uncertainty that leads to anxiety will always occur among states.

No claimant states had expected the rising of the tension in between 2007 and 2009. Since then, uncertainty has dominated the climate in the SCS. However, there is no sign of war, and war is certainly not the predestined or even predicted fate of the region. The reality is that the smaller states in the region are anxious about China's increasing assertiveness in the SCS, while China is also suspicious of other claimant states' intentions of undermining its sovereignty and of their closeness to the US.

Another element of the security dilemma is a lack of malign intention. Despite the prevalent suspicion among the SCS claimant states, there is no evidence that any state harbours expansionist ambition. Every state is meant to defend what they perceive as their legitimate rights in the SCS. This research argues that the Philippines, Vietnam, Malaysia, and Brunei are not expansionists and they adopt cooperative attitude towards China. In contrast, the debate on China's nature will be much more intensive and vigorous. This is because China has been accused of being assertive, aggressive, and abrasive in the SCS, whereas other claimants have seldom been accused of such things.

The task to prove that China's initial motive in the SCS was defensive realist has been done in Chaps. 3, 4 and 5. These chapters argue that from the perspective of China's claim, interests, and behaviour, it was initially a defensive realist state. However, the seizure of the Scarborough Shoal in 2012 and the massive construction of artificial islands in 2014–2015 demonstrate China's offensive realist framework of behaviour.

The last element of the security dilemma is paradoxical or self-defeating policy. This is true for China since China's effort to improve its security has resulted in more insecurity. Nowadays, the sense of insecurity in the region is noticeably prevalent. The claimant states are made anxious by China's growing military power and aggressive activities in the region. Since the end of the 2000s, China has been increasing its patrols and activities (carried out by the Chinese Coast Guard and People's Liberation Army Navy [PLAN]) to assert its maritime rights within the nine-dash line.[10] China's operations have raised alarm among other claimant states who regard these activities as a real threat to their maritime rights.

Regarding power accumulation, since the 1990s, China has been increasing its military spending by double digit increments almost annually.[11] The country's military budget has risen eightfold in 20 years.[12] Comparative figures in terms of increases during 2003–2012 are 175% for China and 32% for the US, and for 2011–2012, the figures are 7.8% for China and –6% for the US.[13] Also, China has the world's second largest naval fleet after the US, and the world's largest number of military personnel.

Countries in Southeast Asia have also been attempting to upgrade their military capability. Malaysia's defence spending has more than doubled since 2000.[14] In March 2014, the Philippines purchased military infrastructure, including 12 FA-50 fighter jets from South Korea, 8 combat utility helicopters, and 2 anti-submarine helicopters, which are worth at least USD 671 million.[15] The US pivot to Asia post 2010, which has projected 50%–60% of US air and naval power into Asia, exacerbates the arms race in the region.[16]

It is obvious that China's military build-up, which is aimed at increasing its security, in fact, propels the insecurity of its neighbours and eventually brings about balancing behaviour. China has been insistently rejecting any external power's presence in Asia, that is, the US involvement. Washington is perceived as the main obstacle to China gaining prominence in the region.[17] China has also been attempting to encourage its Southeast Asian neighbours to dismiss the China threat theory by providing assistance during the regional financial crisis and being involved in regional security agreements to maintain stability in the region. However, the country's continuous military build-up worries its neighbouring countries. Its smaller, weaker southeast neighbours eventually implemented a balancing strategy in response to China by purchasing military infrastructure and forming an alliance with the US. They obviously prefer to balance China instead of bandwagoning it. The reason is clear: they are concerned about China's intentions about their security, especially over the issue of territorial disputes in the SCS. Without a doubt, the increasing military power has not brought about heightened security for China; on the contrary, it threatens China's interests and security in the region. This situation leads to a security dilemma between China and other SCS claimants.

Since other claimant states are militarily weaker than China, they have attempted to balance China's assertiveness by military cooperation with external countries. The US and Japan have welcomed the military initiatives by the Philippines and Vietnam. The US and the Philippines have intensified the *Balikatan*—the two countries' joint military cooperation scheme. Japan supplies the Philippines with military equipment.[18] In addition to that, in March 2016, the US lifted the arms embargo on Vietnam.[19] Overall, Chinese activities meant to secure its maritime domain only invite balancing from extra-regional powers and create a more difficult situation in the SCS, eventually making China less secure to a certain extent.

6.3 Conflict of Interest

In modern international relations, states are not fighting for a *lebensraum* or new space at the expense of other states. The world is now in the era of defensive realism where conquest is no longer easy or even allowed.[20] States hardly can solely depend on military power to grab other states' territory since they are constrained by international law, norms, and long-term interests. Conflicts of interest become a factor that generally precedes a security dilemma. A conflict of interest is a disaccord of interests between two states or two alliances of states when they cannot enjoy the same thing at the same time.[21] As mentioned earlier, even though a conflict of interest in most cases precedes a security dilemma, it does not necessarily lead to one. A conflict of interest according to defensive realism has both an objective and subjective side.[22] The conflicts of interest in the SCS are objectively reconcilable and subjectively irreconcilable. As explained in the Sect. 2.7, a conflict of interest that is objectively reconcilable and subjectively irreconcilable lays the foundation for the application of the security dilemma.

The first conflict of interest—between China and regional rival claimants in the SCS—is objectively reconcilable because of various reasons. First, the maritime rights disputes in the SCS should not be a big issue if all parties adhere to international law, that is, the UNCLOS. Even though all claimants in the SCS disputes have ratified UNCLOS—the Philippines (1986), Vietnam (1994), Malaysia (1996), and Brunei (1996), and China (1996)—which regulates peaceful dispute resolution, not all of them uphold the rule of law.

In particular, China has failed to clarify its maritime rights claim in the SCS according to the UNCLOS. Its nine-dash line covers 90% of the body of water in the SCS, and it overlaps with other claimants' territorial water and maritime rights. The UNCLOS Tribunal rendered its award on 12 July 2016 which gives more clarity on the issue. According to the Award of the UNCLOS Tribunal, China has "no legal basis to claim historic rights of resources within the sea areas falling with the nine dash line".[23] The status of the award itself is legally binding for all parties, including China. Since China's ratification of the UNCLOS in 1996, it has agreed to be bound by any decision of such a compulsory third-party determination according to Article 296 of UNCLOS and Article 11 of Annex VII.[24] Therefore, if all parties concerned in the SCS uphold the UNCLOS, the maritime rights disputes can be resolved and tension can also be managed.

Second, the SCS should not be considered a "gold mine" for claimant states. Regarding energy security, China's main threat is its uncontrollable energy consumption without enhancing its energy efficiency.[25] In other words, domestic consumption is the primary issue for China's energy security. The SCS resources do not have the capacity to offset the declining domestic production and the growing demand for energy in all claimant states[26] which are all in various stages of development. The assumption that the hydrocarbon resources in the SCS can alleviate the energy security problems of China and other claimant states is a misperception. All claimant states should cooperate to boost energy efficiency and develop alternative energy sources. China, for instance, no matter how enormous its resources are, will never be able to satisfy its energy needs, while it ignores the urgency of improving its energy efficiency.

Third, the SCS should be seen as a common property which no state can monopolise. Historically, the SCS has been a ground of trade and exchange where no nation or group claims ownership.[27] The iteration that a nation claims sovereignty since ancient time or time immemorial is baseless. The UNCLOS Tribunal affirms that there was no evidence whatsoever that China has exercised exclusive jurisdiction over the waters of the SCS or used it exclusively by precluding other states from accessing the resources.[28] This undoubtedly applies to other claimant states as well. In the case of Scarborough Shoal, for instance, the Tribunal rules that both China and the Philippines enjoy traditional fishing rights at the shoal and it would be unlawful to halt access for either Filipino or Chinese fishermen to fish near the Shoal.[29]

These are the reasons showing that conflicting interest in the SCS is objectively reconcilable. There are no objectively irreconcilable elements if all parties can keep composed and avoid seeing the SCS from the perspective of a zero-sum game. The thing that leads to the severity of the conflict of interest in the SCS is the subjective perspective and the selfish pursuit of so-called national interest.

The conflict of interest in the SCS becomes subjectively irreconcilable primarily because it involves excessive nationalism. For China, the SCS issue is a part of the national humiliation narrative. As dictated by the regime's propaganda, the SCS is perceived by many in China as "the lost territory". The patriotic education in China—particularly on sovereignty-related issues—becomes entwined with the aim of boosting the Communist regime's legitimacy. It depicts China historically as a victim of other powers' oppression and containment, and the Beijing government as the benevolent entity which still pursues nothing but self-defence. This only makes Chinese people over-sensitive to sovereignty issues, demanding the government to have a harsher attitude towards outside powers and this unfortunately creates a huge impediment to managing tensions in the SCS.[30]

The Chinese demand that the world understand the sensitiveness of their territorial sovereignty issue since they have been invaded and humiliated by imperialists throughout their history.[31] However, this perspective demonstrates a self-centred and overly inward-looking attitude, given that China is not the only nation that has experienced the bitterness of imperialism. Moreover, a history of humiliation cannot constitute a sound reason to demand a privilege or special treatment on the issue of sovereignty and maritime rights claim under international law.[32]

The subjective irreconcilability should not hinder China to manage the tension and to adjust its maritime rights claim in the SCS according to UNCLOS. Section 4.1.5. has shown that China has the capability to control its disgruntled segments of population as evident in the case of the dispute over the Senkaku/Diaoyu Islands. Any compromise made in the SCS might tarnish the Chinese Communist Party's (CCP) reputation, but it is unlikely to lead to its collapse.

The UNCLOS Tribunal in its press release emphasises that different understandings of the respective rights under the provision of the UNCLOS are at the heart of the dispute in the SCS between China and the Philippines.[33] In particular, even though China ratified the UNCLOS in 1996, Beijing has interpreted and applied the provision of the convention according to its historical and cultural perspective.[34] This confirms that what is irreconcilable in the SCS dispute is a subjective view of the UNCLOS by the respective claimants.

The above-mentioned explanation supports the argument that the conflict of interest in the SCS between China and Southeast Asian claimants is objectively reconcilable and subjectively irreconcilable. This situation has led to the application of security dilemma between the two sides.

6.4 The Continuum of the Security Dilemma

It is important to recall Fig. 2.1 of the security dilemma continuum in Sect. 2.8 to have a big picture of the development of the security dilemma process. In the preliminary phase of the security dilemma, states begin to harbour suspicion among themselves due to the accumulation of power.

China's growing military power did not necessarily activate the security dilemma since China adopted a good neighbour policy to alleviate its neighbours' suspicions. This was successful to de-escalate tension in the SCS.

However, the success was limited since it did not lead to any genuine cooperation. Except for the Vietnam-People's Republic of China (PRC) agreement for the Gulf of Tonkin that came into force in 2014, no bilateral or multilateral fisheries agreement has been reached by the claimant states.[35] The Southeast Asian claimants hold to UNCLOS to negotiate or conduct joint development, whereas China tends to avoid the UNCLOS and prefers to have a bilateral agreement as the basis for the joint development. China's joint development proposals have been driven by various intentions. First, it wishes to legitimise its nine-dash line claim which includes two other claimant states' Exclusive Economic Zones (EEZs). Second, it aims to prevent the legalisation of dispute to international legal mechanism. Third, it wants to avoid the negotiation via a Code of Conduct (CoC) which is regarded as a constraint for China's behaviour. Finally, its goal is to exclude any extra-regional powers from meddling in the dispute.[36]

Other claimants, especially the Philippines and Vietnam, have become increasingly suspicious of China's joint development proposal in that it may tacitly legitimise Beijing's claim to their EEZs, which lacks basis according to international law. The fact that Beijing has been unilaterally exploring and exploiting hydrocarbon resources with its deep-water exploration technology and increasing assertiveness, which involves the harassment of survey vessels, frequent arrests of fishermen, and cable cutting, makes the Southeast Asian claimants' priority the negotiation of a CoC rather than considering Beijing's joint development proposal.

Another reason for SCS claimants' reluctance to consider China's joint development proposal is Beijing's failure to clarify its claim in the SCS according to international law, that is, the UNCLOS.[37] To sum up, during the period of de-escalation, even though the situation was relatively stable, no genuine cooperation agreement in the SCS has been reached. In fact, the waters of scepticism and suspicion run very deep.

Below are the events that take the activated security dilemma in the SCS into a spiral phase (Table 6.1).

The incidents mentioned above are clear evidence that China and other claimants entered the stage of the spiral as depicted in Fig. 2.1 in Sect. 2.8. The spiral is a model that explains how states—driven by their anxiety and

Table 6.1 Source of the activation of the security dilemma in the SCS

2007

- In April 2007, China denounced Vietnam for violating its sovereignty by giving permission to British Petroleum to develop two gas fields in the Con Basin, 230 miles off the Vietnam coast.[38]
- In the summer of 2007, China discouraged foreign oil and gas companies to stop exploration projects with their Vietnamese counterparts in the SCS in an area claimed by Hanoi as within their EEZ.[39]
- China established the city of Sansha to administer the Paracel and Spratly Islands in December.[40]
- In 2006 and 2007, several Vietnamese fishermen were injured or killed by Chinese patrol vessels.[41]
- In December 2007, the NPC passed new legislation entrusting the administration of the Paracel and Spratly Islands to Sansha city in Hainan Province, provoking a series of anti-China protests in Vietnam.[42]

2008

- In July, China warned Exxon Mobile Corp. to call off an exploration deal with Vietnam, decrying it as a violation of Chinese sovereignty, whereas a Vietnamese Foreign Ministry spokesman said that the exploration deal fell entirely within Vietnam's sovereignty.[43]

2009

- A joint submission was made by Vietnam and Malaysia in May to the UN Commission on the Limits of the Continental Shelf (CLCS).[44]
- In response to Vietnam and Malaysia's joint submission, China submitted a nine-dash line map to the UN Commission on the Limits of the Continental Shelf (CLCS) in May 2009.[45]
- China expanded the duration of its summertime unilateral fishing ban.[46]

2010

- In 2009 and 2010, there was a more significant presence of Chinese paramilitary in the SCS than ever.[47]
- China intensified naval exercises in the SCS, beginning in 2010.[48]
- In July, at the East Asian Summit in Hanoi, US Secretary of State Hillary Clinton iterated that the US has an interest in the SCS.[49]

(*continued*)

Table 6.1 (continued)

2011

- According to Chinese sources, from 1989 to 2011, there were over 360 cases of harassment, robberies, detainment or arms firing with 25 Chinese fishermen killed or missing.[50]
- In May, Haikou Municipal Government, Hainan Province imposed a unilateral fishing ban in the SCS from 16 May to 1 August.[51]
- Vietnam lodged a protest against the patrol of Chinese Fishery Administration Vessel, *Leizhou* 44261 in the water adjacent to Paracel Islands in May.[52]
- On May 26, China Maritime Surveillance Ship No. 84 cut a Vietnamese cable towing a seismic monitoring device.[53]
- On 9 June, Chinese fishing boat No. 62226, cut the cable of the *Viking II* seismic survey ship in the vicinity of Vanguard Bank.[54]
- China launched a major military drill which involved the North Sea Fleet and the East Sea Fleet into the SCS in August.[55]
- In August, the US and Vietnam entered a new stage of military cooperation—beginning with military medical cooperation.[56]
- In September, the US and Vietnam signed a memorandum of understanding (MoU) on bilateral defence cooperation.[57]
- In November, the US Secretary of State Hillary Clinton and the Philippine Secretary of Foreign Affairs Albert del Rosario signed the Manila Declaration to enhance the two countries' cooperation for maritime security, by maintaining freedom of navigation and resolving maritime disputes according to international law.[58]

2012

- The US granted the US Coast Guard Cutter Hamilton (now the BRP Gregorio Del Pilar) to the Philippine Navy and provided advanced training assistance and communication advice to the Philippine Coast Guard. Manila simplified the clearance procedures for US military vessels and aircraft to enhance military cooperation.[59]

the uncertainty of others' motives—become involved in a continuous action-reaction dynamic of power display.[60] Butterfield and Jervis suggested that spirals take place due to security seekers' consideration that the other side knows they are defensively driven and so read any enmity as an offensive indication.[61] The exact time that China and other claimants in the SCS entered the spiral stage is unclear. Fu Ying and Wu Shicun mentioned that the tension was rising as early as 2003 when Vietnam—the party which they call "the most active violator of the 2002 DoC"—convened a commemoration of the 28th anniversary of the "Liberation of the Nansha (Spratly) Islands".[62] In the same year, the Philippines also held a similar event to celebrate the 25th anniversary of the inauguration of the Kalayaan Municipality in Zhongye (Thitu) Island.[63] However, according to Fu Ying and Wu Shicun, the tension in the SCS was relatively under control until 2009—the year Vietnam and Malaysia presented a joint submission to the UN CLCS in May.[64] By 2009, it was undoubted that China and other claimants in the SCS had entered to the deep spiral of a security dilemma.

In the context of the SCS, a spiral could take place because of several reasons. First, there was an absence of agreed dispute resolution. Since China and the Southeast Asian claimants are not on the same page in resolving the dispute, what they can do is to avoid conflict. However, conflict avoidance is very fragile; it can easily turn into the activation of a security dilemma and spiral by any claimant state. China accused other claimant states' activities in the SCS of being provocations. Other claimant states accuse China of militarising the SCS and attempting to change the status quo in its favour.

The second reason is the increasing strategic value of the SCS to China and other claimant states. As described in Chap. 4, the SCS has become very important to China, especially in terms of strategy and security. Recently, China has also been building maritime awareness and has become more resolute in defending its near seas. The notion that a country's future depends on its maritime power is also shared by other SCS littoral states. This undoubtedly makes the SCS very prone to tension.

It does not matter which party started to escalate the tension in the SCS, because the absence of a dispute resolution process and the increasing significance of the SCS for all claimant states lead to an inevitable heightening of tension. The action-reaction dynamic of power in the SCS creates a sense of victimisation—in which all claimant states consider their actions as merely a response to others' provocation. Small claimant states see themselves as victims of China's bullying; whereas China believes it has been considerably restrained against what it perceives as "small countries bullying the big power" in the SCS.[65]

Every event in the spiral mode only brings about the deepening of tension. However, strategically no one event is more significant than the other. For a more in-depth analysis, an incident that signifies a change in the SCS security dilemma continuum to the point of defection needs to be determined. Spirals last as long as there is any chance of believing that a state is a security seeker[66]; but the point of defection puts an end to this, because the state involved has shifted from defensive realism to start adopting offensive realism.

The incident that signifies the point of defection should be something that is more than an element of the action-reaction dynamic of the power struggle in the SCS. Section 5.5 discusses the definition of defection and indicates two defections on the part of China in the SCS: the seizure of the Scarborough Shoal in 2012 followed by the blockade of Philippine fishermen to enter the Shoal; and the massive construction of artificial islands in 2014–2015. The detail of these defected behaviours has been discussed in Chap. 5.

6.5 The Rationale of China's Defection in the SCS

Why did China defect from defensive realism? Defensive realism suggests that there are material and psychological regulators that change the course of the security dilemma.[67] Regarding material regulators, China is very dissatisfied with the fact that it only controls a minority of features in the SCS, compared to Vietnam and the Philippines. Since the Mischief Reef incident in 1995, for a period of time, all claimants had been restraining themselves from occupying or controlling new features in the SCS. The term "status quo" is often reiterated by the Philippines and Vietnam. In the Spratly Islands, Vietnam occupies 21 features, the Philippines 9, China 6, Malaysia 5, and Taiwan 1.[68] China's occupation of the SCS features is disproportionate to its status as the biggest and most advanced military power among the SCS claimant states. This fact surely is not favourable to China, because what other claimants regard as the status quo is considered by China to be an illegal occupation of Chinese territory.[69] China perceives other claimants' legal actions, exemplified in Malaysia and Vietnam's joint submission to the UN Commission on Limits of Continental Shelf and the Philippines' House Bill 3216 which includes Scarborough Shoal and Kalayaan Island Group as its territory, as a challenge to its territorial sovereignty.[70]

It has already been established that China is also displeased by its view that it loses about 20 million tons of oil per year, or 40% of total offshore production in the SCS, as estimated by Song Enlai, chairman of the board of supervisors of the China National Offshore Oil Cooperation (CNOOC).[71]

In regard to a psychological regulator, China perceived that the US experienced an economic and financial slowdown in 2008 which led to its decline in power and influence, especially in Asia. Therefore, China expected to shift the balance in its favour. This perspective was translated into a determination to protect China's territory from others' provocations in its maritime domain.[72] Moreover, many in Beijing express their frustration about the adoption of shelving the dispute and the joint development policy at the expense of China's territorial sovereignty and interests in the SCS.[73]

There is a strong feeling of dissatisfaction in Beijing about other rival claimants taking for granted China's generosity in the period of de-escalation. China gained nothing from its image building during the de-escalation period and many think that the "China Threat Theory" will always preoccupy its rivals, no matter what.[74] Given this situation, it is logical to say that China would rather quit bearing the political cost of the status quo in the SCS.

In addition to that, there is strong indication that China has lost trust towards other claimants, especially the Philippines. There is an increasing concern about its amicable policy in the past which is perceived as having failed to protect its sovereignty against foreign "encroachment".[75] Fu Ying and Wu Shicun mentioned the Scarborough Shoal incident as the "last straw that broke the camel's back" that provoked Beijing to exert full control over the Shoal.[76]

There are two further questions for this: Why did China do this in the Scarborough Shoal? And why was this carried out in 2012? The answer for the first question lies in Scarborough Shoal's geopolitical significance for China. In terms of its claim, China divides the SCS features into four divisions: *Xisha Qundao* (Paracel Islands), *Dongsha Qundao* (Pratas Islands), *Zhongsha Qundao* (Macclesfield Bank), and *Nansha Qundao* (Spratly Islands). In the Declaration of the Government of the People's Republic of China on China's Territorial Sea, promulgated in September 1958, it is stated that:

> The breadth of China's territorial sea shall be twelve nautical miles, that the straight baselines method shall be employed to determine the baseline of the territorial sea and that such provisions shall apply to all territories of the People's Republic of China, including Dongsha Qundao, Xisha Qundao, Zhongsha Qundao, Nansha Qundao and all other islands belonging to China.[77]

The Republic of China (Taiwan), the territory of which the People's Republic of China believes it inherited after winning the civil war in 1949, also perceives the SCS islands as belonging to four groups. Taipei states that:

> The Nansha (Spratly) Islands, Xisha (Paracel) Islands, Zhongsha (Macclesfield Bank) Islands, and Dongsha (Pratas) Islands (together known as the South China Sea Islands) were first discovered, named, and used by the ancient Chinese, and incorporated into national territory and administered by imperial Chinese governments.[78]

In other words, the division of the SCS Islands into four groups signifies the continuation of preserving the claim throughout history and there is a shared perspective of Chinese claim in the SCS between two straits (Taiwan and Mainland).

China has exerted full control over *Xisha Qundao* (the Paracels) since 1974 after a series of clashes with the Republic of Vietnam (South Vietnam) and has had partial control over *Nansha Qundao* (the Spratlys). *Dongsha Qundao* (the Pratas Islands) is controlled by Taiwan and China has no intention to change this. However, China does not have a presence in *Zhongsha Qundao* (the Macclesfield Bank Islands). Scarborough Shoal is the only feature in the *Zhongsha Qundao* that is a high-tide elevation—which can generate 12 nm territorial sea.[79] By seizing the Scarborough Shoal, China meant to maintain a permanent presence at the *Zhongsha Qundao*. Therefore, China established a presence in three of the SCS island groups, even though not controlling all the features. The control over Scarborough Shoal suggests a step forward in substantiating China's SCS claim.

In terms of resources, Scarborough Shoal is a rich fishing ground which attracts both Filipino and Chinese fishermen. Domestically, according to the Food and Agriculture Organization (FAO), China's fish consumption per capita was more than 36 kg in 2010—which is almost double the global average—and its annual growth in fish consumption is 8%. In addition to that, the Chinese fisheries employ nearly 15 million people.[80] To meet the fishery demand, China needs to secure its "fishing ground" in the SCS, and for which the role of fishermen is crucial. According to Zhang Hongzhou of Singapore's Nanyang Technological University, Beijing perceives fishermen as "important tools" in expanding China's presence and claim in the SCS.[81] This is also Beijing's strategy to bolster its "traditional fishing ground" claim and increase its control over the SCS. Alan Dupont, a security expert at the University of New South Wales calls this strategy "fish, protect, occupy and control".[82] This is how the Scarborough Shoal incident shifted from a fishery incident to China having full control over the feature.

Given the significance of the Scarborough Shoal and China's strategic move in 2012, it is almost inconceivable that it was not premeditated. China's move to seize the Scarborough Shoal to some extent resembles its tactic in occupying the Paracel Islands in 1974.[83] Both conflicts were initially triggered by Chinese fishing boats which acted in the disputed area with the intention of asserting China's claim. These operations were backed up by the PLAN. In the 2012 Scarborough Shoal incident, the Philippine Navy attempted to arrest the Chinese fishermen (this navy was later replaced in the area by the Philippine Coast Guard and Bureau of Fisheries). This action gave an opportunity for China to launch a "counter-attack in self-defence" which resulted in the two-month standoff and ended up with China's control over the shoal.

It remains to answer the second question posed above: Why was the Scarborough Shoal incident carried out in 2012? Since Chinese policy making is very secretive, it is hard to discover the rationale for China's seizure of the Scarborough Shoal. Therefore, this chapter incorporates the metaphor of the smoking gun to interpret China's behaviour.

First, 2012 marked the last year of Hu Jintao's administration. Despite the fact that the SCS tension was rising during his term, Hu Jintao and Wen Jiabao (the Premier) were known as weak and put excessive emphasis on stability.[84] During his leadership, Hu maintained a collective policy-making process and institutionalisation of the party process instead of a one-man show of leadership. However, foreign policy making is fractured and the actors are varied.[85] This gives a sense that Hu Jintao needed to compromise and accommodate many voices before making an important decision.

In particular, Hu Jintao was restrained by some of Jiang Zemin proxies like Xu Caihou and Guo Boxiong and did not have absolute control over the People's Liberation Army (PLA).[86] Hu was also challenged by Bo Xilai, a controversial figure and the disgraced former Party Secretary of Chongqing. Being the son of Bo Yibo—a prominent Communist revolutionist, a former Vice Premier under Zhou Enlai and a member of the politburo under Deng Xiaoping—makes Bo Xilai enjoy the status of a princeling. Bo was known to have close ties with high level military officials, regularly hosting them at his residence in Chongqing and criticising leaders in Beijing for being too lenient.[87] His close relationship with PLA generals and his habit of criticising the Hu-Wen administration raised suspicion at the Zhongnanhai. In March 2012, Beijing dismissed Bo as Chongqing party chief—making it one of the most high-profile scandals in recent Chinese politics.

Following this political turmoil, China faced the Scarborough Shoal incident in April. Hu Jintao understood that being tough serves political stability in the crucial period ahead of the leadership succession in late 2012. He needed to leave a better legacy rather than having been thought of as "a weak leader". The Scarborough Shoal standoff provided an opportunity to demonstrate Hu's toughness towards a small country's bullying, appeasing the PLA and some hawkish elements in Beijing who happened to be his critics, and bringing about more cohesion in the Chinese leadership. Therefore, the option of no retreat at the standoff sounded very reasonable in that situation.

A second element in China's move to defection is the Xi Jinping factor. Since his ascendance to the Politburo Standing Committee in 2007, Xi had already been seen as the General Secretary of the Central Committee of the CCP in waiting. Xi Jinping is the son of Xi Zhongxun, a senior Communist veteran—who was a Vice Premier and Vice Chairman of the National People's Congress. Xi Zhongxun's senior position makes Xi Jinping another princeling in Chinese politics. Whereas it is uncertain if this privilege plays a big role in Xi Jinping's leadership, it is widely known that Xi Jinping is more hawkish than his predecessor. Jin Canrong of Renmin University marks the Xi Jinping leadership as a shift from maintaining stability to maintaining rights.[88] In particular, Xi Jinping's view is that China should be more proactive in defending its maritime rights.

Xi Jinping's attitude in defending sovereignty is evident from a speech he made after he began to hold two top positions in key Chinese institutions. On 16 December 2012, one month after he became the General Secretary of the Central Committee of the CCP and the Chairman of the Central Military Commission, Xi delivered a speech titled "Fostering the Awareness of Struggle, Crisis and Mission". In this speech, he stated:

> Some Asian countries formulate an expansive maritime strategy; they continuously make provocations in Diaoyu (Senkaku) Island or the SCS Islands. We resolutely adopt counter-attack measures, persist in defending our country's

> sovereignty and maritime rights, and protect the stability of diplomatic relations. These countries keep making provocations, violating our interests. The struggle of maritime dispute seems to last for a long period of time. To meet the challenges of our territorial integrity, we cannot turn back; instead we must fiercely take up the challenges and fight for every inch. I was urged by one of our senior veteran leaders that we as governing comrades must have these three things at heart: do not lose five thousand years of civilization; do not ruin the political system built by the former generations; do not shrink the territory left by the ancestors. We must uphold these objectives.[89]

Seven days after Manila initiated an arbitral proceeding at the UNCLOS Tribunal in January 2013 and two months before Xi Jinping became the President, he made a statement in which he included phrases about refusing to give up China's legitimate rights or to sacrifice its core interests. He warned that no country should expect China "to eat the bitter fruits of sacrificing its core interest—sovereignty, security and development".[90]

Less than a month after becoming the President of the People's Republic of China and on the one-year anniversary of the Scarborough Shoal standoff, Xi made a high-profile visit to Hainan Island in early April 2013. In Hainan Island, Xi visited Tanmen Township of Qionghai City, where he met and greeted "maritime militia" who played a significant role in the 2012 Scarborough Shoal confrontation. This maritime militia comprises the fishermen who receive financial and logistic assistance to protect China's interest in the SCS.[91] On that occasion, Xi extended warm regards from the party and government, asked the fishermen to prioritise safety and wished them to have an abundant harvest.[92] According to Yang Qingfu, an elderly figure in Tanmen and a former fishing captain, the maritime militia's primary duty is not to fish but rather to uphold Chinese sovereignty in Spratlys.[93] During his visit to Hainan Island, Xi also visited the navy base in Sanya, inspecting 11 warships, including *Jinggangshan*—one of the most advanced vessels in the PLAN.[94] He emphasised that sovereignty and security should be the highest priority, instructing about measures to defend maritime rights, and urged the building of a defence system in the Chinese maritime boundary.[95] The Hainan visit by Xi Jinping in his first month of presidency demonstrates the Chinese leader's serious concern over maritime rights and particularly perceived Chinese sovereignty in the SCS.

The above-mentioned speeches and gestures reveal Xi Jinping's attitude and determination in defending maritime rights and his concern over the SCS in particular. Even though Xi Jinping officially exercises supreme authority since November 2012, he has played a prominent role in decision making before his ascendance to the party leadership.[96] In mid-2012, around the time when China seized the Scarborough Shoal, Xi assumed top leadership of the Leading Small Group (LSG) on Maritime Rights Protection. The roles of this LSG are (1) to develop strategic measures to serve China's maritime rights and interests[97] and (2) to coordinate the job of 17 maritime-related governmental agencies, such as the State Oceanic Administration, Foreign Ministry, Public Security Ministry, and Agriculture Ministry.[98]

This was not the first time that Xi Jinping headed a most strategic group in decision making. Since his ascendance to the Politburo Standing Committee in 2008, Xi Jinping has led the LSGs on Hong Kong and Macau Affairs, and on Party Building Affairs.[99] LSGs are more significant than the ministries and supersede all other governmental bodies in Chinese political hierarchy.[100] Their recommendations are generally accepted with minimum or no adjustment, and taken as a consensus.[101]

This practice has much to do with overcoming the shortcomings of Jiang Zemin's governance and Hu Jintao's leadership style. In Hu's era, he promoted a collective leadership and the general secretary was merely a primus inter pares instead of the centre of political decision making.[102] Hu Jintao was willing to share his power and authority, particularly to Xi Jinping who was on track to assume the top leadership.[103] The role of Xi Jinping in Hu Jintao's second term was considered to be enormous.[104] His ascendance to head the Maritime Rights LSG might have contributed to the decision to seize the Scarborough Shoal after months of standoff.

The control of the Scarborough Shoal also marks the new normal in the SCS which was signified by another defection thereafter, the massive construction of artificial islands. The huge extent of this building of artificial islands also has the same rationale as China's action in seizing the Scarborough Shoal.

The above-mentioned discussion on Xi Jinping's leadership also explains the rationale behind China's massive building of artificial islands. The artificial island build-up was massively conducted in 2014–2015; however, the work at four reefs has already started after Xi Jinping assumed the highest power in 2012.[105] Xi leads China to a deep conviction that China should be respected and accommodated internationally.[106] In Southeast Asia, this conviction is reflected in Xi's authorization of building artificial islands in the SCS massively that prepares China to project its power in a scale that no other claimant states can match.[107]

The massive building of artificial islands also signifies the shift in China's strategic thinking in controlling the SCS. China no longer thinks that exerting control of more features from other claimants is the only way to strengthen its position in the SCS. The seizure of features from other claimants bears heavy political cost. The UNCLOS Tribunal was initiated by the Philippines in the aftermath of the 2012 Scarborough Shoal incident which created serious diplomatic setback for China. From this lesson, China learns that the optimization of the function of its controlled feature instead of grabbing new features is more effective in enhancing its presence and controlling the sea lane in the SCS. This paradigm is reflected from Beijing's emphasis that the activities of artificial island build-up are conducted "within the scope of China sovereignty, which are lawful, reasonable and justified."[108]

The massive building artificial islands is China's way of changing the command in the SCS. This command is not held by the state which occupies or controls a majority of features in the SCS, but it is assumed by the state which is able to project its power even though it only controls a minority of SCS features.

6.6 How Can China Mitigate the Security Dilemma?

The continuum of the security dilemma is reversible. The conditions can turn into a mitigated dilemma or at worst, a military conflict. However, one of the important operational codes of a defensive realist state is its willingness to adopt an engagement strategy. Such a strategy incorporates three major components: reassurance, invitation to cooperate, and hedging against the possibility that the other side is an aggressor.[109] Engagement strategy can serve five critical purposes simultaneously: (1) to assure the other side of one's good intentions, (2) to gauge the other side's real intentions, (3) to deter the other side from aggressive behaviour, (4) to change the other side's intentions to cooperative or at least more moderate behaviour, and (5) to buy time for power consolidation in case the other side really has an expansionist ambition.[110] Normally, a strategy of engagement is adopted by a defensive realist state and is reciprocated by other defensive realist states. Reassurance is the beginning.

Concretely, China can mitigate the course of the security dilemma if it reverses its behaviour from offensive realist to defensive realist by three actions. First, it can give the Philippines access to fishing and exploration activities in the Philippine EEZ. This has been done by giving access for Philippine fishermen to fish at the water near the Scarborough Shoal after President Duterte visited China in October 2016.[111]

Second, China can show its goodwill by demilitarising the islands (including the artificial ones) that it controls. So far, China's promise to avoid militarisation of the SCS is a mere verbal statement which does not convince other states in the region or external powers.

Third, China can adjust its claim according to the ruling by enjoying common maritime rights and giving up asserting exclusive historical rights in the SCS. This sounds difficult but it is not impossible. Russia and India, two regional great powers, have given precedence for this as discussed in Chap. 5. China has made a slight revision on the wording in its statement of claim in the SCS after the UNCLOS Tribunal ruling as discussed in Sect. 3.3.

The primary factor that may have an impact in the situation is China's perspective on the UNCLOS. The ruling from the UNCLOS Tribunal on 12 July 2016 is seen as a massive defeat for China and put the country into a very difficult situation. However, the extent to which China is willing to clarify its SCS claim according to the UNCLOS will contribute to either escalating or mitigating this security dilemma. China has potentials to adopt defensive realist or offensive realist strategy in the SCS.

Notes

1. "Scarborough Shoal Dispute 'Of Concern'," *Viet Nam News*, 26 April 2012, http://vietnamnews.vn/politics-laws/223972/scarborough-shoal-dispute-of-concern.html#X6I5SzoVyyDTmXhG.97 (accessed 12 July 2016).
2. Jerry E. Esplanada, "Malaysia Too Wants Peace in Panatag Shoal," *Inquirer*, 31 May 2012, http://globalnation.inquirer.net/38389/malaysia-too-wants-peace-in-panatag-shoal (accessed 21 June 2016).
3. "Vietnam, Philippines Issue Joint Statement on Strategic Partnership," *Viet Nam News*, 19 November 2015, http://vietnamnews.vn/politics-laws/278770/viet-nam-philippines-issue-joint-statement-on-strategic-partnership.html#79Xbphp3bdvfyHx5.97 (accessed 8 July 2016).
4. "Vietnam Welcomes South China Sea Ruling, Reasserts Its Own Claims," *Reuters*, 12 July 2016, http://in.reuters.com/article/southchinasea-ruling-vietnam-idINKCN0ZS16W (accessed 29 August 2016).
5. Jamandre, "Brunei Snubs ASEAN Spratly Claimant's Meeting to Forge One Stand on China," *VERA Files*, 4 March 2014.

6. Francis Chan, "China Criticised for Apparent Attempt to Divide ASEAN," *The Strait Times*, 26 April 2016, http://www.straitstimes.com/asia/china-criticised-for-apparent-attempt-to-divide-asean (accessed 28 April 2016).
7. Hamilton and Rathbun, "Scarce Differences: Toward a Material and Systemic Foundation for Offensive and Defensive Realism," 436–65.
8. Michael A Glosny, "Heading Toward a Win–Win Future? Recent Developments in China's Policy Toward Southeast Asia," *Asian Security*, 2, no. 1 (2006): 24–57.
9. Shannon Tiezzi, "China's Growing Defense Budget: Not as Scary as You Think," *The Diplomat*, 5 February 2014, http://thediplomat.com/2014/02/chinas-growing-defense-budget-not-as-scary-as-you-think/ (accessed 5 July 2016).
10. Fang Yang and Mingjiang Li, "Comparing China's Claims and Policies in the East and South China Seas: Implications for Regional Security," *Journal of Asian Security and International Affairs*, (2016); Fravel, "China's Strategy in the South China Sea," 292.
11. David Pilling, "Asia Follows China into an Old-Fashioned Arms Race," *Financial Times*, 2 April 2014, http://www.ft.com/intl/cms/s/0/9d83bf62-b9b9-11e3-a3ef-00144feabdc0.html#axzz2yB0Ekgob (accessed 5 August 2016).
12. Ibid.
13. Stephen Harner, "U.S. Policy, Not China Is Driving the Asian Arms Race," *Forbes Asia*, 6 April 2014, http://www.forbes.com/sites/stephenharner/2014/04/06/u-s-policy-not-china-is-driving-the-asian-arms-race/ (accessed 9 March 2016).
14. Pilling, "Asia Follows China into an Old-Fashioned Arms Race," *Financial Times*, 2 April 2014.
15. Raul Dancel, "US$671 m Arm Buys to Upgrade Philippine Military," *Asia News Network*, 17 March 2014, http://www.asianewsnet.net/news-58075.html (accessed 5 May 2016).
16. Harner, "U.S. Policy, Not China Is Driving the Asian Arms Race," *Forbes Asia*, 6 April 2014.
17. Lim, "A Tale of Two Realisms in Chinese Foreign Policy," 299–312.
18. "Japan to Supply Philippines with Military Equipment," *The Japan Times*, 28 February 2016, http://www.japantimes.co.jp/news/2016/02/28/national/japan-to-supply-philippines-with-military-equipment/#.WGxK7FN96Ul (accessed 15 August 2016).
19. Gardiner Harris, "Vietnam Arms Embargo to Be Fully Lifted, Obama Says in Hanoi," *The New York Times*, 23 May 2016, http://www.nytimes.com/2016/05/24/world/asia/vietnam-us-arms-embargo-obama.html?_r=2 (accessed 19 September 2016).

20. Tang, "Social Evolution of International Politics: From Mearsheimer to Jervis," 31–55.
21. *A Theory of Security Strategies for Our Time: Defensive Realism*, 43.
22. Ibid.
23. Permanent Court of Arbitration, "Press Release of the South China Sea Arbitration (The Republic of the Philippines vs the People's Republic of China)."
24. Jerome Cohen, "Like It or Not, UNCLOS Arbitration Is Legally Binding for China," *East Asia Forum*, 11 July 2016, http://www.eastasiaforum.org/2016/07/11/like-it-or-not-unclos-arbitration-is-legally-binding-for-china/ (accessed 20 July 2016); Hao Duy Phan, "Why a Ruling That Cannot Be Enforced Still Matters," *The Strait Times*, 16 July 2016, http://www.straitstimes.com/opinion/why-a-ruling-that-cannot-be-enforced-still-matters (accessed 14 August 2016).
25. Zha, "China's Energy Security: Domestic and International Issues," 179–90.
26. Owen and Schofield, "Disputed South China Sea Hydrocarbons in Perspective," 809–22.
27. Hayton, *The South China Sea: The Struggle for Power in Asia*, 27–28.
28. Permanent Court of Arbitration, "Press Release of the South China Sea Arbitration (The Republic of the Philippines vs the People's Republic of China)."
29. Ibid.
30. Sutter, "China's Self-Absorbed Nationalism," *The Diplomat*, 31 August 2012.
31. Shicun Wu Ying Fu, "South China Sea: How We Got to This Stage," *The National Interest*, 9 May 2016, http://nationalinterest.org/feature/south-china-sea-how-we-got-stage-16118 (accessed 12 May 2016).
32. 游润恬, "九段线停留在历史视角," 联合早报, 2016年5月15日 [Yew Lun Tian, "Understanding the Basis for China's South China Sea Claims," *Lianhe Zaobao*, 15 May 2016], http://www.zaobao.com.sg/node/617117 (accessed 19 May 2016).
33. Permanent Court of Arbitration, "Press Release of the South China Sea Arbitration (The Republic of the Philippines vs the People's Republic of China)."
34. Robert Beckman, "Tribunal Ruling a Game Changer," *The Strait Times*, 14 July 2016, http://www.straitstimes.com/opinion/tribunal-ruling-a-game-changer-south-china-sea (accessed 15 August 2016).
35. Ralf Emmers, "China's Influence in the South China Sea and the Failure of Joint Development," in *Rising China's Influence in Developing Asia* (Oxford: Oxford University Press, 2016).
36. Ibid.

37. Ibid.
38. Chakraborti, "China and Vietnam in the South China Sea Dispute: A Creeping 'Conflict–Peace–Trepidation' Syndrome," 283–301.
39. Scot Marciel, "Maritime Issues and Sovereignty Disputes in East Asia, Statement before the Subcommittee on East Asian and Pacific Affairs Senate Foreign Relations Committee, 15 July 2009," http://www.state.gov/p/eap/rls/rm/2009/07/126076.htm (accessed 27 August 2016); Schofield and Storey, *The South China Sea Dispute: Increasing Stakes and Rising Tensions*, 31; Glaser, "Tensions Flare in the South China Sea."
40. Tran, "Recent Development in the South China Sea: Implications for Regional Security and Cooperation," 7.
41. Ibid.; Glaser, "Tensions Flare in the South China Sea."
42. Schofield and Storey, *The South China Sea Dispute: Increasing Stakes and Rising Tensions.*
43. "China Warns Exxon over Vietnam Deal-Newspaper," *Reuters*, 20 July 2008, http://uk.reuters.com/article/exxonmobile-asia-idUKPEK2626 9420080720 (accessed 17 August 2015).
44. Glaser, "Tensions Flare in the South China Sea."
45. Chan and Li, "New Chinese Leadership, New Policy in the South China Sea Dispute?" 1–16.
46. Fravel, "China's Strategy in the South China Sea," 292.
47. Johnston, "How New and Assertive Is China's New Assertiveness?" 7–48.
48. Fravel, "China's Strategy in the South China Sea," 292; "Maritime Security in the South China Sea and the Competition over Maritime Rights."
49. US Department of State, *Remarks at Press Availability*, 23 July 2010, Hanoi, http://www.state.gov/secretary/20092013clinton/rm/2010/07/145095.htm (accessed 8 July 2016).
50. Greer, "The South China Sea Is Really a Fishery Dispute," *The Diplomat*, 20 July 2016.
51. Carlyle A Thayer, "China's New Wave of Aggressive Assertiveness in the South China Sea," (Paper presented at the Conference on Maritime Security in the South China Sea, sponsored by the Center for Strategic and International Studies, Washington, 2011), 15.
52. Ibid., 16.
53. Ibid.
54. Ibid., 17.
55. Lyle Goldstein, "Chinese Naval Strategy in the South China Sea: An Abundance of Noise and Smoke, but Little Fire," *Contemporary Southeast Asia: A Journal of International and Strategic Affairs*, 33, no. 3 (2011): 320–47.

56. Gregory Poling, "How Deeper US-Vietnam Military Cooperation Starts with Medicine," *Center for Strategic and International Studies (CSIS)*, 18 August 2011, http://cogitasia.com/how-deeper-u-s-vietnam-mil-coop-starts-with-medicine/ (accessed 3 April 2016).
57. Lewis M. Stern William Jordan, Walter Lohman, "US-Vietnam Defense Relations: Investing in Strategic Alignment," *The Heritage Foundation*, 18 July 2012, http://www.heritage.org/research/reports/2012/07/us-vietnam-defense-relations-investing-in-strategic-alignment#_ftn3 (accessed 6 April 2016).
58. "US Department of State, *Manila Declaration on US–Philippine Alliance*, 16 November 2011, http://translations.state.gov/st/english/texttrans/2011/11/20111116141458su0.2878338.html#axzz4FaWayzlm (accessed 5 July 2016).
59. US Department of State, *Toward a Deeper Alliance: United States-Philippines Bilateral Cooperation*, 27 January 2012, http://www.state.gov/r/pa/prs/ps/2012/01/182689.htm (accessed 14 November 2016).
60. Booth and Wheeler, *The Security Dilemma: Fear, Cooperation and Trust in World Politics*, 45–46.
61. Kydd, *Trust and Mistrust in International Relations*, 66.
62. Ying Fu, "South China Sea: How We Got to This Stage," *The National Interest*, 9 May 2016.
63. Ibid.
64. Ibid.
65. Zhang, "China's Growing Assertiveness in the South China Sea: A Strategic Shift?" 21.
66. Kydd, *Trust and Mistrust in International Relations*, 66.
67. Tang, *A Theory of Security Strategies for Our Time: Defensive Realism*, 66–69.
68. According to the UNCLOS Tribunal, no feature in the Spratly Islands is island; therefore no one can claim a 200 nm of EEZ. See "Press Release of the South China Sea Arbitration (The Republic of the Philippines vs the People's Republic of China)."
69. Wang Wen, "Debunking 10 Myths about China and the South China Sea," *South China Morning Post*, 10 July 2016, http://www.scmp.com/comment/insight-opinion/article/1986732/debunking-10-myths-about-china-and-south-china-sea (accessed 16 August 2016).
70. Thayer, "China's New Wave of Aggressive Assertiveness in the South China Sea," 3.
71. Ibid.
72. Chong-Pin Lin, "Behind Rising East Asian Maritime Tensions with China," *Asian Survey*, 55, no. 3 (2015): 478–501.

73. Zhang, "China's Growing Assertiveness in the South China Sea: A Strategic Shift?" 19, 22; Goldstein, "Chinese Naval Strategy in the South China Sea: An Abundance of Noise and Smoke, but Little Fire," 320–47.
74. "Chinese Naval Strategy in the South China Sea: An Abundance of Noise and Smoke, but Little Fire," 320–47.
75. Jian Zhang, "China's Growing Assertiveness in the South China Sea: A Strategic Shift?" in *The South China Sea and Australia Regional Security Environment*, 2 October 2013 (Canberra: National Security College, Australian National University), 19.
76. Ying Fu, "South China Sea: How We Got to This Stage," *The National Interest*, 9 May 2016.
77. *China Adheres to the Position of Settling Through Negotiation the Relevant Disputes Between China and the Philippines in the South China Sea (People's Republic of China Response to the 12 July 2016 ruling on the South China Sea territorial claims by the UNCLOS Tribunal)*, Beijing, 2016, http://usa.chinadaily.com.cn/epaper/2016-07/14/content_26088896.htm (accessed 15 July 2016).
78. Foreign Ministry of the People's Republic of China, *Position Paper on Republic of China South China Sea Policy* Beijing, 2016, http://multilingual.mofa.gov.tw/web/web_UTF-8/South/Position%20Paper%20on%20ROC%20South%20China%20Sea%20Policy.pdf (accessed 2 April 2016).
79. François-Xavier Bonnet, "Geopolitics of Scarborough Shoal," *Irasec's Discussion Papers*, 14 (2012).
80. Denyer, "China's Fishermen on the Front Line in the South China Sea," *The Sydney Morning Herald*, 16 April 2016.
81. Ibid.
82. Ibid.
83. Graham, "South China Sea History Lesson: Parallels from the Paracels?" *The Interpreter*, 31 March 2016.
84. Jaime A. FlorCruz, "Checkered End-of-Term Report Card for Hu Jintao," *CNN*, 9 November 2012, http://edition.cnn.com/2012/11/08/world/asia/china-hu-jintao-report-card-florcruz (accessed 16 August 2016).
85. Linda Jakobson and Dean Knox, *New Foreign Policy Actors in China* Stockholm International Peace Research Institute, 2010), 48–49.
86. Minnie Chan, "Hu Jintao's Weak Grip on China's Army Inspired Xi Jinping's Military Shake-Up: Sources," *South China Morning Post*, 11 March 2015, http://www.scmp.com/news/china/article/1734663/hu-jintaos-weak-grip-chinas-army-inspired-president-xi-jinpings-military (accessed 28 October 2016).

87. Lingling Wei Jeremy Page, "Bo's Ties to Army Alarmed Beijing," *The Wall Street Journal*, 17 May 2012, http://www.wsj.com/articles/SB10001424052702304203604577398034072800836 (accessed 26 July 2016).
88. "中国维护海洋权益:从维稳到维权的转折," 人民日报海外版,2014年06月28日, [China Defends Maritime Rights: The Shift from Maintaining Stability to Maintaining Rights, *People's Daily* overseas edition, 28 June 2014], http://news.xinhuanet.com/politics/2014-06/28/c_1111359109.htm (accessed 8 August 2016).
89. "回顾习近平治军 老领导曾叮嘱习近平的三件事," 和讯新闻,2015年8月2日 [Reviewing Xi Jinping Governing Military Old Leaders Had Warned of Xi Jinping's Three Points, *Hexun News*, 2 August 2015], http://news.hexun.com/2015-08-02/178025271.html (accessed 15 August 2016).
90. "南海争端如何应对?习近平都将清楚了," 凤凰资讯,2016年7月1日 [How to Deal with the South China Sea Dispute? Xi Jinping has Spoken Clearly, *Phoenix New Media*, 1 July 2016], http://finance.ifeng.com/a/20160701/14550831_0.shtml (accessed 8 September 2016).
91. Philip Wen, "South China Sea: Sleepy Port Town Is Base for Beijing's 'Little Blue Men'," *The Sydney Morning Herald*, 12 July 2016, http://www.smh.com.au/world/south-china-sea-sleepy-port-town-is-base-for-beijings-little-blue-men-20160630-gpv84r.html (accessed 7 August 2016).
92. "习近平赴潭门看望海上民兵连 鼓励大更多的鱼打大鱼," 南海网, 2013年4月9日 [Xi Jinping Visited Tanmen, Met with Maritime Militia Encouraged Them to Trawl for More and Bigger Fish, *Hinews*, 9 April 2013], http://www.hinews.cn/news/system/2013/04/09/015590106.shtml (accessed 15 August 2016).
93. "South China Sea: Sleepy Port Town Is Base for Beijing's 'Little Blue Men'," *The Sydney Morning Herald*, 12 July 2016.
94. Baijie An, "Xi Visits Fleet, Praises Sanya Sailors," *China Daily USA*, 12 April 2013, http://usa.chinadaily.com.cn/2013-04/12/content_16397947.htm (accessed 10 August 2016).
95. "南海争端如何应对?习近平都将清楚了," 凤凰资讯, 2016年7月1日 [How to Deal with the South China Sea Dispute? Xi Jinping has Spoken Clearly, *Phoenix New Media*, 1 July 2016].
96. Linda Jakobson and Ryan Manuel, "How Are Foreign Policy Decisions Made in China?," *Asia & the Pacific Policy Studies*, 3, no. 1 (2016): 98–107.
97. Bonnie S Glaser, "China's Maritime Right Protection Leading Small Group—Shrouded in Secrecy," *Asia Maritime Transparency Initiative*, 11 September 2015, https://amti.csis.org/chinas-maritime-rights-protection-leading-small-group-shrouded-in-secrecy/ (accessed 25 August 2016).

98. "中国已成立中央海权办 系涉海高层次协调机构," 中国网, 2013年3月2日 [China has Established Maritime Protection Leading Small Group, a Top Level Coordinating Body on Maritime Affairs, *China.com.cn*, 2 March 2013], http://ocean.china.com.cn/2013-03/02/content_28105606.htm (accessed 8 September 2016).
99. Alice Miller, "The CCP Central Committee's Leading Small Groups," *China Leadership Monitor*, 26 (2008): 1–21.
100. Cary Huang, "How Leading Small Groups Help Xi Jinping and Other Party Leaders Exert Power," *South China Morning Post*, 20 January 2014, http://www.scmp.com/news/china/article/1409118/how-leading-small-groups-help-xi-jinping-and-other-party-leaders-exert (accessed 21 September 2016).
101. Ibid.
102. Miller, "The CCP Central Committee's Leading Small Groups," 1–21.
103. Interview with a Chinese Academy of Social Sciences (CASS) Scholar, Beijing, 5 November 2015.
104. Interview with a Chinese Academy of Social Sciences (CASS) Scholar, Beijing, 5 November 2015.
105. Julian E. Barnes Jeremy Page, "China Expands Island Construction in Disputed South China Sea," *The Wall Street Journal*, 18 February 2015, http://www.wsj.com/articles/china-expands-island-construction-in-disputed-south-china-sea-1424290852 (accessed 17 September 2016).
106. Jeffrey A Bader, *How Xi Jinping Sees the World... and Why* (Brookings Institution, 2016). https://www.brookings.edu/wp-content/uploads/2016/07/xi_jinping_worldview_bader-1.pdf (accessed 21 November 2016).
107. Ibid.
108. "China to Complete Land Reclamation of Construction on Some Nansha Islands Soon," *China Daily*, 16 June 2015, http://www.chinadaily.com.cn/china/2015-06/16/content_21017939.htm (accessed 13 May 2016).
109. Tang, *A Theory of Security Strategies for Our Time: Defensive Realism*, 102.
110. Ibid.
111. Hunt and Quiano, "China Allows Philippines Fishermen Access to Disputed Shoal in South China Sea," *CNN*, 31 October 2016.

CHAPTER 7

Security Dilemma Between China vis-à-vis the United States of America in the South China Sea

The security dilemma in the South China Sea (SCS) does not merely apply to China and other Southeast Asian claimants. This dilemma also takes place between China and a non-claimant state, that is, the US. The US role in the SCS is not limited to that of an external power which was invited by Southeast Asian claimants to balance against China's assertiveness. The US is definitely not a backstage actor in the SCS and is actively involved in the security dilemma with China as the rising regional power. The series of standoffs between the two countries' naval ships—like the EP-3 reconnaissance plane incident and the 2009 *Impeccable* incident—demonstrates this prominent role in the SCS.

As with the previous chapter, this chapter also relies on the theoretical framework of security dilemma as discussed in Chap. 2. It starts with examining the qualities of the security dilemma (uncertainty, lack of malign intention, and paradoxical/self-defeating policy) as this has panned out in the SCS, analysing the relationship between China and the US. It is then shown that the conflict of interest in the SCS is basically subjectively irreconcilable and objectively reconcilable. This is followed by a discussion of the operation of the security dilemma between two great powers: China and the US.

Unlike the security dilemma between China and the other SCS claimants, the security dilemma between China and the US differs in some points. First, the Sino-US security dilemma (SUSD) has a wider context of rivalry between the two countries as it relates to dominating the Asian region. The SCS is merely a reflection of these two great powers' rivalry.

K. H. Raditio, *Understanding China's Behaviour in the South China Sea*, https://doi.org/10.1007/978-981-13-1283-0_7

Second, as elaborated in this chapter, the SUSD has not yet reached the point of defection and is still around the stage of the spiral. There are some reasons why the SUSD differs from the security dilemma between China and other SCS claimants. This chapter elaborates the development of the SUSD in the SCS and attempts to shed some light on the rationale for China's behaviour.

7.1 The Elements of a Security Dilemma

The first element of any security dilemma is uncertainty. According to defensive realist theory, security-seeking states have issues in reading other states' motivation, in other words they seek to understand to what extent a state harbours an expansionist ambition or is merely pursuing its security. Every state claims it is a security seeker, however, when all states keep developing their power, it becomes difficult to understand other states' intentions since every state has its own idea on what accumulating the appropriate amount of power may be.

This happens with China. A skyrocketing development in the last three decades after the opening-up and reformation initiated by Deng Xiaoping has led China to become an economic power house. According to Ni Lexiong, a Chinese strategist at the Shanghai University of Political Science and Law, these two steps have transformed China from an "inward-looking economy" to an "outward-looking economy". China has become dependent on international trade and one-seventh of its employment is related directly or indirectly to foreign trade. In other words, China's economic development relies on the ocean.[1] Specifically, Ni indicates that the main route of China's growth lies along the SCS—Malacca Strait—Gulf of Aden.[2] This route serves both China's commercial trade and energy supply, which also underlines its Achilles heel. First, its oil imports from Africa and the Middle East have to pass some volatile regions that are beyond the PLAN's reach.[3] Second, China always worries about the so-called economic neo-containment by the West, which is deeply rooted in the belief that the West, especially the US, will do everything to hinder China's development.[4] This second point is the most concerning for China which regards dependency on "international cooperation" to some extent equals relying on the US.[5] Its leadership feels extremely reluctant to be in this position since its moves with regard to the Taiwan issue have been constrained by the role of the US in the region.[6]

Hence, China feels compelled to alleviate this vulnerability by establishing control around its periphery. Here lies the importance of the SCS as part of the "maritime vein" that needs to be secured. If the SCS is controlled by the US and its allies, China's future is far from optimistic.[7] The inability to develop within the constraint of Western powers will have several crucial impacts. As described at length previously, one is the reputation of the ruling Communist Party. During the whole of Chinese history, the legitimacy of the ruling regime has been judged by its ability to protect its borders and sovereignty. In modern China, that demand has also progressed to include the ability to guarantee national development. From Beijing's perspective, the SCS is predominantly about these issues.

To cope with its anxiety, China has been building its military power—especially its navy which is discussed in Sect. 4.1.2. On the other hand, the US perceives China's rapid navy development with great suspicion. Particularly during 2008–2009 when the US experienced economic and financial slow-down, China's accelerated growth in many aspects, especially in the military contributed to a significant amount of worry and distrust towards China.[8] The US' greatest reservation about China's growing military power is the lack of transparency, making it suspicious of Beijing's intention.[9] From the US perspective, China's prominent military power is not good news for its allies and endangers its leading position in the region.

The US-China suspicion in the SCS is part of the bigger picture of the rivalry between these great powers. The US considers China's opaque policy-making process and human rights issues render the country untrustworthy. Whereas Beijing regards Washington to harbour ill intentions to undermine its regime and legitimacy.[10] This mutual suspicion has always haunted bilateral relations. Since China perceives the SCS as another chance to advance[11] and the US regards itself as the defender of freedom of navigation (FON), the SCS becomes a field for a struggle for power between these two countries. In particular, the US believes that China's primary motive is to dominate Asia in the maritime realm and expel the US influence, whereas China believes that the US intends to contain China's development to maintain its hegemonic power.

The second element of any security dilemma is the lack of malign intention. As no state can be sure about other states' intentions, this is at the root of uncertainty underlining the security dilemma. According to Tang Shiping, lack of malign intention is the essential element for a security dilemma to apply.[12] This means the states that are involved in a security dilemma are security seekers or defensive realist states, not expansionists. The states engaged in the security dilemma must be that which believe that security can be attained by accumulating proportional power instead of maximising their power. They must accept the constraint of other states' behaviour and/or common agreements.

Beijing always maintains that it has behaved in the SCS out of defensive motives in that the SCS lies within China's national interest and is related to its survival.[13] In order to secure the SCS and advance its development, China considers it must build its navy and becomes a maritime power.[14] Three missions underline China's naval development. First, to deter Taiwan from proclaiming independence and anticipate the US naval force coming to Taiwan's rescue which was evident during the 1995–1996 crisis. Second, to protect China's sea route for international trade, especially for energy imports which pass many volatile regions. Third, to project its power in the western Pacific as a deterrent against the US in case a crisis takes place.[15] These motives show that China's interest in the SCS is primarily defensive realist.

To gauge whether the US is a defensive realist state, one needs to analyse each administration. Tang Shiping suggests that different administrations have different attitudes towards foreign policy, for instance, the US under the George W. Bush administration was an offensive realist state.[16] Since the tension in the SCS has taken place mostly during the Obama administration, it is essential to find out the nature of his foreign policy.

It is unsure whether Obama's foreign policy can be defined as "defensive realist" in nature. Obviously, the Obama administration differed from George W. Bush's. It did not adhere to offensive realist precepts and was definitely lacking in expansionist ambition. There are some reasons for this argument.

First, Obama does not believe that American troops should be put at great risk overseas—even for humanitarian purposes—unless there is a security threat against the US.[17] Between 2010 and 2016, Washington continued to cut its defence budget by over 14% in real terms and by 30% as a percentage of GDP.[18] Former Secretary of Defence Robert Gates called this cut "a sign that the US is not interested in protecting its global interest".[19] This undoubtedly raised concern in Manila and Hanoi over whether the US is committed to the SCS in light of such budget cuts.[20]

Second, Obama is less interventionist and has little interest in striking other countries. In Syria, although Obama himself stated that Assad should step down, he did not do much militarily to make it happen.[21] This policy has really upset US allies in the Middle East.

Third, he believes that armed conflict or external attacks—including by those perpetrated by fundamentalist groups like ISIS—are not the biggest threat to the US. Obama perceives climate change as a dire threat not only for the US but also for the entire world.[22]

Fourth, particularly towards China, Obama believes that a weakened and threatened China creates more harm to the US than a thriving and prosperous China.[23] He prefers to mobilise Asian countries and strengthen US ties with its allies in the region to contain China's growing assertiveness.[24]

Hillary Clinton, the then Secretary of State, who carried out the pivot to Asia in 2011 stated that the US "has no territorial ambition".[25] She added that Asia is crucial to America's interest and its presence and leadership are not only welcomed, they are longed for by the states in the region.[26] Clinton also assured China that the US rejects the view that China's progress is a threat and maintained that its successful development is beneficial for America.[27]

The reasons above may lead us to arrive at a conclusion that the US under the Obama administration was not preoccupied with a malign intention towards China. In fact, it is more precise to surmise that it too was worried about China's growing assertiveness and has been in the throes of a dilemma: either to take a strong measure—which may end up with unnecessary conflict, or to stay passive—seen as abandonment by its regional allies.[28]

The third element of any security dilemma is paradoxical or self-defeating policy. Due to a sense of insecurity in the ocean, China has developed a blue water navy capability which aims to project its power in the near and high seas. Over the past two decades, China's naval development has become the biggest rival to the US in the western Pacific since the end of World War II.[29] This rapid and significant development is attributed to several reasons. First, as China's economy grew, so did its defence budget; second, China shifted its focus from land to maritime domain with the collapse of the Soviet Union as its major threat; third, military technology from Russia and the former Soviet states was made available to China.[30]

In particular, it is noteworthy to discuss China's construction of its naval base on Hainan Island which is home to dozens of nuclear submarines. The instalment of the nuclear base is a response to the implementation of the Monroe Doctrine to dominate nearby waters and constitutes part of China's contingency plan if it has to be involved in a military conflict with the US.[31] Overall, Hugh White has assessed that China's military achievement makes the country pose serious challenge to the US. The key developments are: first, China owns nuclear-powered attack submarines which are not necessarily more advanced than the US but enough to challenge the US operation in the East Asian seafront. Second, China has developed a large fleet of fourth generation Soviet-based technology combat aircraft which are intended to defend its maritime domain. This fleet hampers the US aircrafts from prevailing over the Taiwan Strait. Third, China has built anti-ship ballistic missiles for attacking aircraft carriers. Fourth, China has upgraded its surveillance system which can target US warships' operations in its near seas.[32]

These developments pose a great challenge for the US, especially due to China's assertiveness in the SCS. The US worries about China's motive in developing its military power, a concern exacerbated by China's failure to clarify its nine-dash line claim in the SCS. The nine-dash line map which China submitted to the UN in 2009 was dismissed by the UNCLOS Tribunal ruling on July 2016, a decision which China strongly opposes. China's defiance has created more suspicion from the US. The primary issue is that China will someday deny US forces access to operate without restriction in China's near seas, access considered vital for the US and its allies' security.[33]

In addition to all these points, China's assertive behaviour since between 2007 and 2009 has created grave concern among Southeast Asian claimants and Japan who perceives the SCS as its key maritime route. These countries expect the US to play a bigger role in the region to balance China's assertiveness. In response to the various Chinese developments above, the US force came to the region under the foreign policy of "Pivot to Asia". In late 2011, the US announced the rotational deployment of 2500 marines in Darwin, Australia, followed by the deployment of 4 of its littoral combat ships in Singapore.[34] Furthermore, in June 2012, Secretary of Defence Leon Panetta declared that 60% of the US naval and air power will be projected into the Pacific Ocean by 2020.[35]

The Obama administration has assured China that its pivot to Asia has no motivation to contain China. However, Beijing retains deep distrust of the US intention, since its navy and air force have intensified their surveillance operations in China's proximities. Beijing views these actions as deliberate provocation since no country in today's world receives such great pressure from US activities.[36]

Apart from enhancing the military ties with its regional allies like Japan and the Philippines, Washington has also enhanced its strategic relationship with two countries that are either China's rival claimant (Vietnam) or strategic rivals in Asia (India). Beijing perceives the US behaviour in Asia as similar to the US military deployment in Darwin, Australia. The closer relations with Myanmar, the lifting of the arms embargo on Vietnam, and the enhanced military cooperation with the Philippines are all viewed as containment against China and meddling in the SCS disputes. In particular, the US initiative to conduct FONOPs in the SCS is perceived as an "abuse" of international law.[37]

US FONOPs are meant to challenge not only actual claims in the maritime domain but also potential claims which are considered excessive.[38] This becomes relevant in the context of the SCS since China maintains strategic ambiguity in its claim, especially regarding the nine-dash line claim.

The US navy ships operations in the SCS are not meant only to defend the FON; they are intended to gather intelligence data regarding China's military development, especially at the Yulin naval base on Hainan Island. In 2009, the US and China were involved in a series of warship skirmishes in the SCS when the USS *Impeccable* was interrupted by a Chinese naval warship. Similar incidents also occurred with the USS *Bowditch* (2003), USS *Lassen* (2015), USS *Curtis Wilbur* (January 2016), and USS *William Lawrence* (May 2016). Superficially, the skirmishes between the US and Chinese warships are attributed to different interpretations of international law, that is, the UNCLOS.[39] However, these repeated incidents underline the lack of trust in these bilateral relations stemming from China's striking military development and the US anxiety about it.[40] Another issue is the military gap between the two countries. The US surveillance operations on Yulin naval base in Hainan is supported by advanced technology that China does not possess in order to retaliate with. China feels it is being stymied by the US and is greatly disturbed by this action, which is why Beijing expresses grave objections and calls the US activities in the SCS "unfriendly".[41]

These facts demonstrate how China experiences a paradox in the SCS. China—operating on the premise that its naval development and assertive behaviour can provide more security—is in fact becoming less secure with the US' stronger presence in the region. Some Chinese scholars criticise Beijing's actions in the SCS as counterproductive. Shi Yinhong of Renmin University suggests Chinese leadership should reflect on whether its behaviour boosts US popularity in the region.[42] Zhu Feng of Nanjing University has advised Beijing to stop blaming external factors and begin to reflect on its blunders.[43] These statements are in line with the

US Deputy Secretary of State Anthony Blinken who suggested that China's assertive behaviour is the primary reason for the countries in the region to enhance their military ties with the US.[44]

On the US side, a paradox is also experienced. The US pivot to Asia is seen by Beijing as a strategic containment for China. The Asian pivot which is meant to strengthen US influence faces strong opposition from Beijing. China's disappointment with the US behaviour has emboldened the country to act more resolutely in defending what it perceives as its legitimate rights in the SCS.

In other words, the two events that have strengthened China's strategic presence in the SCS have been attributed by China to the US "meddling" in the region. The first is the seizure of the Scarborough Shoal from its US ally, that is, the Philippines, in 2012 which changed the status quo in the region and heightened tension. The Scarborough Shoal incident marked a new development in the SCS where China added another feature to its scope of control. The second is China's massive island construction in 2014–2015 which is perceived as a potential threat to the FON, since, according to Peter Dutton, it may turn the SCS into a Chinese "strategic strait".[45] If the so-called Chinese strait in the SCS is realised, US naval activities in the region will be severely hampered.

Here, one can see that the US pivot to Asia to balance China's assertiveness in fact could not deter China from being assertive, let alone stabilise the SCS. The more the US involves itself in the SCS, the more resolute Beijing is in asserting its claim there. According to Ouyang Yujing, the Director General of the Department of Boundary and Ocean Affairs of China's Ministry of Foreign Affairs, China will bounce back to the US more powerfully, as it feels pressured.[46] This makes the US mission to secure its interest in the SCS more challenging.

7.2 Conflict of Interests

On the level of the security dilemma between China and the US and its allies, the conflict of interest is also characterised by the combination of objectively reconcilable and subjectively irreconcilable differences. Unlike the conflict of interest between China and its rival SCS claimants, the conflict of interest between China and the US and its allies is not about overlapping territory or rights, but rather about the rivalry of leadership in Asia. The SCS maritime dispute itself is only a reflection of this rivalry but not the source of the conflict of interest per se.

The conflict of interest between two sides is objectively reconcilable because the rising of a great power does not inevitably lead to war or military conflict. Whereas China's assertive behaviour towards the SCS claimants began in 2007, the Sino-US strategic rivalry dates back as early as 1999 when Beijing reassessed the US ambition to expand its influence in Central Asia and the Persian Gulf and undermine Russia, which prompted China to accelerate its military build-up.[47] This strategic rivalry has led to a Sino-US conflict of interest which is subjectively irreconcilable yet objectively reconcilable.

7.2.1 Maritime Access

The aspects of this Sino-US conflict of interest in the SCS are many and varied. The first point concerns access. The SCS is one of the world's most important sea routes. Particularly for China, the SCS is the main transportation route servicing its economy and a major security bulwark against a potential foreign enemy. Beijing is reluctant to trust its transportation vein for economic development to "international cooperation" and perceives losing sole access as a surrender to US domination.[48] China's fate in the SCS is either "losing face by accepting foreign warranty" or "accepting the burden and risks of self-determination".[49] Ni Lexiong of Shanghai University of Political Science suggests that due to the Chinese culture and ethos, China will inevitably choose the latter option.[50] By so doing, China does not merely control its own fate but also dominate Japan's maritime security.[51]

Beijing is preoccupied with a strategy to prevent the US from expanding its influence in Asia at China's expense. In the western Pacific, China has suggested the idea of the separation of a sphere of influence with the US—where China dominates Taiwan and its near seas; and the US dominates the rest of the western Pacific.[52] This idea is not welcomed by the Obama administration, since the US cannot operate its sphere of influence under China's scheme. More importantly, if the US subscribes to China's idea of separate spheres of influence in the western Pacific, this will severely undermine the US alliance with Japan and South Korea.[53] This has convinced Washington that China's intention in the SCS is to expel the US presence and dominate Asia.[54]

The respective interpretations of China and the US subjectively are irreconcilable. However, objectively the conflict of interest can be reconciled to some point. The strategic rivalry between China and the US is real; however this does not necessarily lead to a military conflict. The first step to avoid tragic consequences in the SCS is to address some misperceptions which these two strategic rivals have.

China is unlikely to block access in the SCS, since this will go against its interest. The FON in the SCS serves China's interest and any attempt to impede it will create a backlash from the international community. In particular, Beijing is really concerned about relations with its southeast neighbours. Amicable relations with these countries, under ASEAN, are a key element in advancing Beijing's top-level agenda of a Maritime Silk Road and Belt and Road Initiative (BRI).[55] These two initiatives are crucial for China's future development and if they are not implemented successfully, it will be very difficult for China to advance.

China will make a rational choice by performing as a benevolent power whose rise is not at any country's expense. Since the US is attempting to build stronger economic ties with ASEAN in the context of the TPP, the Maritime Silk Road and BRI have to succeed to secure China's strategy for the future. In addition to that, to make the Maritime Silk Road and BRI successful, China will not seek full control over the whole body of water of the SCS by declaring the nine-dash line as a maritime boundary since it is against China's declaration of the territorial baselines in the Paracels.[56]

Objectively, affirming the FON in the SCS is the key to alleviating the conflict of interest between China and the US. China should not take action that can be seen as impeding the FON, since doing so is against its interest. On the other hand, the US Senate should permit the US to become a party to the UNCLOS in order to have an authoritative voice in upholding the FON.[57] Furthermore, another significant step to reduce the tension would be voluntarily closing military facilities in the SCS and halting the US intelligence operations there.[58]

7.2.2 *China's Rise and the US' Global Position*

The second element of the conflict of interest is dealing with China's rise. China's assertive posture—in its foreign policy in general and in the SCS issue in particular—is often attributed to a misperception of its position in world politics. Many in Beijing believe that the recent series of China's successes in the global arena—for example, coping with the financial crisis at the end of 1990s and the 2000s and even surpassing Japan as the second largest economy; holding world-class events like the 2008 Summer Olympics and the 2010 Shanghai Expo—have led the country to be a first-class superpower.[59] China draws great self-confidence from these achievements and does not credit them to the US or the existing order.[60] Furthermore, China perceives that the US is declining and marred with many issues such as its unemployment rate, budget deficit and financial disorder, and its status as the world's superpower is seriously challenged.[61] China is optimistic about replacing the US as the number one in the world in the near future.[62] As a consequence, Beijing believes that the US is trying very hard to contain China's rise in order to maintain its hegemonic position. This is evident in the open statements by high-ranking Chinese officials in the military and the Communist Party that consider the US as China's primary security threat.[63]

In the maritime domain, China perceives control over the SCS as a strategic step to attain global power.[64] More subjectively, the SCS has become China's "last opportunity to advance".[65] According to General Peng Guanqian, Deputy Secretary General of China's National Security Forum, the SCS is the litmus test of whether China can achieve national rejuvenation.[66] Therefore, China is determined to increase its presence and control in the SCS. The US involvement in the SCS dispute and its direct activities are viewed suspiciously by Beijing as containment. This idea of US containment against China resonates very well in Beijing, much more so than the concern in Washington about China's rise.[67] This is likely due to the ubiquitous national humiliation narrative.[68]

The subjectivity of China and the US in the SCS issue is manifested in the zero-sum attitude, as if the SCS can only accommodate one of the great rival powers' interests. In particular, China is also very suspicious about the US pivot to Asia since Secretary Clinton conveyed the idea in 2011. It is without question that the US has become anxious about China's growing military power and assertiveness vis-à-vis its rival claimant states in the SCS, particularly during the 2009–2010 period, and considers this as a serious threat to FON and the US power projection into Asia.[69] Nevertheless, Chinese officials and scholars who realise that China's behaviour contributes to the escalation of tension in the SCS constitute tiny minority.[70] Even though Beijing maintains a restrained attitude towards commenting on the US pivot to Asia strategy, there were some statements voiced by the People's Daily.[71] One report stated that this strategy was directed towards containing Beijing and preserving US hegemony in the Asia region. Furthermore, it also warned the US of the "zero-sum game with China" if it continued to see China as a challenge to its hegemonic ambition.[72]

To address the issue objectively, one needs to make an accurate judgement on China's rise. Although China's skyrocketing development in the last decades is undoubtedly impressive, China should not be overconfident about overtaking the US as the number one superpower. There is no strong correlation between rapid economic growth and military power. The GDP is only one indication that cannot wholly represent a country's wealth. According to the UN, a state's wealth lies in its manufactured capital (infrastructure), human capital (skills, health, education, and research), and natural capital (below earth resources, and environment).

The US owns nearly USD 144 trillion of this wealth or 4.5 times China's USD 32 trillion.[73] In the coming years, China's growth rate is expected to plummet from 8% in 2015 to 4%, and if the US has the same growth rate, China needs many decades to catch up.[74] In other words, the US is much richer and far more capable of converting its wealth into military power.[75] Although China is capable of producing nuclear-based submarines, its technology relies on Russia and it is only comparable to the US navy as it was commissioned in the 1950s.[76]

The other reason for China to give up its soon-to-be-number one superpower illusion is that the US does not rely solely on military might in maintaining its global position. Washington has built friendships and alliances with many countries in all regions, particularly with the first world economies, which reduce the cost of supporting the US-led world order[77] whereas China has no ally, except for North Korea, which brings more trouble than advantage for Beijing. All these factors combined make the US position as a global power unchallenged. To perceive that China will take over the US position in the near future is unfounded.[78]

Instead of containing China, the primary intention of the US in the region is to balance it.[79] China's rapid growth does not pose threats to the US; it worries the US regional allies and the SCS claimant states. Even though China's claim in the SCS traces back before the founding of the People's Republic of China in 1949, China's assertive behaviour in the SCS is to some extent supported by its huge growth in economic and military power. However, Beijing itself has failed to clarify its SCS claim based on international law.

Hedley Bull contends that the main function of this balancing is to preserve the international order and ensure the operation of international law.[80] Since China has been benefiting from the international order, the US balancing in Asia should not be seen in a negative way. The US rebalancing sustains order and since China has no capability or intention to take the US global role, Beijing should give up its misperception of the US presence in the region as containment against its rise.

On the other hand, Washington needs to adjust its foreign policy when dealing with the rise of China. The US needs to accept China's growing power, role, and interests in the international system as the new normal. The status quo policy will not serve the dynamic of power relations and interests in the international system.[81] Since status quo diplomacy only serves the perpetuation of the existing system, such a policy tends to perceive China's growing power in a zero-sum way. The US needs to pay heed to China's concern about its core interests—the survival of China's political system, its territorial integrity, and its sustainable development—no matter how ambiguous they are.

China's peaceful rise will depend on other countries, especially the US attitude towards China.[82] Additionally, China should not expand its core interests and become too demanding in its relations with the US. The SCS issue, for instance, should not be upgraded to a core interest.[83] China should keep it open for negotiation and rule out the use of force to resolve it.

7.2.3 *The Asymmetrical Interests Between Two Great Powers in the Asian Context*

The third aspect is the asymmetrical interests between the US and China in the context of Asia. Unlike the US, China is not a global power; its interests primarily lie in the Asian mainland and the East Asian coast in the western Pacific.[84] The US has to allow China to play a larger role in Asia, at the same time maintaining its stronger presence in the region.[85] China also needs to cooperate with the US and abandon the ambition to dominate Asia, since it is against the wishes of many Asian countries.[86] In particular, the SCS has a very significant meaning for China's security and future development. It relates to the Communist regime's legitimacy before the Chinese people—which is one of the Chinese core interests. For the US, defending FON in the SCS is not a primary national interest that is related to the country's political system or survival.[87] The US presence to sustain order and law in the SCS is needed, but this mission should not lead to conflict with China.

On top of that, despite so many discrepancies in the interests of China and the US in the SCS, the two countries agree that the SCS issue is best addressed diplomatically rather than militarily and they have been in support of ASEAN managing the conflict and maintaining stability.[88] What they do not agree on is the mechanism for resolving the dispute. China prefers negotiation with states directly concerned and the US is in support of the international legal mechanism.[89]

The US position will need Washington's consistency. If it wants to maintain international law and protect the FON, the US should eliminate hypocrisy by becoming party to UNCLOS. Top policy makers in Washington such as all former secretaries of states and secretaries of defence, and even the business community—which relies heavily on the FON—believe that the US accession to the UNCLOS serves the national interest.[90] Becoming part of the UNCLOS will give the US more legitimacy to maintain FON and expect all parties to adhere to it.

7.3 The Continuum of Security Dilemma

Unlike the security dilemma between China and other SCS claimants, the security dilemma between China and the US in the SCS is a mere reflection of the two great powers' rivalry. This security dilemma was activated with the US involvement in the region. The US role in the SCS is not merely limited to supporting China's rival claimants; it directly confronts China in surveillance activities and FONOPs. Currently, the security dilemma has reached the spiral stage (see Fig. 2.1 in Sect. 2.8). This stage began when China and the US became involved in the series of seemingly unending actions and counteractions in pursuing their respective interests. The development of this security dilemma to this current spiral stage is a result of the series of events presented in Table 7.1.

The evidence presented in this chapter indicates that the security dilemma between China and the US in the SCS has not reached the defection stage. In other words, even though the two countries are embroiled in a series of action-reaction dynamics, no country has defected and altered the status quo.

In the context of the security dilemma between China and the US, the application of the concept of defection is, in effect, different from that which would be applicable for China and its other neighbouring SCS claimants. This is because of three major reasons. First, China has no territorial disputes with the US in the SCS. Second, as discussed in the previous section, there is asymmetry in the conflict of interests between China and the US in the SCS. For China, the SCS is significant in many aspects—security, geopolitics, national integrity, and the Chinese Communist Party (CCP) legitimacy—as discussed in Chap. 4. Yet, for the US, the significance

Table 7.1 The differences between the two security dilemmas

Dimensions	*China and other SCS claimants*	*China and the US*
Conflict of interest	The territorial dispute pivots on maritime rights in the SCS	Strategic rivalry: China needs to dominate its near seas to secure its development. The US needs to strengthen its presence in Asia and the western Pacific
The US role	The US is a balancing factor against China and in favour of other claimant states	The US is the primary rival
Definition of status quo	The status quo is the situation when there is no permanent change in territorial control	The status quo is when the SCS is a neutral zone with no power dominating it permanently. The US also hints that building (and militarising) the Scarborough Shoal is the line which should not be crossed.
Dynamic/ process	China has defected by controlling the Scarborough Shoal in 2012 and blocking access for Philippine fishermen. Massive artificial islands building has been conducted in 2014–2015	The status quo is still maintained
Control/ resource	China is the centre of the gravity	The US has more resources to regulate the development of the security dilemma

of the SCS to its national interest is relatively low. Third, unlike China and ASEAN states, the US and China do not have any official agreement regarding the SCS. Because of this absence of a clear principle by which to measure such a potential defection, it becomes difficult to assess one (Table 7.2).

A defection could take place if one of the parties deliberately violates the other's interests and changes the status quo in the SCS, for instance, if China really hampers the US FON or makes it difficult to sail in the SCS. The US itself has admonished China about the line that should not be crossed in the SCS. During the Nuclear Security Summit on 31 March 2016, Obama reminded Xi Jinping not to aim at the Scarborough Shoal or declare an air defence identification zone (ADIZ) in the SCS.[100] On the other hand, if the US navy ships deliberately harm China's military or maritime law enforcement ships in the SCS, this also could be perceived as a defection.

Table 7.2 Sources of the activation of the security dilemma between China and the US

2001

- In April, the US Navy EP-3 reconnaissance plane and a Chinese PLAN F-8 inceptor fighter jet were involved in a mid-air collision 104 km southeast of Hainan Island. The US crew made an emergency landing on Hainan Island and China detained the 24 crew members for 11 days.[91]

2002

- In September, the US naval ship *Bowditch* conducting oceanographic surveillance in the Yellow Sea was confronted by Chinese patrol vessels for "violating China's EEZ".[92]

2009

- In March US naval ship *Impeccable* was interfered with by a Chinese ship while conducting surveillance activities in international waters 75 miles south of Hainan Island.[93]

2010

- In July, Secretary Clinton asserted the US national interest in the SCS at the ASEAN Regional Forum in Hanoi.[94]

2013

- From December 2013 until October 2015, China built artificial islands on seven coral reefs in the Spratlys with a total area of 3000 acres.[95]

2015

- In October, the USS *Lassen* conducted a FONOP by deliberately transiting within 12 nautical miles of five maritime features in the Spratly Island, including Subi Reef which is occupied by China. China expressed its objection, called the operation "illegal" and stated it "threatened China's sovereignty and security interests".[96]

2016

- In January, the USS *Curtis Wilbur* transited in innocent passage within 12 nautical miles of Triton Island in the Paracels amidst Beijing's strong protest of "violating the relevant Chinese law and entering China's territorial sea without authorization".[97]
- In May the USS *William Lawrence* conducted an FONOP near Fiery Cross of the Spratly Islands which is occupied by China, transiting within 12 nautical miles. Beijing responded to this with two fighter jets and three warships shadowing the USS *William Lawrence*, followed by the Chinese Foreign Ministry's protest.[98]
- In July, the US, Japan, and Australia issued a joint statement, urging China and the Philippines to abide by the UNCLOS Tribunal ruling of July 12, calling it "final and legally binding".[99]

Regarding China's massive construction of islands in the Spratlys, Peter Dutton argues that this "fundamentally changed regional political and security dynamics".[101] China's island building is indeed an aggressive attempt to exert control over the SCS and increase the risk of military conflict. It may also develop to turn the SCS into China's "strategic strait".[102] Even though island building potentially threatens to alter the status quo, China has never directly impeded FON or harmed the US interest in the SCS. This research argues that the status quo would be altered in the SCS if China changed the status of the SCS into a "Chinese lake" or "strategic strait" by impeding the sea lanes in it and/or deliberately harming the US interest in the SCS, that is, attempting to kick out the US from the SCS by using force.

The series of incidents between China and the US regarding the US surveillance activities and FONOP cannot be seen as China's defection to alter the status quo in its favour for two main reasons. First, Washington cannot ignore the difference of interpretation of UNCLOS with regard to military activities within a coastal state's EEZ. China as well as Vietnam opposes military operations within their EEZs based on their interpretation of UNCLOS. In other words, FONOP may increase tension in the region because China's and Vietnam's interpretation of allowed military operations in the EEZ is different from the US. On the other hand, the US FONOP is not a militarisation and does not alter the status quo in the SCS. Despite the difference of interpretation regarding military activities within the EEZ, FONOP serves the function of challenging both actual and potential excessive claims which China has refused to clarify according to international law.[103]

Second, the US is not a party to UNCLOS and refuses to accede to it. Therefore, it is unreasonable for the US to expect China to abide to UNCLOS and its Tribunal ruling. Neither is it reasonable to even challenge China's interpretation of UNCLOS.

Neither China nor the US has defected in the SCS security dilemma because of three reasons. First, Washington and Beijing are well aware that Sino-US relations are the world's most important bilateral ties. The two countries need each other to tackle many issues ranging from terrorism to climate change. It is not worth it to sacrifice these bilateral relations for the SCS issue. However, the situation is completely different with the security dilemma between China and other Southeast Asian claimants. In this case, China's defection by seizing the Scarborough Shoal prompted Manila to initiate an arbitration tribunal. As a country with backward military power, the Philippines' activation of "lawfare" is the last resort for it to launch an attack towards China, even though this has deteriorated Sino-Philippine bilateral relations as a consequence. Facing the US, China has adopted a different approach in order to avoid trouble at its expense. Since the US is the world's biggest military power and not a party to the UNCLOS, if China defects, the US will not pursue "lawfare" to deal, it will have a reason to retaliate and cause China considerable damage. If war erupts, the outcome could be detrimental as both countries are nuclear powers.

Second, Washington and Beijing's interests in the SCS are asymmetrical. For China, the SCS is an opportunity to strengthen its prominent position in Asia. It also means saving China's face and, if perceived in the context of its economic development and the legitimacy of the Communist Party, the SCS is a core interest. The US interest in the SCS is not as urgent as China's. The concern of the US is FON for its commercial and military ships. The US is indeed perturbed about how Chinese activities and its assertive behaviour in the SCS seriously threaten other claimant states' interests, some of which have alliance relationships with the US while others have in recent years formed security partnerships with it. This leads to a credibility issue for the US if Washington is reluctant to act. However, the US can maintain or increase its presence in the region. Its interests do not need to be defended with a military clash.[104]

To some extent, the logic is the same as that of Russia's invasion into Crimea. Even though Obama is unhappy with Russia's incursion, he avoids a military clash. Obama acknowledged the asymmetrical interests between two countries: Ukraine is Russia's core interest and the US has not much at stake there.[105] The situation is complex for the White House since the Ukraine is not a NATO member country. Instead of military conflict, Obama suggested imposing sanctions against Russia through the United Nations Security Council.[106]

Third, China and the US realise the reconcilability of the security dilemma in the SCS. Regardless of the heated tension between the two countries, the SCS will not impede the whole context of bilateral relations. The two sides are still in the process of formulating a model for their bilateral relations, yet this project has not been fruitful. In 2009, President Obama initiated the idea of a "G2" with China. This was soon off the table because Hu's administration was of the view that China was still a developing country and had many problems domestically. In 2013, Xi's administration proposed the idea of "new type of major power relations". This time, Obama was unresponsive to China's proposal.

The main gap in formulating the bilateral relations model successfully is that the US perceives that it should be a framework to find a solution for global problems, whereas China sees it as a means to get the US acknowledgement of itself as an equal superpower.[107] The US is also cautious that China's proposed "new type of major power relations" is a "trap" to make the US bend to China's core interest, especially in the East China Sea and the SCS.[108] In the word of Fu Ying, chairperson of the Foreign Affairs Committee of China's National People's Congress Standing Committee, the US has limited experience in dealing with China as it is neither ally nor foe while China as a growing power is still in figuring out to build a relationship with the global superpower.[109] However, no matter how big the discrepancies between the two, Beijing and Washington are both aware that conflict is not inevitable. Obama and Hu Jintao in 2011 have assured each other that the US "welcomes a strong, prosperous and successful China that plays a greater role in world affairs. China welcomes the US as an Asia Pacific nation that contributes to peace, stability and prosperity in the region."[110] This task is undoubtedly arduous, yet possible.

7.4 How Far Can China Go?

China has adopted different behaviours towards SCS claimants compared with how it behaves towards the US. In the security dilemma with the SCS claimants, China has defected from a defensive realist stance to adopting offensive realism, yet China avoids defecting vis-à-vis the US. Why has China not adopted offensive realism towards the US?

First, China is the less secure state vis-à-vis the US and does not have sufficient control over its relations with the latter. China is not confident about an issue that it perceives as one of its core interests. Only a couple of months after State Councillor Dai Bingguo asserted China's three core interests: the continuity of China's political system; sovereignty and territorial integrity; and sustainable economic and social development, at the 2009 China-US Strategic and Economic Dialogue, Obama's administration authorised arms sales to Taiwan and receive the Dalai Lama at the White House. China perceived these as a violation of its interest, while the US saw them as a commonplace practice.

Regardless of how China was disappointed with the US moves, it failed to retaliate by imposing sanctions such as threats against US companies involved in the arms sales to Taiwan.[111] Despite the heated tension with the US, Hu Jintao still made a compromise by attending the Nuclear Non-proliferation Summit in Washington, DC, in April 2012.[112] This demonstrates that China does not have control over its relations with the US. Despite its grave dissatisfaction with the US move regarding one of its core interests, Beijing has no choice but to keep its relations with Washington stable.

Overall, in its relations with the US China is often left with limited options. Behaviour that is perceived as a defection in the SCS, for instance, an open military clash with the US, will eventually be resolved at China's expense. Moreover, China has no control over managing its relations with the US because it is not resourceful enough to initiate reassurance with the US.

Second, it is important to note that the essence of the defection is the lack of trust.[113] China decided to seize the Scarborough Shoal because it had insufficient trust towards the Philippines, considering that the Philippine occupation of its perceived territory should be ended.[114] In the words of Fu Ying and Wu Shicun, the 2012 Scarborough Shoal incident became the "straw that broke the camel's back" for China.[115] Moreover, there is a fear that restraint on China's part will be misunderstood by other claimant states as tolerance—which would eventually lead other claimants to become more demanding.[116] China does not acknowledge other SCS claimants' definition of the "status quo" of their occupying features which China perceives as sovereign to it.[117] In contrast, despite many disappointments, China still maintains a certain level of trust towards the US, especially under the Obama administration. Given the moderate approach of Obama's foreign policy towards China, China has no reason to lose trust in the US.

Third, China is aware that it is unlikely to become a dominant power in the region without facing significant resistance from other powers.[118] This applies in the SCS as well because the area is too important to be dominated by China alone. States like Japan, India, and even Indonesia will support the US to push China from making the SCS subject to its command. This is the balancing strategy that limits China's hegemonic ambition.

Japan is in bitter rivalry with China. It will not surrender the SCS—which it also considers to be its own economic vein—to Chinese hands. Japan's leaders have a deep suspicion that China's rising will be not peaceful and harmless to its interests.[119] Therefore, Japan has been supporting the US FONOP and assisting other SCS claimant states to counter China.[120]

Even though India's relations with China are not as bitter as Japan's, it also shares a similar anxiety. India's strategy in Asia is to work with the US to contain China, though it will not serve the US ambition at the expense of its own regional role.[121] In the SCS, which India also perceive as the strategic route for its development and encounters with the Southeast Asian region, India has joined Japan in expressing its concern over China's assertive behaviour.[122]

Unlike India and Japan, Indonesia is not a competitor or rival to China. However, it cannot conceal its concern over China's assertive behaviour in the SCS. In as early as July 2010, Indonesia suggested that China's SCS claim—in the form of the nine-dash line—lacked a basis in international law and was inconsistent with the UNCLOS.[123] In addition to that Indonesia—together with Japan, Singapore, and Thailand, became an observer of the Philippines-initiated UNCLOS Tribunal. Indonesia most likely will adopt a hedging strategy which would avoid leaning towards either China or the US and thus succeed in keeping the balance of power in the Southeast Asian region.

These are the factors that explain why China does not defect from its defensive realist track when dealing with the US. The logic consists of factors which amount to more than mere consideration of its relative power; China still treats its relations with the US as one of its foreign policy priorities and has no reason to alter the order that has helped it rise so swiftly.

However, the US has signalled its opposition to China's intention to build a military fortress at the Scarborough Shoal. During the Nuclear Security Summit on 31 March 2016, Obama reminded Xi Jinping not to aim at the Scarborough Shoal or declare an ADIZ in the SCS.[124] Building a military outpost at Scarborough Shoal only 120 nautical miles from the Philippine coast would be a threat for Philippine (and US) security. Announcing the ADIZ will also hamper FON, since civilian planes will have to make long and costly detours to avoid risking encounters with the PLA Air Force.[125] A Chinese military fortress at the Scarborough Shoal will accommodate Chinese fighter jets to reach Manila, the Clark Base, and Subic Base within a short time.[126] By sending this signal to China, the US is trying to draw a line. If China crosses this line, the US will perceive this as a defection and as a consequence it will make a move against China.

The US determination is supported by The Hague Tribunal's award on July 2016 that invalidates China's claim and activities in the SCS. Obama has clearly indicated that "there will be consequences" if China violates international law.[127] The US still needs to prove its credibility if China really crosses that line. Despite the pivot to Asia, the deployment of US marines in Darwin and enhanced military ties with the Philippines, Obama has been very restrained towards China in the SCS. China has much greater control over the SCS than it enjoyed at the beginning of Obama's presidency.[128] This fact really makes the Philippines sceptical of the US firmness over its position.[129]

7.5 The Future of Sino-US Rivalry in the SCS

This research has attempted to present a picture of the future of Sino-US rivalry in the SCS, based on developments on the ground. Since the US (under the Obama administration) and China are not expansive states and are aware of the reconcilability of their conflict of interest, the future of these great powers' rivalry depends on the success of their efforts in managing the gap in their expectations. In the light of the defensive realist framework, success in the management of this gap can be seen from each state's restraint to defect.

Unlike the security dilemma between China and other SCS claimants (especially the Philippines), the SUSD has not yet developed to a point at which the status quo has been altered. However, even though military conflict is avoidable, distrust and misperception between the two countries still runs very deep.

This chapter has argued that conflict in the SCS is not inevitable—as offensive realism may suggest. The theory would be inapplicable if China sustainably accepts the US presence and leadership in Asia not only in words but primarily in deeds.[130] There is no clear evidence that this standard has been met by China. However, this does not mean that there is no tendency towards China's acceptance of the US presence. The biennial rim of the Pacific (RIMPAC) naval drill may offer a clue on the US and China effort to reduce to alleviate the security dilemma.

The RIMPAC has taken place near the Hawaiian Islands since 1971 and includes navy drills such as damage control, gunfire, anti-piracy, search and rescue, diving and submarine rescue.[131] In 2012, Beijing protested its exclusion from the RIMPAC to the US, calling it a US attempt to contain and pressure China.[132] Due to US invitation, China has been involved in the RIMPAC since 2014. According to US law, China is only involved in humanitarian assistance elements, not in any combat-related exercises.[133]

In 2014, the RIMPAC involved 23 nations, 47 ships, 200 aircraft, and 25,000 troops.[134] China sees the navy drill as a good opportunity to make its power and intentions known to other navies, and also to welcome the US engagement.[135] The 2016 RIMPAC marks the 25th anniversary of the naval drill. China has expanded its involvement in the exercise with the inclusion of the missile destroyer *Xi'an*, the hospital ship *Peace Ark*, the submarine rescue vessel *Changdao*, the supply ship *Gaoyuhu*, three helicopters, a diving squad, a marine squad, and 1200 personnel in total.[136] According to Deputy Navy Commander Wang Hai, China's participation is significant for promoting the "new type of major power relationship" between China and the US—a term that has become part of Xi Jinping's foreign policy dictum.[137]

China's involvement in the RIMPAC under the US invitation is evidence of the defensive realist state's operational code to indicate its benign intentions and represents a means of gauging other's motivations simultaneously.[138] The US invitation demonstrates that Obama does not adopt a zero-sum attitude towards China. He is willing to engage China in the drill to show that the US has no intention to counter or contain China. By involving China, Obama has also attempted to soften China's assertiveness in the region. As Secretary Carter mentioned, China's participation in the RIMPAC contributes to "relationships that are critical to ensuring safety and security and peace of the region's sea lanes".[139] By contrast, some Washington politicians—with a zero-sum game mindset—criticised the Obama administration for inviting China to the naval drill, given its assertiveness in the East China Sea and the SCS. One of them is the Senate Armed Services Committee Chairman Senator John McCain, who argued that China's militarisation in the SCS disqualifies itself from participating in the RIMPAC.[140]

China's response of the US invitation in the RIMPAC is also a benign signal. Tang suggests that reassurance is a strategy to encourage cooperative behaviours from a security-seeking state that is insecure.[141] In this reassurance project, China's attitude is "wait and see" instead of being proactive, because China is the more insecure country in the SUSD. Normally, an insecure state will not initiate reassurance, although it does not have a malign intention. The initiative is more likely made by less insecure state since the likelihood of bearing a destructive outcome from another state's defection is lower.[142]

China is the more insecure state in this security dilemma because of several reasons. First, there is an asymmetry of interests between China and the US in the SCS. China has more at stake in the SCS since the SCS is directly related to its security and core interests. Therefore, losing control over the SCS will be more detrimental for China, whereas for the US, the SCS—apart from the context of the FON—does not directly relate to its national interests.

Second, China's military power is inferior to the US. The 2009 *Impeccable* incident as well as other incidents involving US military ships highlights the issue of China's military weakness. The US has made China very insecure by uncovering the gap of military technology between two countries. The Chinese leadership is deeply disturbed by the fact that it cannot retaliate to the US surveillance operations on its naval base in Yulin, Hainan Island, since its technology is still far behind.[143]

Third, as Kenneth Lieberthal and Wang Jisi suggest, the strategic distrust, or, in other words, the sense of rivalry between these two great powers appears to be more popular in Beijing than in Washington.[144] Lieberthal and Wang attribute this to the century of humiliation narrative—which is that China is preoccupied by its history of invasion and degradation at the hands of foreign powers due to its own weakness. The above-mentioned factors—the security issue, the unbalance in military power, and the historical perspective—make China becomes a more fearful and insecure state in its security dilemma with the US.

Finally, RIMPAC is evidence of the superiority of defensive realism in explaining the complexity of the SUSD. RIMPAC creates a hope that reassurance is possible to alleviate the security dilemma. This points to the idea that US willingness to share leadership in both Asia and China's accommodation of the US presence in the region is possible.

Notes

1. 倪乐雄, "中国"海上生命线"问题凸显," [Ni Lexiong, "The Emerging of China's 'Maritime Life Line' Problem," *Tongzhou Gongjin*], 16–17.
2. Ibid.
3. Andrew S. Erickson and Gabriel Collins, "China's Maritime Evolution: Military and Commercial Factors," *Pacific Focus*, 22, no. 2 (2007): 47–76.
4. Lanteigne, "China's Maritime Security and the 'Malacca Dilemma'," 143–61.
5. 倪乐雄, "发展强大的海上力量,非为霸权," *领导文萃*, [Ni Lexiong, "Developing Maritime Power Is Not Hegemonic," *Lingdao Wencui*], no. 7 (2006).
6. Ibid.
7. "国家海权战略的当代转型与威慑作用,"[Ni Lexiong, "The Modern Transformation and Deterrence Function of Maritime Strategy," *Guoji Guancha*].
8. Kenneth Lieberthal and Jisi Wang, "Addressing US-China Strategic Distrust," *John L. Thornton China Center Monograph Series*, no. 4 (2012): 1–50.
9. Jihyun Kim, "Possible Future of the Contest in the South China Sea," *The Chinese Journal of International Politics*, (2016): pow001.

10. Lieberthal and Wang, "Addressing US-China Strategic Distrust," 1–50.
11. Jun Zhan, "China Goes to the Blue Waters: The Navy, Seapower Mentality and the South China Sea," *The Journal of Strategic Studies*, 17, no. 3 (1994): 180–208.
12. Tang, *A Theory of Security Strategies for Our Time: Defensive Realism*, 49–54.
13. Zhang, "Sea Power and China's Strategic Choices," 17–31.
14. Robert S. Ross, "China's Naval Nationalism: Sources, Prospects, and the U.S. Response," *International Security*, 34, no. 2 (2009): 46–81.
15. Leszek Buszynski, "The South China Sea: Oil, Maritime Claims, and US—China Strategic Rivalry," *The Washington Quarterly*, 35, no. 2 (2012).
16. Tang, *A Theory of Security Strategies for Our Time: Defensive Realism*, 87, 180.
17. Jeffrey Goldberg, "The Obama Doctrine," *The Atlantic*, April 2016, http://www.theatlantic.com/magazine/archive/2016/04/the-obama-doctrine/471525/ (accessed 8 September 2016).
18. Mac Thornberry and Andrew F. Krepinevich, "Preserving Primacy: A Defense Strategy for the New Administration," *Foreign Affairs*, September/October 2016 Issue, https://www.foreignaffairs.com/articles/north-america/2016-08-03/preserving-primacy (accessed 2 November 2016).
19. Ibid.
20. Ralf Emmers, "The US Rebalancing Strategy: Impact on the South China Sea," *The South China Sea and Australia's Regional Security Environment, National Security College Occasional Paper*, 5 (2013): 41–44.
21. Goldberg, "The Obama Doctrine," *The Atlantic*, April 2016.
22. Ibid.
23. Ibid.
24. Ibid.
25. Hillary Clinton, "America's Pacific Century," *Foreign Policy*, 11 October 2011, http://foreignpolicy.com/2011/10/11/americas-pacific-century/ (accessed 5 September 2016).
26. Ibid.
27. Ibid.
28. Bader, "The US and China's Nine-Dash Line: Ending the Ambiguity," The Brookings Institute; Eric Hyer, "Here's How the South China Sea Ruling Affects US Interests," *The Washington Post*, 11 August 2016, https://www.washingtonpost.com/news/monkey-cage/wp/2016/08/11/heres-how-the-south-china-sea-ruling-affects-u-s-interests/ (accessed 18 September 2016).
29. White, *The China Choice: Why America Should Share Power*, 68.

30. Ibid., 67.
31. Kaplan, "The Geography of Chinese Power," 22–41.
32. White, *The China Choice: Why America Should Share Power*, 71–72.
33. Lieberthal and Wang, "Addressing US-China Strategic Distrust," 1–50.
34. Emmers, "The US Rebalancing Strategy: Impact on the South China Sea," 41–44.
35. Ibid.
36. Lieberthal and Wang, "Addressing US-China Strategic Distrust," 1–50.
37. "Angry China Shadows US Warship near Man-Made Islands," *Reuters*, 27 October 2015, http://www.reuters.com/article/us-southchinasea-usa-idUSKCN0SK2AC20151027 (accessed 10 August 2016).
38. Lynn Kuok, "The US FON Program in the South China Sea: A Lawful and Necessary Response to China's Strategic Ambiguity," in *East Asia Policy Paper 9* (Center for East Asia Policy Studies, The Brookings Institution, 2016), 19.
39. China and 20 other developing countries, including Vietnam believe that military activities, such as surveillance and reconnaissance in another country's EEZ should be undertaken with the permit of the relevant states, whereas the US maintains that military operations fall within freedom of navigation and are guaranteed by the international law.
40. Valencia, "The Impeccable Incident: Truth and Consequences," 22–28.
41. Ibid., 28–29.
42. Bonnie Glaser and Brittany Billingsley, "US-China Relations: US Pivot to Asia Leaves China off Balance," *Comparative Connections*, 13, no. 3 (2011): 29.
43. Ibid.
44. Alexander Neill, "Managing a New Security Dilemma," *The Strait Times*, 3 June 2016, http://www.straitstimes.com/opinion/managing-a-new-security-dilemma (accessed 21 June 2016).
45. Dutton, "A Maritime or Continental Order for Southeast Asia and the South China Sea?" 5.
46. Li Xue and Yanzhuo Xu, "How the US Misjudged the South China Sea, Part II," *The Diplomat*, 5 August 2016, http://thediplomat.com/2016/08/how-the-us-misjudged-the-south-china-sea-part-ii/ (accessed 19 August 2016).
47. Josef Gregory Mahoney and Maximilian Mayer, "How to Make the South China Sea More Secure—for Both China and Its Neighbours," *South China Morning Post*, 9 August 2016, http://www.scmp.com/comment/insight-opinion/article/2000901/how-make-south-china-sea-more-secure-both-china-and-its (accessed 11 December 2016).
48. 倪乐雄, "发展强大的海上力量,非为霸权,"[Ni Lexiong, "Developing Maritime Power is Not Hegemonic," *Lingdao Wencui*].

49. "中国"海上生命线"问题凸显," [Ni Lexiong, "The Emerging of China's 'Maritime Life Line' Problem," *Tongzhou Gongjin*], 16–17.
50. Ibid.
51. Ibid.
52. Buszynski, "The South China Sea: Oil, Maritime Claims, and US–China Strategic Rivalry."
53. Ibid., 148.
54. Lieberthal and Wang, "Addressing US-China Strategic Distrust," 1–50.
55. Xue and Xu, "How the US Misjudged the South China Sea, Part II," *The Diplomat*, 5 August 2016.
56. Ibid.
57. Jeffrey A. Bader, "What the United States and China Should Do in the Wake of the South China Sea Ruling," *The Brookings Institute*, 13 July 2016, https://www.brookings.edu/2016/07/13/what-the-united-states-and-china-should-do-in-the-wake-of-the-south-china-sea-ruling/ (accessed 8 September 2016).
58. Walter C. Clemens Jr., "How to Avoid War in the South China Sea," *The Diplomat*, 21 July 2016, http://thediplomat.com/2016/07/how-to-avoid-war-in-the-south-china-sea/ (accessed 29 October 2016).
59. Lieberthal and Wang, "Addressing US-China Strategic Distrust," 1–50.
60. Ibid.
61. Ibid., 9.
62. Ibid., 36.
63. Ibid., 13.
64. Kim, "The South China Sea in China's Strategic Thinking," 369–87.
65. Zhan, "China Goes to the Blue Waters: The Navy, Seapower Mentality and the South China Sea," 180–208.
66. Robert Lawrence Kuhn, "Candid Thoughts on South China Sea Disputes," *China Daily*, 6 August 2016, http://www.chinadaily.com.cn/opinion/2016-08/06/content_26367442.htm (accessed 18 August 2016).
67. Lieberthal and Wang, "Addressing US-China Strategic Distrust," 1–50; David J. Firestein, "The US-China Perception Gap in the South China Sea," *The Diplomat*, 19 August 2016, http://thediplomat.com/2016/08/the-us-china-perception-gap-in-the-south-china-sea/ (accessed 28 August 2016).
68. Lieberthal and Wang, "Addressing US-China Strategic Distrust," 1–50.
69. Michael D Swaine, "Chinese Leadership and Elite Responses to the US Pacific Pivot," *China Leadership Monitor*, 38 (2012): 1–26.
70. Yang and Li, "Comparing China's Claims and Policies in the East and South China Seas: Implications for Regional Security."

71. These voices can be considered as "quasi–official," since they appear on the Communist mouthpiece—which means they do not necessarily express the government's official stance, but at least they are not against or in many cases they are supportive to the official position.
72. Zhong Sheng, "Goals of US 'Return-to-Asia Strategy Questioned," *People's Daily*, 18 October 2011, http://en.people.cn/90780/7620216.html (accessed 24 August 2016).
73. Stephen G Brooks and William C Wohlforth, "The Once and Future Superpower: Why China Won't Overtake the United States," *Foreign Affairs*, 95 (2016): 91.
74. Reza Varjavand, "Will China surpass US as World's Superpower?" *Chicago Tribune*, 2 October 2015, http://www.chicagotribune.com/suburbs/daily-southtown/opinion/ct-sta-varjavand-china-st-1004-20151002-story.html (accessed 24 August 2016).
75. Brooks and Wohlforth, "The Once and Future Superpower: Why China Won't Overtake the United States," 91.
76. Ibid., 96.
77. Ibid., 98.
78. White, *The China Choice: Why America should Share Power*, 4.
79. Li Xue and Yanzhuo Xu, "How the US Misjudged the South China Sea, Part I," *The Diplomat*, 4 August 2016, http://thediplomat.com/2016/08/how-the-us-misjudged-the-south-china-sea-part-i/ (accessed 19 August 2016).
80. Hedley Bull, *The Anarchical Society: A Study of Order in World Politics*, vol. 4 (Basingstoke: Palgrave Macmillan, 2012), 103–04.
81. Kai He and Huiyun Feng, "Debating China's Assertiveness: Taking China's Power and Interests Seriously," *International Politics*, 49, no. 5 (2012): 633–44.
82. Ibid.
83. Ibid., 641.
84. White, *The China Choice: Why America Should Share Power*, 69.
85. Ibid., 5.
86. Ibid., 61.
87. Bilahari Kausikan, "Pavlovian Conditioning and 'Correct Thinking' on the South China Sea," *The Strait Times*, 1 April 2016, http://www.straitstimes.com/opinion/pavlovian-conditioning-and-correct-thinking-on-the-south-china-sea (accessed 9 June 2016).
88. Emmers, "The US Rebalancing Strategy: Impact on the South China Sea," 41–44.
89. Ibid.
90. Bader, "What the United States and China Should Do in the Wake of the South China Sea Ruling," *The Brookings Institute*, 13 July 2016.

91. Shirley A Kan et al., "China-US Aircraft Collision Incident of April 2001: Assessments and Policy Implications," (paper presented at the CRS Report for Congress, 2001).
92. Erik Eckholm, "China Complains US Navy Violated 200-Mile Zone," *The New York Times*, 26 September 2002, http://www.nytimes.com/2002/09/26/international/china-complains-us-navy-violated-200mile-zone.html (accessed 20 July 2016).
93. Richard Weitz, "Maritime Confrontation Highlights Troubled State of China-US Defense Diplomacy," *The Jamestown Foundation*, *China Brief*, Volume 9 Issue 9, 30 April 2009, http://www.jamestown.org/single/?tx_ttnews%5Btt_news%5D=34923&no_cache=1#.V7lgUvl96Uk (accessed 15 August 2016).
94. US Department of State, *Remarks at Press Availability*, 23 July 2010, Hanoi, http://www.state.gov/secretary/20092013clinton/rm/2010/07/145095.htm (accessed 8 July 2016).
95. Matthew Southerland, *China's Island Building in the South China Sea: Damage to the Marine Environment, Implications, and International Law* (2016).
96. Kuok, "The US FON Program in the South China Sea: A Lawful and Necessary Response to China's Strategic Ambiguity," 15.
97. Ibid., 17.
98. Ibid., 18.
99. "Joint Statement of the Japan-United States-Australia Trilateral Strategic Dialogue," *US Department of State—Office of the Spokesperson*, 25 July 2016, http://www.state.gov/r/pa/prs/ps/2016/07/260442.htm (accessed 23 July 2016).
100. Jane Perlez, "A US Admiral's Bluntness Rattles China, and Washington," *The New York Times*, 9 May 2016, http://m.cn.nytimes.com/asia-pacific/20160509/c09harris/en-us/ (accessed 20 October 2016).
101. Dutton, "A Maritime or Continental Order for Southeast Asia and the South China Sea?," 5.
102. Ibid., 8.
103. Kuok, "The US FON Program in the South China Sea: A Lawful and Necessary Response to China's Strategic Ambiguity," 19.
104. Kausikan, "Pavlovian Conditioning and 'Correct Thinking' on the South China Sea," *The Strait Times*, 1 April 2016.
105. Goldberg, "The Obama Doctrine," *The Atlantic*, April 2016.
106. Dan Roberts, "Obama Suggests Further Sanctions Against Russia over Ukraine Incursion," *The Guardian*, 29 August 2014, https://www.theguardian.com/world/2014/aug/28/obama-ukraine-russia-more-sanctions-invasion (accessed 10 August 2016).

107. Dingding Chen, "Defining a 'New Type of Major Power Relations'," *The Diplomat*, 8 November 2014, http://thediplomat.com/2014/11/defining-a-new-type-of-major-power-relations/ (accessed 17 July 2016).
108. Cheng Li and Lucy Xu, "Chinese Enthusiasm and American Cynicism over the 'New Type of Great Power Relations'," *Brookings Institution*, 4 December 2014, https://www.brookings.edu/opinions/chinese-enthusiasm-and-american-cynicism-over-the-new-type-of-great-power-relations/ (accessed 9 August 2016).
109. Fu Ying, "What Are the U.S. and China Fighting Over?" *BloombergView*, 1 September 2016, https://www.bloomberg.com/view/articles/2016-09-01/what-are-the-u-s-and-china-fighting-over (accessed 8 September 2016).
110. Henry A. Kissinger, "The Future of US-Chinese Relations: Conflict Is a Choice, Not a Necessity," *Foreign Affairs*, (2012): 44–55.
111. Kai He and Huiyun Feng, "China's Bargaining Strategies for a Peaceful Rise: Successes and Challenges," *Asian Security*, 10, no. 2 (2014): 168–87.
112. Ibid.
113. Kydd, *Trust and Mistrust in International Relations*, 183.
114. Zhang, "China's Growing Assertiveness in the South China Sea: A Strategic Shift?," 19.
115. Ying Fu, "South China Sea: How We Got to This Stage," *The National Interest*, 9 May 2016.
116. Fangyin Zhou, "Between Assertiveness and Self-Restraint: Understanding China's South China Sea Policy," *International Affairs*, 92, no. 4 (2016): 869–90.
117. Wen, "Debunking 10 Myths about China and the South China Sea," *South China Morning Post*, 10 July 2016.
118. White, *The China Choice: Why America Should Share Power*, 61.
119. Ibid., 86.
120. Emiko Jozuka, "Japan to Join US in South China Sea Patrols," *CNN*, 16 September 2016, http://edition.cnn.com/2016/09/15/asia/japan-south-china-sea-patrols/ (accessed 14 November 2016); Robin Harding and Michael Peel, "Japan Provides Ships for Philippines to Help Counter China at Sea," *Financial Times*, 7 September 2016, https://www.ft.com/content/6bdb1cdc-7422-11e6-b60a-de4532d5ea35 (accessed 14 November 2016).
121. White, *The China Choice: Why America Should Share Power*, 89.
122. Nandini Krishnamoorthy, "India Will Not Become Japan's 'Pawn' to Contain Beijing in South China Sea, China's State-Run Paper Says," *International Business Times*, 12 November 2016, http://www.ibtimes.co.uk/india-will-not-become-japans-pawn-contain-beijing-south-china-sea-chinas-state-run-paper-says-1591202 (accessed 21 November 2016).

123. United Nations, *Indonesian Diplomatic Note to the Secretary General of the United Nations No. 480/POL-703/VII/10*, 2010, http://www.un.org/depts/los/clcs_new/submissions_files/mysvnm33_09/idn_2010re_mys_vnm_e.pdf (accessed 12 December 2015).
124. Perlez, "A US Admiral's Bluntness Rattles China, and Washington," *The New York Times*, 9 May 2016.
125. Ibid.
126. Michael Sullivan, "In South China Sea Dispute, Filipinos Say US credibility Is on the Line," *National Public Radio*, 17 July 2016, http://www.npr.org/2016/07/17/486240079/in-south-china-sea-dispute-filipinos-say-u-s-credibility-is-on-the-line (accessed 29 November 2016).
127. Jason Miks, "Obama: Consequences If China Violates Rules and Norms," *CNN*, 4 September 2016, http://edition.cnn.com/2016/09/04/us/obama-china-response-zakaria-interview-miks/ (accessed 7 September 2016).
128. Mark Landler and Jane Perlez, "Rare Harmony as China and U.S. Commit to Climate Deal," *The New York Times*, 3 September 2016, http://www.nytimes.com/2016/09/04/world/asia/obama-xi-jinping-china-climate-accord.html (accessed 18 October 2016).
129. Sullivan, "In South China Sea Dispute, Filipinos Say US credibility Is on the Line," *National Public Radio*, 17 July 2016.
130. Xiaoting Li, "Applying Offensive Realism to the Rise of China: Structural Incentives and Chinese Diplomacy Toward the Neighboring States," *International Relations of the Asia-Pacific*, 16, no. 2 (2016): 241–71.
131. "Chinese Naval Fleet Sails Out for 2016 RIMPAC Drills," *Xinhua*, 15 June 2016, http://news.xinhuanet.com/english/2016-06/15/c_135439589.htm (accessed 18 August 2016).
132. Miles Yu, "Inside China: China Upset over RIMPAC Snub," *The Washington Times*, 4 July 2012, http://www.washingtontimes.com/news/2012/jul/4/inside-china-china-upset-over-rimpac-snub/ (accessed 6 August 2016).
133. Kirk Spitzer, "US and China Warships to Participate in Massive Pacific War Games," *The Navy Times*, 28 June 2016, https://www.navytimes.com/story/military/2016/06/28/us-and-china-warships-participate-massive-pacific-war-games/86476962/ (accessed 29 July 2016).
134. "Chinese Ships Set Sail for RIMPAC Naval Drill," *Xinhua*, 10 June 2014, http://news.xinhuanet.com/english/video/2014-06/10/c_133395974.htm (accessed 9 September 2016).
135. Ibid.
136. "Chinese Naval Fleet Sails Out for 2016 RIMPAC Drills," *Xinhua*, 15 June 2016.
137. Ibid.

138. Tang, *A Theory of Security Strategies for Our Time: Defensive Realism*, 141–42.
139. Spitzer, "US and China Warships to Participate in Massive Pacific War Games," *The Navy Times*, 28 June 2016.
140. Bill Gertz, "US Sends Mixed Signals to China by Allowing Participation in RIMPAC: Gertz," *Asia Times*, 19 April 2016, http://atimes.com/2016/04/us-sends-mixed-signals-to-china-by-allowing-participation-in-rimpac/ (accessed 25 August 2016).
141. Tang, *A Theory of Security Strategies for Our Time: Defensive Realism*, 144.
142. Ibid., 156.
143. Valencia, "The Impeccable Incident: Truth and Consequences," 22–28.
144. Lieberthal and Wang, "Addressing US-China Strategic Distrust," 1–50.

CHAPTER 8

Conclusion

8.1 Summary of the Research Findings

This research examines whether a security dilemma applies in the South China Sea (SCS), with a particular focus on China's behaviour. For a security dilemma to apply, three criteria must be met: first, states involved are uncertain of each other's motivation; second, these states must lack a malign intention; third, such states face a paradox of self-defeating behaviour (an endeavour to enhance one's security but results in its reduction).

The mounting evidence demonstrates that China's behaviour in the SCS fundamentally lacks malign intention. History reveals that China's strong presence in the SCS and its claim was made before the founding of the People's Republic of China (PRC). China's SCS claim is unrelated to its growing power since the late twentieth century. Moreover, China's SCS interests in resources, geopolitics, security, Taiwan, and the legitimacy of the Chinese Communist Party (CCP) are mostly defensive. However, there is an indication that the Mahan Doctrine—which is offensive in nature—is gaining more attention among People's Liberation Army (PLA) high officials. If China behaves according to the Mahan Doctrine by attempting to expel US ships from the first and second island chains, it can be considered an offensive realist state.

The fact that the conflict of interests between China and other SCS claimant states is objectively reconcilable and subjectively irreconcilable supports the application of the security dilemma. It is objectively reconcilable

K. H. Raditio, *Understanding China's Behaviour in the South China Sea*, https://doi.org/10.1007/978-981-13-1283-0_8

because (1) if all parties abide by the provision of the United Nations Convention on the Law of the Sea (UNCLOS; although it does not touch the sovereignty issue), the maritime rights dispute can be managed; (2) China's main problem in terms of energy is mostly related to its uncontrollable demand and inefficiency; (3) the SCS has always been common property and never monopolised by any entity; (4) the SCS is not a top priority issue for the Chinese people, and making a compromise in the SCS may tarnish the CCP's reputation and undermine its legitimacy, though it is unlikely to cause its collapse. It is subjectively irreconcilable because it has been connected to excessive nationalism. China's sense of superiority over its Southeast Asian neighbours and of victimhood towards external powers makes the Chinese government reluctant to make any compromise in the SCS.

The security dilemma between China and other SCS claimants began between 2007 and 2009 and gradually shifted with China's defection from defensive realism to offensive realism. Defection is a behaviour of a state attempting to alter the status quo in favour of its interest. Defection also means a state starts to adopt a malign intention and an offensive realist strategy. Defection in the SCS should meet all of these criteria: (1) it must be a move that creates new status in favour of the initiator; (2) it must be a breach of the agreed consensus, either the 2002 DoC or the UNCLOS; (3) it must be a move that has not been conducted during the period of de-escalation (after the 1995 Mischief Reef incident until between 2007 and 2009). Based on these criteria, there are two examples of evidence relating to China's defection. The first of these is the seizure of the Scarborough Shoal in 2012 followed by the blockade of Philippine fishermen to conduct activities in the vicinity of the shoal. Second is China's monumental construction of artificial islands in 2014–2015.

From a strategic point of view, there are several reasons for China's defection which are (1) its dissatisfaction for having minority control of SCS features; and (2) the Scarborough Shoal (Huangyan Dao) has significant impact in substantiating China's claim in the SCS since it is the only high-tide elevation feature in the Zhongsha Islands. From the perspective of the policy makers, the seizure of the Scarborough Shoal took place because Hu Jintao (who was sitting president) needed to show his determination against his critics. Furthermore, Xi Jinping needed to consolidate his leadership by adopting a tough stance in the SCS. Xi Jinping had assumed the top position of the Leading Small Group on Maritime Rights Protection in mid-2012, which was about the same time as the Scarborough

Shoal incident. The extensive construction of artificial islands which took place in 2014–2015 was also motivated by Xi Jinping's intention to cement his leadership and show his determination to both international and domestic audiences.

Besides other SCS claimants, China also faces security dilemma with the US in the SCS. Unlike the former security dilemma, the latter is only a reflection of the strategic rivalry between the two great powers. It is important to note that neither country has defected in the SCS because both parties realise the intractability of the security dilemma. The security dilemma between China and the US exists because they both have a conflict of interest that is subjectively irreconcilable and objectively reconcilable. From the US side, it subjectively perceives that China will block access to the SCS. In addition to freedom of navigation and growing Chinese domination, the US may also be concerned with its reputation as a reliable security provider to its allies and partners, some of which are claimant states in the SCS dispute. From China's side, its subjective view is manifested in: (1) the idea that the US is declining in economic power and that China will supersede the US position in the near future; and (2) the assumption that the escalation of tension in the SCS is mostly provoked by external factors. Furthermore, the conflict of interest between China and the US is not asymmetrical. China is a regional power, whilst the US is a global power. For China, the SCS means survival, whilst for the US the SCS is only one area where it wants to maintain presence. Therefore, objectively, the conflict between China and the US can be avoided as long as each party is willing to accommodate each other's interests to some extent.

The SCS episode continued into the realm of legal dispute when the Philippines initiated the arbitral proceeding against China's SCS claim on 22 January 2013. On 12 July 2016, the UNCLOS Tribunal which was initiated by the Philippines rendered its award which invalidated China's maritime rights claim in the SCS. China's compliance with the Tribunal ruling determines its future behaviour in the SCS as either being defensive realist or offensive realist.

In the aftermath of the Tribunal ruling, China shows a reversal from its offensive realism in two aspects. First is the new wording of its statement of claim in the SCS as explained in Chap. 3. Second, China granted access to the Philippine fishermen to the Scarborough Shoal after the Philippine President Rodrigo Duterte (who started his term in 30 June 2016) travelled to China. These moves demonstrate that the UNCLOS Tribunal ruling has a constraining effect on China's behaviour to some extent.

China's future behaviour in the SCS depends on a combination of domestic and international factors. In brief, domestic factors (leadership rivalry, the sense of exceptionalism, and victimhood) tend to propel China to act in an offensive realist manner as was evident in the 2012 Scarborough Shoal incident and the 2014–2015 massive construction of artificial islands. China's behaviour also depends on international factors such as the US balancing activities against China. Since the Chinese leadership is aware of some regional countries' support for the US role, China is unlikely to adopt an offensive realist approach against the US. However, the nature of the defensive realism world which is supported by the prevalence of international law tends to motivate China to adopt a defensive realist strategy.

8.2 Significance for Theory and Policy

The main findings of this thesis show strong support for defensive realism theory. During the period of de-escalation (1995 until between 2007 and 2009), China had the most advanced military power compared to other SCS claimants. However, instead of using force, China extended its cooperative behaviour which was successful in de-escalating the SCS tension. China demonstrated its serious commitment to stabilising the region by participating in several multilateral agreements: the 2002 DoC, the ASEAN TAC in 2003, and the JMSU in 2005. This fact is at odds with the offensive realism assumption that suggests China will pursue hegemonic ambition to resolve its dispute with other claimants.[1]

Furthermore, the development of the SCS tension corresponds to the security dilemma continuum. Mounting evidence shows that instead of pre-meditated actions, the development of the SCS security dilemma is a result of uncertainty and inadvertency between China and other claimant states. The same applies to the tension between China and the US in the SCS. Uncertainty is one of the key concepts of defensive realism.[2] In contrast, offensive realism suggests that all states aim at power maximisation and regional hegemony, which creates much less uncertainty.[3] This assumption cannot stand before the reality of the states concerned in the SCS.

Evidence in this research also suggests that China is experiencing a self-defeating phenomenon. Self-defeating behaviour is one of the basic tenets of defensive realism which suggests that a state's attempt to enhance its power does not necessarily lead to its increased security. This is particularly apparent in the case of China's Yulin naval base and the US surveillance activities. China's building of the Yulin naval base in Hainan Island is driven by defensive motivation. However, this has raised concerns for the US since the base can be used to launch a nuclear submarine, which in turn threatens US naval ships in the region, leading to the growing frequency of surveillance and intelligence gathering on flights and ships, which is perceived by China as a threat by the US.

Having confirmed the nature of China's defensive realist behaviour in the SCS, this research concludes that China has defected to offensive realism. Chinese defection behaviours show that a state could change from one form of realist strategy to the other. By contrast, offensive realism argues that all states are offensive realist and offensive realism is the only strategy to guarantee a state's survival. This presupposition is not in alignment with China's SCS behaviour.

With regard to China's relations with the US in the SCS, this research finds that China's involvement in the US-led rim of the Pacific (RIMPAC) since 2014 dismisses the offensive realist argument that China will expel the US from the first and second island chains. Offensive realism cannot explain China's participation in enhancing the US-led maritime order in the Pacific. However, according to defensive realism, it is logical for China to accept the existing US-led order.

In terms of policy, this research suggests that China should be given the opportunity to reverse its policy towards other claimants to defensive realism. Dealing with China using the offensive realism perspective will not help to stabilise the region. Evidence shows that China is fundamentally a defensive realist state. However, it can adopt offensive realist measures under some circumstances. This research finds that domestic factors, that is, political rivalry within the CCP's leadership, plays a significant role in China's offensive realist behaviour.

In addition, the Chinese population and its leadership maintain a sense of exceptionalism and superiority towards other countries. This means that they are very sensitive about their own reputation and dignity (*mianzi*). China's sensitivity about its dignity should be accommodated politically but not legally. The rapprochement initiative by the newly installed Philippine President Rodrigo Duterte has proved to be effective in de-escalating the SCS tension. However, the Philippines should not withdraw its submission to the UNCLOS Tribunal or undermine the tribunal ruling on 12 July 2016. This ruling has given legal certainty on a maritime rights dispute in the SCS and the future of the SCS should be shaped based on the ruling of the UNCLOS Tribunal.

Notes

1. Mearsheimer, “Can China Rise Peacefully?” *The National Interest*, 25 October 2014.
2. Hamilton and Rathbun, “Scarce Differences: Toward a Material and Systemic Foundation for Offensive and Defensive Realism,” 436–65.
3. Ibid.

Appendix A: Chinese *Nota Verbale* (CML/17/2009) to the UN Secretary General, 7 May 2009

K. H. Raditio, *Understanding China's Behaviour in the South China Sea*, https://doi.org/10.1007/978-981-13-1283-0

(Translation)

CML/17/2009

New York, 7 May 2009

The Permanent Mission of the People's Republic of China to the United Nations presents its compliments to the Secretary-General of the United Nations and, with reference to the Joint Submission by Malaysia and the Socialist Republic of VietNam dated 6 May 2009, to the Commission on the Limits of the Continental Shelf (hereinafter referred to as "the Commission") concerning the outer limits of the continental shelf beyond 200 nautical miles, has the honor to state the position as follows:

China has indisputable sovereignty over the islands in the South China Sea and the adjacent waters, and enjoys sovereign rights and jurisdiction over the relevant waters as well as the seabed and subsoil thereof (see attached map). The above position is consistently held by the Chinese Government, and is widely known by the international community.

The continental shelf beyond 200 nautical miles as contained in the Joint Submission by Malaysia and the Socialist Republic of Viet Nam has seriously infringed China's sovereignty, sovereign rights and jurisdiction in the South China Sea. In accordance with Article 5(a) of Annex I to the Rules of Procedure of the Commission on the Limits of the Continental Shelf, the Chinese Government seriously requests the Commission not to consider the Joint Submission by Malaysia and the Socialist Republic of Viet Nam. The Chinese Government has informed Malaysia and the Socialist Republic of VietNam of the above position.

The Pennanent Mission of the People's Republic of China to the United Nations requests that this Note Verb ale be circulated to all members of the Commission, all States Parties to the United Nations Convention on the Law of the Sea as well as all Members of the United Nations.

The Permanent Mission of the People's Republic of China to the United Nations avails itself of this opportunity to renew to the Secretary-General of the United Nations the assurances of its highest consideration.

H.E. Mr. BAN KI-MOON

Secretary-General
The United Nations
NEWYORK

Source: http://www.un.org/Depts/los/clcs_new/submissions_files/mysvnm33_09/chn_2009re_mys_vnm_e.pdf

Appendix B: Diplomatic Note from Pham Van Dong to Zhou Enlai (14 September 1958)

K. H. Raditio, *Understanding China's Behaviour in the South China Sea*, https://doi.org/10.1007/978-981-13-1283-0

Diplomatic Note from Pham Van Dong to Zhou Enlai (14 September 1958)

THỦ TƯỚNG PHỦ
NƯỚC VIỆT NAM DÂN CHỦ CỘNG HÒA

Thưa Đồng chí Tổng lý,

Chúng tôi xin trân trọng báo tin để Đồng chí Tổng lý rõ:

Chính phủ nước Việt-nam Dân chủ Cộng hoà ghi nhận và tán thành bản tuyên bố, ngày 4 tháng 9 năm 1958, của Chính phủ nước Cộng hoà Nhân dân Trung-hoa, quyết định về hải phận của Trung-quốc.

Chính phủ nước Việt-nam Dân chủ Cộng hoà tôn trọng quyết định ấy và sẽ chỉ thị cho các cơ quan Nhà nước có trách nhiệm triệt để tôn trọng hải phận 12 hải lý của Trung-quốc, trong mọi quan hệ với nước Cộng hoà Nhân dân Trung-hoa trên mặt bể.

Chúng tôi xin kính gửi Đồng chí Tổng lý lời chào rất trân trọng./.

Hà-nội, ngày 14 tháng 9 năm 1958

PHẠM VĂN ĐỒNG
Thủ tướng Chính phủ
Nước Việt-nam Dân chủ Cộng hoà

Kính gửi:
Đồng chí CHU ÂN LAI
Tổng lý Quốc vụ viện
Nước Cộng hoà Nhân dân Trung-hoa
tại
BẮC-KINH.

Source: Luu Van Loi, *The Sino-Vietnamese Difference on the Hoang Sa and Truong Sa Archipelagoes* (Hanoi: The Gioi Publishers, 1996), 74.

Translation:

"Comrade Prime Minister,

We have the honour to bring to your knowledge that the Government of the DRVN recognizes and supports the declaration dated 4th September, 1958 of the Government of the PRC fixing the width of the Chinese territorial waters. The Government of the DRVN respects this decision and will give instructions to its State bodies to respect the 12-mile width of the territorial waters of China in all their relations in the maritime field with the PRC. I address to you, comrade Prime Minister, the assurance of my distinguished consideration".

Appendix C: "Philippines v. China Arbitration Case: Summary of the Philippines Submissions and Tribunal Awards"

Citation:
Jonathan Spangler and Olga Daksueva (eds.), "Philippines v. China Arbitration Case: Summary of the Philippines' Submissions and Tribunal's Awards," South China Sea Think Tank, July 14, 2016, <http://scstt.org/features/2016/863>.

SOUTH CHINA SEA THINK TANK 南海智庫

On January 22, 2013, the Philippines formally initiated arbitral proceedings against China under Article 287 and Annex VII of the United Nations Convention on the Law of the Sea (UNCLOS).

On February 19, 2013, China rejected and returned the Philippines' Note Verbale initiating the proceedings, stated that it would neither accept nor participate in the arbitration, and provided reasoning to support its position. China has since reiterated and developed its position by means of official government statements. Taiwan, due to its lack of representation in the United Nations, was unable to participate in the arbitral proceedings despite the fact that the Philippines' submissions and arguments sought international legal decisions affecting its maritime territorial claims and interests.

K. H. Raditio, *Understanding China's Behaviour in the South China Sea*, https://doi.org/10.1007/978-981-13-1283-0

The Philippines, in its Memorial presented to the Tribunal on March 30, 2014, requested that the Tribunal issue an Award regarding fifteen submissions related to the status and legal entitlements of certain features in the South China Sea, the conduct of states and other actors in the disputed areas, and the legal legitimacy of China's historical claims. The Philippines, in its testimony during the arbitral proceedings, also requested that the Tribunal address other key issues beyond the scope of its fifteen Submissions.

On July 12, 2016, the Arbitral Tribunal issued its Award. The Philippines' submissions and additional claims, the Tribunal's conclusions contained in its Award on Jurisdiction and Admissibility, and its conclusions made in its final Award are summarized below.

	Philippines' submission or additional claim March 30, 2014; November 30, 2015	*Tribunal's position in Award on Jurisdiction and Admissibility October 29, 2015*	*Tribunal's position in final Award July 12, 2016*
1	China's maritime entitlements in the South China Sea, like those of the Philippines, may not extend beyond those permitted by [UNCLOS]	Reserved consideration	UNCLOS "defines the scope of maritime entitlements in the South China Sea, which may not extend beyond the limits imposed therein." (X, 1203, B, 1)
2	China's claims to sovereign rights and jurisdiction, and to "historic rights", with respect to the maritime areas of the South China Sea encompassed by the so-called "nine-dash line" are contrary to the Convention and without lawful effect to the extent that they exceed the geographic and substantive limits of China's maritime entitlements under UNCLOS	Reserved consideration	China's claims regarding "historic rights, or other sovereign rights or jurisdiction, [within] the 'nine-dash line' are contrary to [UNCLOS and have no] lawful effect [where] they exceed the geographic and substantive limits of China's maritime entitlements under [UNCLOS]" UNCLOS "superseded any historic rights, or other sovereign rights or jurisdiction, in excess of the limits imposed therein." (X, 1203, B, 2)

(*continued*)

(continued)

	Philippines' submission or additional claim March 30, 2014; November 30, 2015	*Tribunal's position in Award on Jurisdiction and Admissibility October 29, 2015*	*Tribunal's position in final Award July 12, 2016*
3	Scarborough Shoal generates no entitlement to an exclusive economic zone or continental shelf	Had jurisdiction	Scarborough Shoal is a rock without EEZ or continental shelf entitlements. (X, 1203, B, 6) It is entitled to territorial waters
4	Mischief Reef, Second Thomas Shoal and Subi Reef are low-tide elevations that do not generate entitlement to a territorial sea, exclusive economic zone or continental shelf, and are not features that are capable of appropriation by occupation or otherwise	Had jurisdiction	Mischief Reef and Second Thomas Shoal are low-tide elevations without territorial sea, EEZ, or continental shelf entitlements. They are not "capable of appropriation." (X, 1203, B, 4) Subi Reef is a low-tide elevation without territorial sea, EEZ, or continental shelf entitlements. It is not "capable of appropriation, but may be used as the baseline for measuring the breadth of the territorial sea of high-tide features situated at a distance not exceeding the breadth of the territorial sea." (X, 1203, B, 5) It is within the 12-nm territorial waters of Sandy Cay, which is a high-tide feature. (X, 1203, B, 3, d)
5	Mischief Reef and Second Thomas Shoal are part of the exclusive economic zone and continental shelf of the Philippines	Reserved consideration	Mischief Reef and Second Thomas Shoal are low-tide elevations without territorial sea, EEZ, or continental shelf entitlements, and "there are no overlapping [EEZ or continental shelf] entitlements ... in the areas." (X, 1203, B, 4)

(*continued*)

(continued)

	Philippines' submission or additional claim March 30, 2014; November 30, 2015	*Tribunal's position in Award on Jurisdiction and Admissibility October 29, 2015*	*Tribunal's position in final Award July 12, 2016*
6	Gaven Reef and McKennan Reef (including Hughes Reef) are low-tide elevations that do not generate entitlement to a territorial sea, exclusive economic zone or continental shelf, but their low-water line may be used to determine the baseline from which the breadth of the territorial sea of Namyit and Sin Cowe, respectively, is measured	Had jurisdiction	Gaven Reef (South) and Hughes Reef are low-tide elevations without territorial sea, EEZ, or continental shelf entitlements. They are not "capable of appropriation, but may be used as the baseline for measuring the breadth of the territorial sea of high-tide features situated at a distance not exceeding the breadth of the territorial sea." (X, 1203, B, 5) Gaven Reef (South) is within the 12-nm territorial waters of Gaven Reef (North) and Namyit Island, which are high-tide features. (X, 1203, B, 3, e) Hughes Reef is within the 12-nm territorial waters of McKennan Reef and Sin Cowe Island, which are high-tide features. (X, 1203, B, 3, f)
7	Johnson Reef, Cuarteron Reef and Fiery Cross Reef generate no entitlement to an exclusive economic zone or continental shelf	Had jurisdiction	Johnson Reef, Cuarteron Reef and Fiery Cross Reef are rocks without EEZ or continental shelf entitlements. (X, 1203, B, 6) They are entitled to territorial waters
8	China has unlawfully interfered with the enjoyment and exercise of the sovereign rights of the Philippines with respect to the living and non-living resources of its exclusive economic zone and continental shelf	Reserved consideration	China "breached its obligations under Article 56" regarding "the Philippines' sovereign rights over the living resources of its exclusive economic zone" by implementing its 2012 South China Sea fishing moratorium and not making "exception for areas of the South China Sea falling within the exclusive economic zone of the Philippines [or] limiting the moratorium to Chinese flagged vessels." (X, 1203, B, 9)

(*continued*)

(continued)

	Philippines' submission or additional claim March 30, 2014; November 30, 2015	*Tribunal's position in Award on Jurisdiction and Admissibility October 29, 2015*	*Tribunal's position in final Award July 12, 2016*
9	China has unlawfully failed to prevent its nationals and vessels from exploiting the living resources in the exclusive economic zone of the Philippines	Reserved consideration	China "breached its obligations under Article 58(3)" by not preventing "fishing by Chinese flagged vessels" at Mischief Reef and Second Thomas Shoal, which are within the Philippines' EEZ, in May 2013. (X, 1203, B, 11)
10	China has unlawfully prevented Philippine fishermen from pursuing their livelihoods by interfering with traditional fishing activities at Scarborough Shoal	Had jurisdiction	China has, since May 2012, "unlawfully prevented fishermen from the Philippines from engaging in traditional fishing at Scarborough Shoal," which "has been a traditional fishing ground for fishermen of many nationalities." (X, 1203, B, 11)
11	China has violated its obligations under the Convention to protect and preserve the marine environment at Scarborough Shoal and Second Thomas Shoal	Had jurisdiction	China "breached its obligations under Articles 192 and 194(5)" because it "was aware of, tolerated, protected, and failed to prevent" environmentally destructive activities by fishermen from Chinese flagged vessels, who "have engaged in the harvesting of endangered species on a significant scale[and] the harvesting of giant clams in a manner that is severely destructive of the coral reef ecosystem" in the South China Sea. (X, 1203, B, 12)

(*continued*)

(continued)

	Philippines' submission or additional claim March 30, 2014; November 30, 2015	*Tribunal's position in Award on Jurisdiction and Admissibility October 29, 2015*	*Tribunal's position in final Award July 12, 2016*
12	China's occupation and construction activities on Mischief Reef (a) violate the provisions of the Convention concerning artificial islands, installations and structures; (b) violate China's duties to protect and preserve the marine environment under the Convention; and (c) constitute unlawful acts of attempted appropriation in violation of the Convention	Reserved consideration	China "breached its obligations under Articles 123, 192, 194(1), 194(5), 197, and 206" because its land reclamation and construction have "caused severe, irreparable harm to the coral reef ecosystem" without cooperating, coordinating, or communicating environmental impact assessments with other countries. (X, 1203, B, 13) China "breached Articles 60 and 80" through its "construction of artificial islands, installations, and structures at Mischief Reef without the authorisation of the Philippines" because the feature is a low-tide elevation not capable of appropriation within the Philippines' EEZ. (X, 1203, B, 14)
13	China has breached its obligations under the Convention by operating its law enforcement vessels in a dangerous manner causing serious risk of collision to Philippine vessels navigating in the vicinity of Scarborough Shoal	Had jurisdiction	China "breached its obligations under Article 94" and "violated Rules 2, 6, 7, 8, 15, and 16 of the Convention on the International Regulations for Preventing Collisions at Sea, 1972" by causing "serious risk of collision and danger to Philippine ships and personnel" through the "operation of its law enforcement vessels" on April 28 and May 26, 2012. (X, 1203, B, 15)

(*continued*)

(continued)

	Philippines' submission or additional claim March 30, 2014; November 30, 2015	*Tribunal's position in Award on Jurisdiction and Admissibility October 29, 2015*	*Tribunal's position in final Award July 12, 2016*
14	Since the commencement of this arbitration in January 2013, China has unlawfully aggravated and extended the dispute by, among other things: (a) interfering with the Philippines' rights of navigation in the waters at, and adjacent to, Second Thomas Shoal; (b) preventing the rotation and resupply of Philippine personnel stationed at Second Thomas Shoal; and (c) endangering the health and well-being of Philippine personnel stationed at Second Thomas Shoal	Reserved consideration	China has aggravated the disputes over "the status of maritime features in the Spratly Islands" as well as those about the countries' "respective rights and entitlements" and "the protection and preservation of the marine environment" at Mischief Reef. (X, 1203, B, 16) China has enlarged the disputes over "the protection and preservation of the marine environment to Cuarteron Reef, Fiery Cross Reef, Gaven Reef (North), Johnson Reef, Hughes Reef, and Subi Reef." (X, 1203, B, 16)
15	Original: China shall desist from further unlawful claims and activities Amended: China shall respect the rights and freedoms of the Philippines under the Convention, shall comply with its duties under the Convention, including those relevant to the protection and preservation of the marine environment in the South China Sea, and shall exercise its rights and freedoms in the South China Sea with due regard to those of the Philippines under the Convention	Requested clarification	China should have abstained from activities with "a prejudicial effect [on] the execution of the decisions to be given" and activities that "might aggravate or extend the dispute during" the arbitral proceedings. (X, 1203, B, 16)

(*continued*)

(continued)

	Philippines' submission or additional claim March 30, 2014; November 30, 2015	*Tribunal's position in Award on Jurisdiction and Admissibility October 29, 2015*	*Tribunal's position in final Award July 12, 2016*
Additional issues			
1	Itu Aba (Taiping) Island is a rock, not an island, under Article 121(1) and 121(3) of UNCLOS. (Itu Aba Island is occupied by Taiwan and is the largest feature in the Spratly Islands.)		Itu Aba (Taiping) Island is a rock without EEZ or continental shelf entitlements because "no maritime feature claimed by China within 200 nautical miles of Mischief Reef or Second Thomas Shoal constitutes a fully entitled island." (X, 1203, A, 2, a)
2	Thitu Island is a rock, not an island, under Article 121(1) and 121(3) of UNCLOS. (Thitu Island is occupied by the Philippines and is the second-largest feature in the Spratly Islands.)		Thitu Island is a rock without EEZ or continental shelf entitlements because "no maritime feature claimed by China within 200 nautical miles of Mischief Reef or Second Thomas Shoal constitutes a fully entitled island." (X, 1203, A, 2, a)
3	West York Island is a rock, not an island, under Article 121(1) and 121(3) of UNCLOS. (West York Island is occupied by the Philippines and is the third-largest feature in the Spratly Islands.)		West York Island is a rock without EEZ or continental shelf entitlements because "no maritime feature claimed by China within 200 nautical miles of Mischief Reef or Second Thomas Shoal constitutes a fully entitled island." (X, 1203, A, 2, a)

Edited by **Jonathan Spangler** and **Olga Daksueva**

South China Sea Think Tank (SCSTT) is an independent, non-profit organization that promotes dialogue, research, and education on South China Sea issues.

SCSTT does not take any institutional position on the South China Sea disputes. Published material does not necessarily reflect the views of its members or contributors, their respective institutions, or the governments involved in the disputes. While SCSTT makes every attempt to provide accurate information, contributors are solely responsible for the content of their own articles. Suggestions, corrections, and article submissions can be sent to research@scstt.org.

Index[1]

[1] Note: Page numbers followed by 'n' refer to notes.

K. H. Raditio, *Understanding China's Behaviour in the South China Sea*, https://doi.org/10.1007/978-981-13-1283-0

The manufacturer's authorised representative in the EU is Springer Nature Customer Service Centre GmbH, Europaplatz 3, 69115 Heidelberg, Germany. If you have any concerns regarding our products, please contact ProductSafety@springernature.com

Printed and bound by CPI Group (UK) Ltd, Croydon, CR0 4YY
25/09/2026
02222897-0003